SECOND EDITION

THE **Keys** TO
Effective
Schools

SECOND EDITION

THE **Keys** TO
Effective
Schools

EDUCATIONAL REFORM AS
CONTINUOUS IMPROVEMENT

EDITED BY

Willis D. Hawley

WITH **DONALD L. ROLLIE**

A JOINT PUBLICATION

PATRICIA A. ALEXANDER ▪ EVA L. BAKER ▪ JAMES A. BANKS ▪ PETER COOKSON
LORNA M. EARL ▪ RICHARD F. ELMORE ▪ MICHAEL FULLAN ▪ GENEVA GAY
JACQUELINE JORDAN IRVINE ▪ KENNETH LEITHWOOD ▪ ANN LIEBERMAN
JUDITH WARREN LITTLE ▪ LYNNE MILLER ▪ P. KAREN MURPHY ▪ FRED M. NEWMANN
SONIA NIETO ▪ JANET WARD SCHOFIELD ▪ WALTER G. STEPHAN ▪ GARY SYKES ▪ LINDA VALLI

CORWIN PRESS
A SAGE Publications Company
Thousand Oaks, CA 91320

For information:

Corwin Press
A Sage Publications Company
2455 Teller Road
Thousand Oaks, California 91320
www.corwinpress.com

Sage Publications Ltd.
1 Oliver's Yard
55 City Road
London EC1Y 1SP
United Kingdom

Sage Publications India Pvt. Ltd.
B-42, Panchsheel Enclave
Post Box 4109
New Delhi 110 017 India

Printed in the United States of America

Library of Congress Cataloging-in-Publication Data

The keys to effective schools : educational reform as continuous
improvement / edited by Willis D. Hawley.—2nd ed.
        p. cm.
"A Joint Publication with National Education Association and Corwin Press."
Includes bibliographical references and index.
ISBN 1-4129-4100-8 or 978-1-4129-4100-6 (cloth)
ISBN 1-4129-4101-6 or 978-1-4129-4101-3 (pbk.)
    1. School improvement programs—United States. 2. Teacher effectiveness—United States.
3. Learning. I. Hawley, Willis D. II. National Educational Association (U.S.)
LB2822.82.K493 2007
    371.200973—dc22   2006014859

This book is printed on acid-free paper.

06   07   08   09   10   10   9   8   7   6   5   4   3   2   1

Acquisitions Editor:	Rachel Livsey
Editorial Assistant:	Phyllis Cappello
Production Editor:	Catherine M. Chilton
Copy Editor:	Carla Freeman
Typesetter:	C&M Digitals (P) Ltd.
Indexer:	Molly Hall
Cover Designer:	Monique Hahn
Graphic Designer:	Audrey Snodgrass

Contents

Introduction to the Second Edition

The National Education Association (NEA) believes that great public schools are a basic right for every child. And we know that when the people who work in our nation's public schools are treated as professionals, and given the support and tools they need to succeed, magical things can happen for our children.

These are the guiding principles that led to NEA's development of the Keys to Excellence for Your Schools (KEYS) Initiative. This high-quality tool allows educators to measure the conditions and climate in their schools to support effective teaching and learning and improve student achievement. In order to more fully describe the conditions a school needs to have in place for students to achieve at the highest levels, NEA proudly presents *The Keys to Effective Schools.*

The contributors to this volume include many of the most respected education researchers in the country. Their expertise is well established—they have spent countless hours in public schools, they understand how schools operate, and they value the point of view of school employees. They offer practical insight and wisdom, based on the philosophy that quality schools are created and sustained by those who work in them.

We hope you will gain many benefits from having this book as a resource.

Sincerely

Reg Weaver
President
National Education Association

Preface

The Problem of Continuous School Improvement

F or decades, a series of cyclical reform efforts have been fueled by doomsday criticism and reports, followed by an intensive search for workable solutions. In most schools, innovations tend to appear and disappear with predictable regularity. Few reform initiatives are systemic, and they result in short-run gains rather than building a capacity for continuous improvement.

Increasingly, educational researchers and policy analysts agree that the organizational structures and cultures of schools can either enhance or hinder their effectiveness. There is growing recognition that quality teaching and conditions that support it, such as supportive leadership that builds learning communities within schools and communities, evidence-based decision making focused on student learning, and collaborative problem solving and action, are essential foundations for continuous school improvement.

This book offers a series of essays by prominent researchers that identify the rationale for strategies that parents, educators, and policymakers can use to create conditions in schools that facilitate the learning of all students. These concise, research-based chapters are written around the framework of the KEYS initiative of the National Education Association (NEA). KEYS, or Keys to Excellence in Your Schools, is a program based on a careful and thorough investigation into how the organizational and cultural characteristics of a school can affect student achievement.

Although this book was originally commissioned to support the adoption and implementation of the KEYS initiative, the lessons in the chapters apply to any effort to improve schools in fundamental ways.

THE KEYS INITIATIVE

From the research that undergirds KEYS, we learned that quality schools consist of many characteristics, and we identified indicators that can be used to measure quality. Ways of identifying how schools measure up provide schools with tools they can use to improve teaching and learning conditions. Schools that consistently display multiple characteristics of quality, which we call *indicators of school excellence,* promote high student achievement. But we also learned that to achieve total quality, all of the characteristics must be present, and in large quantities. These characteristics, or indicators, cluster into six broad factors, which we call *keys.* Each key factor will be addressed in whole or in part by one or more of the chapters that follow. The six keys are as follows:

- Authentic, Learner-Centered Instruction
- Shared Understanding and Commitment to High Goals
- Open Communication and Collaborative Problem Solving
- Continuous Assessment for Teaching and Learning
- Personal and Professional Learning
- Resources to Support Teaching and Learning

The KEYS initiative provides participating schools with a survey and follow-up analysis that enables them to measure conditions in their schools that affect teaching and learning, identify barriers that may be blocking change, and initiate an improvement effort based on systematically collected data. Part of KEYS is a self-assessment tool that helps schools focus on what works, for whom, and under what conditions. Part of KEYS is a school-based improvement strategy concerned with an organization's enabling conditions and relationships, not specific programs. Finally, KEYS is a strategy to involve the NEA in school quality improvement through collegial networking, collective action, and association capacity building. This is an improvement effort that focuses on using NEA resources to lead in establishing the enabling conditions that let schools improve and students learn.

ORIGINS OF THE KEYS INITIATIVE

The NEA, which today represents over 3.2 million teachers and other education employees, has been deeply involved in improving the quality of public education since its inception in 1857. The approaches have varied from highly academic pedagogical studies to practical self-help projects for individual classrooms, but the common goal has remained: to provide effective schooling for America's children.

During the 1980s and into the 1990s, the NEA launched numerous efforts to enhance education quality. Among them were the Mastery in Learning Project and the NEA Learning Laboratories. The primary focus of Mastery in Learning was to enhance learning through school-based reform of teaching and curriculum, emphasizing the importance of making critical decisions as close to the classroom as possible regarding the education of children. The Learning Laboratories project, launched 3 years later, was dedicated to creating a network of school districts engaged in "learning" to improve learning for students and educators. It could be said that the project began to focus on the building of learning communities.

The KEYS initiative built on the NEA's long-standing tradition of innovation. KEYS was NEA's first attempt to quantify dimensions of *school quality* and focus on student achievement. The KEYS initiative demonstrates one of many appropriate roles for teacher unions: achieving conditions in schools that enable school systems and educators to make good decisions in a knowledge-oriented society.

THE RESEARCH-BASED FOUNDATION FOR KEYS

The NEA research that developed the KEYS initiative began with an analysis of recent research on schools as professional communities and other components of effective schools. Key findings provided the building blocks for KEYS, and these are consistent with the findings of more recent research summarized in this book. Of particular importance to the development of KEYS was evidence from several studies of school change indicating that unless school improvement efforts truly touch the minds and hearts of teachers and become manifest in their behavior and attitudes, the ultimate aims of school reform will go unmet. On average, teachers have been teaching 17 years, working in their current districts for almost 14 years, and serving in their current buildings for 10 years. Contrast this to the average stay of a superintendent (3 years) or even a principal (3 to 5 years), and it becomes apparent that in a long-term process like creating a quality school, teachers must play a central role.

NEA RESEARCH SUPPORTING THE KEYS INITIATIVE

Although the development of the KEYS initiative is based on a strong foundation of research by scholars, the NEA has conducted its own research examining the relationship between organizational characteristics of schools and student learning. This research led to the development of the KEYS instrument and provides evidence that the indicators of school quality that are the focus of the KEYS assessment instrument are predictors of high student achievement. The essential findings from this research are the following:

- Quality schools are multidimensional environments, characterized by many factors that, in total, make them quality teaching and learning environments. There is no one aspect that should be the focus of policymakers in attempting to raise the quality of schools or student achievement. Although not every characteristic contributes directly to student achievement, there are indirect effects, as these characteristics are interrelated.
- Student achievement is high when school goals, mission, and objectives are clear, explicit, and continuously developed and shared with all concerned.
- Student achievement is higher in schools in which there is a shared understanding about achievable student outcomes and there is parent and school employee commitment to long-range, continuous improvement.
- Student achievement is high when central and building administration are committed to long-term, continuous improvement.

- Student achievement is higher in schools that exhibit the belief that all students can achieve under the right conditions.
- Student achievement is higher in schools that understand and use assessment of students on a regular basis and use a variety of assessment tools.
- High-performing public schools are places in which teachers are involved in choosing teaching materials and resources.
- High-performing schools are places in which all school employees, students, parents, and the community are involved in seeking, identifying, and eliminating barriers to improvement and academic success.
- High-achieving schools are places in which employee training is based on analysis of student performance and is used to improve job performance. Emphasis is placed on developing teamwork and on improving teaching techniques.
- In high-performing schools, continuing evaluation is focused primarily on the system, not on individuals, and the overall quality of the school is rated.
- In high-achieving schools, two-way, nonthreatening communication is constantly occurring. Emphasis is placed on developing a climate for continual improvement.
- In high-achieving schools, there is concern for the appropriate and cautious use of standardized tests. Multiple forms of assessment are used to identify needs for and strategies of improvement.

In short, an impressive amount of important theory, research, and practice leads one to the conclusion that the organizational characteristics of schools affect the conditions of teaching and learning and, in turn, these conditions significantly influence student achievement.

GUIDELINES FOR SCHOOL IMPROVEMENT

Research by the NEA and others provides several guidelines for actions that provide direction for schools that wish to increase their capacity for continuous improvement:

- Strive for shared understanding about achievable education outcomes. Work collaboratively to define a purpose and goals and to determine quantifiable outcomes along with the best methods, strategies, and actions to achieve those outcomes.
- Involve the total learning community—teachers, education support personnel, administrators, parents, students, and community and business organizations—in quality improvement planning and problem solving the implementation of necessary changes.
- Engage in continuous, ongoing assessment of teaching and learning and base decision making on this assessment. Establish accountability at all levels to motivate and give direction to improvement.
- Emphasize personal and professional learning and development. Create a learning environment for the organization. Establish regular, needs-specific staff development focused on solving problems related to student needs.
- Professional development for teachers and administrators should be an integral part of any plan to decentralize management practices. As much as possible, this training should be designed to meet the needs of students in individual schools.
- Don't play the quality game unless you are willing to keep score. Be ready to show quantifiable "before and after" data on your change efforts. Focus on assessing the system and its programs.
- Build two-way, nonthreatening communication channels among all stakeholders.
- Frequently clarify the expectations, purpose, and progress related to school improvement for the entire learning community.
- Ensure that materials and social support for continuous improvement are provided.

CONCLUSION

Many of those who would reform our schools continue to seek prescriptive, simple, and inexpensive recipes for what works in schools. All too often, they neglect vital structural and cultural characteristics of schools that affect student outcomes. The chapters in this book show that any comprehensive approach to educational improvement needs to address the challenges involved in creating and sustaining conditions in schools that fundamentally influence the quality of teaching and thereby the opportunities students have to achieve at high levels.

—Donald L. Rollie
Quality Schools, Research, and Policy
National Education Association

About the Editors

Willis D. Hawley is Professor Emeritus of Education and Public Policy at the University of Maryland and Scholar in Residence at the American Association of School Administrators. From 1997 to 1999, he was Executive Director of the National Partnership for Excellence and Accountability in Teaching. From 1993 to 1998, he served as Dean of the College of Education at the University of Maryland. From 1980 to 1993, he was Professor of Education and Political Science at Vanderbilt University. He served as Dean of Peabody College at Vanderbilt from 1980 to 1989 and then as Director of the Center for Education and Human Development Policy at Vanderbilt Institute for Public Policy Studies. He received his PhD in political science, with distinction, from the University of California, Berkeley, in 1970. He taught at Yale and Duke Universities before going to Vanderbilt.

He has published numerous articles, book chapters and software dealing with school reform, urban politics, political learning, organizational change, school desegregation, educational policy, teacher education and professional development, policies affecting teaching quality, the costs and benefits of racially and ethnically diverse schools, and school restructuring and effectiveness.

Hawley has served on the boards of several scholarly and professional publications and as consultant to numerous public agencies, as well as many state and local governments, professional associations, and foundations. From 1977 to 1978, he served as Director of Education Studies, President's Reorganization Project, Executive Office of the President of the United States. He also organized and directed The Common Destiny Alliance, a coalition of national organizations and scholars interested in improving intergroup relations.

Donald L. Rollie. Since the publication of the first edition of *The Keys to Effective Schools* (2002), Don Rollie has passed away. Don was an important force for the National Education Association's (NEA) work devoted to creating higher-quality schools. He regularly asked his colleagues the "To what end?" question: "So what difference will this make for student achievement?" His long and distinguished career spanned every level: local, state, and national. During the course of that career, he served as the Executive Director for two state associations and was Manager of the Quality Schools, Research, and Policy unit at NEA. Don believed in the NEA/KEYS Initiative as the path by which all schools could practice "continuous improvement." Don also believed that school staffs need both knowledge and license to make the decisions by which all students attain high achievement. Don's humor and humanity will be missed by his colleagues at NEA and by all of the people he touched.

About the Contributors

Patricia A. Alexander is Professor and Distinguished Scholar-Teacher in the Department of Human Development at the University of Maryland. She has held leadership positions in the American Psychological Association (APA) and the American Educational Research Association, is a Fellow of the APA, and was a Spencer Fellow of the National Academy of Education. Since receiving her PhD from the University of Maryland, in 1981, she has published more than 170 articles, books, or chapters in the area of learning and instruction and has also presented more than 160 papers or invited addresses at national and international conferences. Her research addresses topics such as learning; individual differences; and the interaction of knowledge, interest, and strategic processing. Her recent publications have focused on the nature of academic development, particularly as it relates to domain-specific knowledge and to learning from text. Currently, she serves as the editor of *Contemporary Educational Psychology* and *Instructional Science* and sits on editorial boards for numerous journals, including *Reading Research Quarterly, Journal of Educational Psychology, Educational Psychologist, American Educational Research Journal,* and *Journal of Literacy Research.*

Alexander has received various national, university, and college awards for teaching. Recently, she was named one of the 10 most productive scholars in educational psychology and was the 2001 recipient of the Oscar S. Causey Award for outstanding contributions to literacy research from the National Reading Conference. She is also the 2006 recipient of the E. L. Thorndike Award for

Career Achievement in Educational Psychology from APA Division 15.

Eva L. Baker is Distinguished Professor of Education, UCLA Graduate School of Education & Information Studies. She is codirector of the National Center for Research on Evaluation, Standards, and Student Testing (CRESST) and director of the Center for the Study of Evaluation (CSE). She teaches classes in assessment policy and design and in technology. Her research centers on the integration of measurement, training, and accountability systems. She has studied the uses of technology-based measures of complex performance in experimental and large-scale environments for both military and public education and training. She was chair of the Board on Testing and Assessment of the National Research Council and a cochair of the Joint Committee on the revision of the *Standards for Educational and Psychological Testing* (published in 1999), sponsored by the American Educational Research Association (AERA), the American Psychological Association (APA), and the National Council on Measurement in Education. She has held elected office in the APA and the AERA. She is a Fellow in APA and the Association for Psychological Science. She is president-elect of the AERA and is a Certified Performance Technologist.

James A. Banks is Russell F. Stark University Professor and Director of the Center for Multicultural Education at the University of Washington, Seattle. His books include *Educating Citizens in a Multicultural Society; Cultural Diversity and Education: Foundations, Curriculum and Teaching; Diversity and Citizenship Education: Global Perspectives;* and *Race, Culture, and Education: The Selected Works of James A. Banks.* He is a past president of the American Educational Research Association (AERA) and the National Council for the Social Studies (NCSS). He is also a member of the National Academy of Education and holds honorary Doctorates of Humane Letters from four universities. He is a Spencer Fellow at the Center for Advanced Study in the Behavioral Sciences at Stanford for the 2005–2006 academic year.

Peter Cookson is Dean of the Graduate School and Professor of Educational Administration at Lewis and Clark College, in Portland, Oregon. He has been president of Teachers College Innovations at Columbia University. He has taught in public and private schools. His research and numerous publications deal with applications of educational technology, educational policy, reform, and school choice.

Lorna M. Earl, PhD, is Director, Aporia Consulting, Ltd., and a recently retired Associate Professor in the Theory and Policy Studies Department and Head of the International Centre for Educational Change at OISE/UT. Her career has spanned research, policy, and practice in school districts, provincial government, and academe. After 25 years as a Research Officer and Research Director in school districts, she was the first Director of Assessment for the Ontario Education Quality and Accountability Office. From there, she moved to OISE/UT. She is a teacher and a researcher with a background in psychology and education and a doctorate in epidemiology and biostatistics. She has worked for more than 20 years in schools and on school boards and, as a leader in the field of assessment and evaluation, has been involved in consultation, research, and staff development with teachers' organizations, ministries of education, school boards, and charitable foundations in Canada, England, Australia, Europe, and the United States.

Throughout her career, Earl has concentrated her efforts on policy and program evaluations, as a vehicle to enhance learning for pupils and for organizations. She has done extensive work in the areas of literacy and the middle years but has concentrated her efforts on issues related to evaluation of large-scale reform and assessment (large-scale and classroom) in many venues around the world. Some of her recent publications are *Leading in a Data Rich World: Harnessing Data for School Improvement; Large-Scale Reform: Life Cycles and Implications for Sustainability; The National Literacy and Numeracy Strategies in England: Building an Infrastructure for Sustainable Change; Changing Secondary Schools Is Hard;* and *Leadership for Large-Scale Reform.*

Richard F. Elmore is Gregory R. Anrig Professor of Educational Leadership at Harvard University and a Director of the Consortium for Policy Research in Education. His research focuses on the effects of federal, state, and local policy on accountability and the capacity of schools to deliver high-quality instruction. He has also conducted research on school choice, school restructuring, and how changes in teaching and learning affect school organizations. He has served as an advisor to numerous agencies at local, state, and federal levels of government.

Michael Fullan is the former Dean of the Ontario Institute for Studies in Education of the University of Toronto. Recognized as an international authority on educational reform, he is engaged in training, consulting, and evaluating change projects around the world. His ideas for managing change are used in many countries, and his books have been published in many languages. He led the evaluation team that conducted the 4-year assessment of the National Literacy and Numeracy Strategy in England, from 1998–2003. In April 2004, he was appointed Special Advisor to the Premier and Minister of Education in Ontario. His widely acclaimed books include the *What's Worth Fighting For* trilogy (with Andy Hargreaves); the *Change Forces* trilogy; *The New Meaning of Educational Change*, third edition; *Leading in a Culture of Change* (awarded the 2002 Book of the Year Award by the National Staff Development Council); *The Moral Imperative of School Leadership;* and *Leadership and Sustainability: System Thinkers in Action.*

Geneva Gay is Professor of Education at the University of Washington-Seattle, where she teaches multicultural education and general curriculum theory. She is the recipient of the Distinguished Scholar Award, presented by the Committee on the Role and Status of Minorities in Educational Research and Development of the American Educational Research Association; the first Multicultural Educator Award, presented by the National Association of Multicultural Education; and the 2004 W. E. B. DuBois Distinguished Lecturer Award, presented by the Special Interest Group on Research Focus on Black Education of the American Educational Research Association. She is nationally and internationally known for her scholarship in multicultural education, particularly as it relates to curriculum design, staff development, classroom instruction, and intersections of culture, race, ethnicity, teaching, and learning. Her writings include numerous articles and book chapters. She was coeditor of *Expressively Black: The Cultural Basis of Ethnic Identity* (Praeger, 1987); author of *At the Essence of Learning: Multicultural Education* (Kappa Delta Pi, 1994) and *Culturally Responsive Teaching: Theory, Practice, & Research* (Teachers College Press, 2000); and editor of *Becoming Multicultural Educators: Personal*

Journey Toward Professional Agency (Jossey-Bass, 2003). *Culturally Responsive Teaching* received the 2001 Outstanding Writing Award from the American Association of Colleges for Teacher Education (AACTE). She also is a member of the authorship team of the Scott Foresman New Elementary Social Studies Series. Her professional service includes membership on several national editorial review and advisory boards. International consultations on multicultural education have taken her to Canada, Brazil, Taiwan, Finland, Japan, England, Scotland, and Australia.

Jacqueline Jordan Irvine is Professor of Urban Education Emeritus at Emory University. Her research deals with the cultural context of teaching and learning and professional development of urban teachers. She is the founding Director of the Center for Urban Learning/Teaching and Urban Research in Education and Schools, which has been recognized by the U.S. Department of Education as a model of effective professional development practice, and she is currently codirector of the Southern Consortium for Educational Research in Urban Schools. Her widely cited books include *Black Students and School Failure, Growing Up African American in Catholic Schools, Culturally Responsive Teaching, Critical Knowledge for Diverse Learners,* and *Educating Teachers for Diversity: Seeing with a Critical Eye.* She has received numerous awards for her professional contributions, including recognition by the American Association of Colleges of Teacher Education; the Association for Supervision, Curriculum, and Development; and the American Educational Research Association.

Kenneth Leithwood is Professor of Educational Administration and Director of the Centre for Leadership Development at the University of Toronto (OISE). Leithwood's interests include understanding the consequences of alternative visions of leadership, the cognitive and emotional processes of leaders, leadership development, organizational leadership, and school reform. His most recent studies deal with leadership in highly accountable policy contexts and in schools serving diverse populations. He is the senior editor of the International Handbook on Educational Leadership and Administration. Some of his other recent books include *Understanding Schools as Intelligent Systems; Changing Leadership for Changing Times; Organizational Learning in Schools* (with Karen Seashore Louis); *Expert Problem Solving: Evidence*

From School and District Leaders; and *Making Schools Smarter.* He is responsible for the design and implementation of school leadership development programs at the University of Toronto (OISE) and consults with many other leadership development agencies as well.

Ann Lieberman is Emeritus Professor from Teachers College, Columbia University. She is now Senior Scholar at the Carnegie Foundation for the Advancement of Teaching and Visiting Professor at Stanford University. She was president of the American Educational Research Association (AERA) in 1992. She is widely known for her work in the areas of teacher leadership and development, collaborative research, networks and school-university partnerships, and, increasingly, the problems and prospects of educational change.

Judith Warren Little is Professor at the Graduate School of Education, University of California, Berkeley. Her research focuses on teachers' work and careers, the contexts of teaching, and policies and practices of professional development. In her current research, she is investigating how teachers' interactions with one another in ordinary workplace settings and in more formal professional development contexts supply resources for teacher learning and the improvement of practice.

Lynne Miller is Professor of Educational Leadership and Coexecutive Director of the Southern Maine Partnership at the University of Southern Maine (USM), where she holds the Russell Chair in Philosophy and Education. Before joining the USM faculty in 1987, she held a variety of teaching and administrative positions in public schools in Pennsylvania and Indiana. In addition, she served as Assistant Professor of Education at the University of Massachusetts, Amherst, where she was the liaison to the Worcester Teacher Corps and to the Boston desegregation effort. As a scholar, she has she written widely in the fields of professional learning and school reform; most recently, she completed two books with Ann Lieberman, *Teachers Caught in the Action* (Teachers College Press, 2001) and *Teacher Leadership* (Jossey-Bass, 2004). She is currently engaged in connecting high school and college faculty in efforts to prepare more students for success in higher education.

P. Karen Murphy is Associate Professor of Educational and School Psychology and Special Education at Pennsylvania State University. She is interested in the processes underpinning students' learning and how cognition and motivation impact these processes. Her current research projects pertain to the impact of students' and teachers' knowledge, beliefs, and interest on learning; student learning in particular domains (e.g., mathematics); the impact of technology in classroom learning; and the linking of philosophy and psychology in educational psychology. Murphy's research has been recognized as exemplary by the American Psychological Association and the International Reading Association.

Fred M. Newmann, Emeritus Professor of Curriculum and Instruction, University of Wisconsin–Madison, directed the National Center on Effective Secondary Schools and the Center on Organization and Restructuring of Schools. With 30 years' experience in school reform research, curriculum development, and teacher education, he contributed new curriculum in the analysis of public controversy and community-based learning. His research has addressed higher-order thinking in social studies, student engagement in secondary schools, authentic achievement and assessment, and professional development to build capacity in low-income schools.

Sonia Nieto, a researcher, teacher, lecturer, and writer, is Professor Emerita of Language, Literacy, and Culture in the School of Education, University of Massachusetts, Amherst. She has taught students at all levels, from elementary grades through graduate school, most recently preparing teachers and teacher educators. Her research focuses on multicultural education and on the education of Latinos, immigrants, and students of diverse cultural and linguistic backgrounds. Her books include *Affirming Diversity: The Sociopolitical Context of Multicultural Education* (fourth edition, 2004); *What Keeps Teachers Going?* (2003); and two edited volumes, *Puerto Rican Students in U.S. Schools* (2000) and *Why We Teach* (2005), among others. She has also published dozens of book chapters and articles in journals, such as *Educational Leadership, Harvard Educational Review, Multicultural Education,* and *Theory Into Practice.* She serves on several national advisory boards that focus on educational equity and social justice and has received many awards for scholarship, advocacy, and activism, including two honorary doctorates, one in Humane Letters from Lesley University in Cambridge, Massachusetts (1999), and the other in Intercultural Relations from Bridgewater State College, Massachusetts (2004). She was an Annenberg Institute Senior Fellow from 1998 to 2000 and was awarded a monthlong residency at the Bellagio Center, in Italy, in 2000.

Janet Ward Schofield is Professor of Psychology and Senior Scientist at the Learning Research and Development Center at the University of Pittsburgh. She has also served on the faculty of Spellman College and as a visiting scholar at the Social Science Research Center in Berlin. She earned a BA magna cum laude at Harvard University, where she was elected to Phi Beta Kappa, and received her PhD from Harvard in 1972. She is a social psychologist whose research has focused on social and technological change in school settings. She has published more than 90 papers on topics ranging from school desegregation to peer relations in diverse school environments to computer use in schools. She has also authored or coauthored four books, including *Black and White in School: Trust, Tension, or Tolerance?* which was awarded the Society for the Psychological Study of Social Issues–Gordon Allport Intergroup Relations Prize. She was elected to serve as a member of the American Psychological Association's governing body, the Council of Representatives. A fellow of both the American Psychological Association (APA) and the Association for Psychological Science (APS), she has served as a consultant to school districts, to foundations, and to policymakers at the local, state, and national levels, as well as on boards and committees at the National Academy of Sciences.

Walter G. Stephan is Emeritus Professor of Psychology at New Mexico State University. His publications include *Intergroup Relations* (with Cookie Stephan), *Improving Intergroup Relations* (with Cookie Stephan), and *Education Programs for Improving Intergroup Relations* (with Paul Vogt). His lifelong interest in this and related topics continues.

Gary Sykes is Professor in the Departments of Educational Administration and Teacher Education, Michigan State University, where he studies educational policy issues related to teachers and teaching, teacher education, school choice, and school districts. Recent books include *Choosing Choice* (with David Plank) and *Teaching as the Learning Profession* (with Linda Darling-Hammond).

Linda Valli is Associate Professor of Education in the Department of Curriculum and Instruction at the University of Maryland, College Park. She has also been a junior and senior high school teacher, a director of teacher education, and an associate dean. Her research interests include teacher preparation, professional development, school improvement, and cultural diversity. She has published numerous book chapters as well as articles in journals, such as *Teaching and Teacher Education*, *Journal of Teacher Education*, and *Action in Teacher Education*, and has authored or edited three books, including *Reflective Teacher Education: Cases and Critiques*.

CHAPTER ONE

Educational Reform as Continuous Improvement

Michael Fullan

T he chapters in this book are relevant to virtually any comprehensive effort aimed at creating the conditions in schools
that promote continuous improvement. The book was initially
prepared to serve as a resource document for the National
Education Association's (NEA, 1997) KEYS project. KEYS is an
acronym for "Keys to Excellence in Your Schools." Through
reviews of research and in consultation with prominent scholars,
NEA has identified numerous factors essential to effective schools
and has developed a survey instrument designed to gather data on
these items, and, in turn, to feed back the data to participating
schools. The items cluster into six main domains:

1. Knowledge of teaching and learning

2. Shared understanding and commitment to high goals

3. Open communication and collaborative problem solving

4. Continuous assessment for teaching and learning

5. Personal and professional learning

6. Resources to support teaching and learning

The KEYS project is one example of the larger effort to transform the teaching profession. The National Commission on Teaching and America's Future (NCTAF, 1996) documented the problem as follows:

Low expectations for student performance

Unenforced standards for teachers

Major flaws in teacher preparation

Painfully slipshod teacher recruitment

Inadequate induction for beginning teachers

Lack of professional development and rewards for knowledge and skill

Schools structured for failure rather than success (p. 24)

This is not the first time that the reform of schools has brought teaching to the forefront (Fullan, Galluzzo, Morris, & Watson, 1998). Such a focus on teaching needs to start with the recruitment and professional development of effective and committed teachers. As we have argued in our study, *The Rise and Stall of Teacher Education Reform* (Fullan et al., 1998), a comprehensive sustained initiative should incorporate the following:

- A stronger knowledge base for teaching and teacher education
- Plans for attracting able, diverse, and committed students to the career of teaching
- Redesigning of teacher preparation programs field of practice so that the links to both arts and sciences and to the field of practice are strengthened
- Reform in the working conditions of schools
- Development and monitoring of external standards for progress as well as for teacher development

- Candidates and teachers on the job
- A rigorous and dynamic research enterprise focusing on teaching, teacher education, and assessment and monitoring of strategies (p. 58)

We have also said that teachers, ranging from the individual teacher in the classroom to the most visible union leader, must "help to recreate the profession." Hargreaves and I concluded in *What's Worth Fighting for Out There* (1998) that the teaching profession has not yet come of age and that the next decade, furthermore,

> will be a defining era for the teaching profession. Will it become a stronger learning profession? Will it become a force for societal change and social practice? Can it develop its own visions of and commitments to educational and social change, instead of simply vetoing and reacting to the change agendas of others? (p. 103)

More recently, the National Academy of Education systematically mapped out a comprehensive curriculum for preparing teachers for a changing world (Darling-Hammond & Bransford, 2005; National Academy of Education, 2005). The KEYS initiative and the chapters in this book are written in the spirit of changing the conditions under which teachers work, so that continuous improvement is built into the culture of the school and the infrastructure that supports it.

The KEYS project, with its survey instrument, feedback, action planning, and online professional development in the schools and districts participating in the program, is engaged in very difficult work. The ultimate goal is to mobilize thousands of schools and districts in transforming professional development and organizational learning. The KEYS project by itself will not accomplish such fundamental reform. It can, however, have a significant impact by connecting the powerful concepts in the KEYS instrument with the content priorities embedded in the new teaching and learning curricula being developed across the nation; these are premised on an understanding that systematic, evidence-driven professional development, a focus on teaching and learning, the development of learning schools and school districts, and success for all students are closely intertwined.

What we need, then, is to consolidate the knowledge base about what makes for continuous improvement and, correspondingly, to mobilize sets of actions among educators, in partnership with others, to engage in reform initiatives that are based on this knowledge base.

The chapters in the book align with the themes in the KEYS project as follows:

Knowledge of teaching and learning: P. Karen Murphy and Patricia A. Alexander (Chapter 2)

Shared understanding and commitment: Fred M. Newmann (Chapter 3)

Communication and problem solving: Judith Warren Little (Chapter 4)

Assessment for teaching and learning: Eva L. Baker (Chapter 5); Lorna M. Earl (Chapter 6)

Personal and professional learning: Ann Lieberman and Lynne Miller (Chapter 7); Willis D. Hawley and Linda Valli (Chapter 8)

Supportive requirements: Kenneth Leithwood (Chapter 9); Willis D. Hawley and Gary Sykes (Chapter 10); James A. Banks, Peter Cookson, Geneva Gay, Willis D. Hawley, Jacqueline Jordan Irvine, Sonia Nieto, Janet Ward Schofield, and Walter G. Stephan (Chapter 11); Richard F. Elmore (Chapter 12)

The assumption of KEYS is that schools and districts that focus on the six clusters—and do so in a way that closely connects these themes to particular curriculum priorities—will increase their capacity to achieve coherence and focus and will affect learning for all students within the system.

In this introductory chapter, first, I start with the core argument that professional development, pedagogical improvement, and student learning need to be tightly interwoven for schools to be effective. The chapters by Newmann, Little, Baker, and Earl form the basis of this conclusion. Murphy and Alexander summarize research that identifies essential knowledge about student learning.

Second, I reinforce the argument by examining personal and professional learning. These ideas are founded on the chapters by Valli and Hawley, and Lieberman and Miller.

Third, you can't have learning organizations without having schools and districts as learning systems and without having teaching as a learning profession. The last section focuses on districts as learning systems and on teaching as a profession. Elmore, Leithwood, Hawley and Sykes, and Banks et al. provide the conditions and requirements necessary for continuous learning to be embedded.

DEEP UNDERSTANDING OF HOW PEOPLE LEARN

The fundamental goal of school improvement is, of course, improved student learning, especially raising the bar and closing the gap so that all students can learn at high levels. Quality teaching is the key determinant of student learning. In the last several years, research on learning has significantly altered traditional understanding of how people learn, and this research is changing the definition of high-quality teaching. Murphy and Alexander were commissioned by the American Psychological Association to synthesize and summarize research on learning and to identify implications of this research for how we think about teaching. Their chapter in this book provides a succinct but authoritative review of research on teaching and learning that is relevant to the development of strategies to restructure schools as learning organizations for both students and teachers. Darling-Hammond and Bransford (2005) have more recently provided a comprehensive knowledge base for what teachers will need to know and do, individually and collectively, in the 21st century, including the following: knowledge of theories of learning; developmentally appropriate teaching to fit the individual needs of students; knowledge of curriculum and subject matter; assessment; classroom management; and, equally important, how teachers develop and learn both in preservice and once they enter the profession.

PROFESSIONAL COMMUNITY, PEDAGOGICAL IMPROVEMENT, AND STUDENT LEARNING

Newmann's chapter makes the case, strongly backed up by research he conducted with his colleagues, that three core

elements must come together in a highly interactive and systematic way if a school is to become effective. First, there must be a
professional learning community in which teachers and others
develop (as a result of continuous interaction) shared understanding and commitment to achieve high-level outcomes for all
students. Second, this joint work must focus on critically assessing
and adopting new instructional practices that are best suited for
accomplishing high-level outcomes for all students. Third, in turn,
shared systematic use of data for learning, so that changes in
teaching are keyed to what students are learning or not learning,
is crucial for success. In brief, these three factors—professional
community, instructional practice, and assessment of student
work—feed on each other to create new synergies tantamount to
continuous improvement.

Little's chapter establishes the theoretical underpinnings
relative to Newmann's findings on shared understanding. Little
indicates why professional development, communication, and collaboration must go together and shows how this cluster affects the
"culture" of schools. Hargreaves and I have called this the need to
reculture school professional relationships away from isolating,
balkanized, and superficial collegiality toward strong forms of
collaboration (Fullan & Hargreaves, 1996; Hargreaves & Fullan,
1998). Similarly, Little talks about three supporting conditions for
culture building: (1) shared interests and shared responsibility,
(2) opportunity to interact and learn, and (3) resources. Little
concludes with a point that we will return to in the last section,
that collaboration does not mean agreement and does not mean
absence of conflict. As I shall argue later, the more people collaborate, the more they have to disagree about.

Until recently, student assessment was not carefully examined
in the work on collaborative cultures. It has now become clear, as
the chapters by Baker and Earl demonstrate, that assessment of
student work and corresponding planning for improvement are
essential for school effectiveness. In a recent compendium, professional learning communities and assessment for learning have
been closely linked, to demonstrate how students benefit (DuFour,
Eaker, & DuFour, 2005).

Baker takes up the issue of improving the learning of students
who are tested by involving students in reflecting on their work
and by engaging teachers in altering their teaching in order to
help students reach academic goals. Earl extends these ideas by

claiming that "classroom assessment has been shown to be one of the most powerful levers for enhancing student learning." Earl concludes,

> In the long run, teachers develop agreement about the nature and quality of their assessment and of the students' work. By sharing the decisions about how to assess, there are fewer discrepancies in student assessment standards and procedures between grades and/or classes; they develop a deeper understanding of curriculum and of individual students; and they engage in the intense discussions about standards and evidence that lead to a shared understanding of expectations for students, more refined language about children and learning, and consistent procedures for making and communicating judgments.

As Hargreaves and I have also said, teachers must become "assessment literate" for two reasons (Hargreaves & Fullan, 1998). One is that external assessment and accountability are here to stay. The "out there" is now "in here," and educators need to "move toward the danger" and learn to hold their own in the politically contentious arena of debating how well students are doing. Second, becoming assessment literate is absolutely essential for examining and improving one's own teaching practices in order to get better results. Examining student work with other teachers is a powerful strategy for enhancing teaching and learning. Thus, professional learning community, instructional practices, and student learning go hand in hand.

PERSONAL AND PROFESSIONAL LEARNING

In their chapter, Valli and Hawley consolidate learning about professional development in 10 basic principles or "essentials" of effective teacher learning:

1. Professional development should be based on collaborative analyses of the differences between (a) actual student performance and (b) goals and standards for student learning.

2. Professional development should be primarily school based and built into the day-to-day work of teaching.

3. Professional development should involve teachers in the identification of what they need to learn and in the development of the learning experiences in which they will be involved.

4. The content should reflect the best research on the given topic (e.g., how to enhance the literacy of adolescents).

5. The content of professional development should focus on what students are to learn and how to address the different problems students may have in learning that material.

6. Professional development should provide experiential opportunities to gain an understanding of and reflect on the research and theory underlying the knowledge and skills being learned.

7. The way teacher learning is facilitated should mirror the instructional approaches they are expected to master and allow teachers to experience the consequences of newly learned capabilities.

8. Professional development should be continuous and ongoing, involving follow-up and support for further learning, including support from sources external to the school that can provide necessary resources and new perspectives.

9. Professional development should be connected to a comprehensive change process focused on specific goals for improving student learning.

10. Evaluation of professional development should incorporate multiple sources of information on (a) outcomes for students and (b) instruction and other processes that are involved in implementing the lessons learned.

Similarly, in their chapter, Lieberman and Miller conclude that professional development must be transformed to encompass (a) teacher career development, (b) organizing schools to support ongoing learning communities, and (c) education reform networks that support teacher learning. Thus, personal learning, organizational (school-based) learning, and broader education reform networks (subject matter collaborative, school-university partnerships, and other reform networks) are all playing roles in building new learning communities and reshaping professional development.

THE SCHOOL AND DISTRICT AS LEARNING ORGANIZATIONS

A great deal of lip service is given to the concept of the *learning organization*, but what does it really mean in concrete terms? At the general level, the concept means continually acquiring new knowledge, skills, and understanding to improve one's actions and results. Thus, the previous sections, in which professional development, collaboration, pedagogical improvement, and student learning interact over time, provide an example of organizational learning at the school level.

Elmore raises the question of how entire school districts—large sets of schools—can become learning systems. His discussion is founded on the ideas in the chapters reviewed so far. As he puts it,

> The single most persistent problem of educational reform in the United States is the failure of reforms to alter the fundamental conditions of teaching and learning for students and teachers in schools in anything other than a small-scale and idiosyncratic way.

The challenge is to do for entire school districts what Newmann and our other authors have done for individual schools, namely, establish systemwide frameworks of accountability, support teachers and others in analyzing their instructional practices together in light of what students are learning, and establish processes of continuous learning within and across schools. This is something that has not normally happened.

There are however, several examples in the literature of successful attempts at turning school districts into learning organizations, including Elmore's (1996) study of District #2 in New York

City; the four urban districts in the Rockefeller Foundation's professional development infrastructure initiative (Fullan, Watson, & Kilcher, 1997); the Durham School District in Ontario, Canada (Fullan, Alberts, Lieberman, & Zywine, 1996); and the York Region school district, also in Ontario (Sharratt & Fullan, in press). Only recently has districtwide improvement been the focus of reform strategies and corresponding research; so much more needs to be done in this domain.

Both Elmore's and Leithwood's chapters in this volume are particularly relevant to the role of districts in leading and supporting systemwide reform. Elmore reiterates his long-standing criticism that most education reforms do not get at the instructional core of teaching and therefore are superficial in their affects. He shows that No Child Left Behind legislation puts additional direct pressure on large-scale reform but does not result in the instructional focus that would be necessary for reform to occur within classrooms. His argument for internal accountability (within schools) as a necessary condition for external accountability to be effective is compelling.

For internal accountability to occur, new capacities will be required, a subject that Leithwood as well as Hawley and Sykes tackle in their chapters. Leithwood describes several sets of conditions that must be met: focusing on workload complexity, student grouping, school conditions, and parent and community relationships. The value of the Elmore and Leithwood chapters is that they add specificity to the agenda and therefore enable us to concentrate on the detailed conditions for improving schools.

Finally, Hawley and Sykes as well as Banks and his colleagues provide essential perspectives that cut across the whole process of reform. Hawley and Sykes argue that continuous improvement involves four interrelated sets of actions: (1) developing consensus on goals, standards, and assessment; (2) continuously assessing student performance; (3) collaborative, evidence-based problem solving; and (4) implementation of promising practices. Banks et al. reinforce the perspective on reform by showing how continuous improvement must serve the needs of a multicultural society. Their 12 principles make a compelling case and provide a powerful framework for equity-based action and corresponding results.

CONCLUSION

In summary, there are new developments in the field of educational reform that are based on three interrelated forces. One is the knowledge base, which is becoming more and more precise in identifying the characteristics that make for continuous improvement in schools and school systems. The second is the moral imperative of raising the bar and closing the gap for all students, not just the 50% who are now served by our school systems. The third related force is the increasing commitment to achieve reform on a larger scale. In the next few years, we expect to see more and more large-scale reform initiatives build on this knowledge base. Two examples that I have been involved in are (1) the attempt to achieve *Breakthrough* results (for example, 90%-plus success in literacy), using our knowledge base to design more powerful systems of reform (Fullan, Hill, & Crevola, 2006), and (2) going beyond *Turnaround Leadership* to achieve deep, equitable reform outcomes (Fullan, in press). In the meantime, the chapters in this book provide a plethora of good ideas for pressing for greater reform results in the immediate future.

REFERENCES

Darling-Hammond, L., & Bransford, J. (2005). *Preparing teachers for a changing world.* San Francisco: Jossey-Bass.

DuFour, R., Eaker, R., & DuFour, R. (2005). *On common ground.* Bloomington, IN: National Education Service.

Elmore, R. (1996). *Staff development and instructional improvement in Community School District #2, New York City.* Cambridge, MA: Consortium for Policy Research in Education, Harvard University.

Fullan, M. (in press). *Turnaround leadership.* San Francisco: Jossey-Bass.

Fullan, M., Alberts, B., Lieberman, A., & Zywine, J. (1996). *Report of Country Expert Commission Canada/United States of America.* Carl Bertelsmann Prize.

Fullan, M., Galluzzo, G., Morris, P., & Watson, N. (1998). *The rise and stall of teacher education reform.* Washington, DC: American Association of Colleges for Teacher Education.

Fullan, M., & Hargreaves, A. (1996). *What's worth fighting for in your school . . .* New York: Teachers College Press.

Fullan, M., Hill, P., & Crevola, C. (2006). *Breakthrough*. Thousand Oaks, CA: Corwin Press.

Fullan, M., Watson, N., & Kilcher, A. (1997). *Building infrastructures for professional development*. New York: Rockefeller Foundation.

Hargreaves, A., & Fullan, M. (1998). *What's worth fighting for out there*. New York: Teachers College Press.

National Academy of Education. (2005). *A good teacher in every classroom*. Washington, DC: Author.

National Commission on Teaching and America's Future. (1996). *What matters most: Teaching for America's future*. Washington, DC: Author.

National Education Association. (1997). *KEYS project: Study and implementation of quality conditions of teaching and learning*. Washington, DC: Author.

Sharratt, L., & Fullan, M. (in press). The school district that did the right things right. *Journal of School Leadership*.

CHAPTER TWO

Contextualizing Learner-Centered Principles for Teachers and Teaching

P. Karen Murphy and Patricia A. Alexander

It seems that each new decade comes with its own set of educational reform initiatives. These initiatives arise from internal sources (e.g., teachers or school administrators) as well as external constituents (e.g., parents and policymakers). In just the latter half of the 20th century, for example, reform efforts produced alternative conceptualizations of teachers as knowledge transmitters, scientists, and technicians and of teaching as scaffolding, apprenticing, and a persuasive practice (e.g., Murphy & Mason, in press; Palincsar & Brown, 1984; Rogoff, 1990). Such initiatives serve to capture the prevailing philosophical orientations toward teaching, as well as signal developing trends in research and practices of the time. More often then not, however, these initiatives are short-lived. As a result, very few teaching or learning initiatives are around long enough to produce broad and durable outcomes (Alexander, Murphy, & Woods, 1996).

Within the last 25 years, there have been several significant calls for educational reform, most manifesting in the form of federal legislation. The first such call for educational reform was *A Nation at Risk*, the report of the National Commission on Excellence in Education, published in 1983, by the U.S. Department of Education. Six years later, this report was followed by a summit meeting of the nation's governors and President George H. W. Bush. The outcomes of this summit highlighted national concerns about education and what would be needed to improve the current educational system, in the form of eight educational goals to be achieved by the year 2000. These goals were signed into law by President Clinton in 1994 as the Goals 2000: Educate America Act. The most recent educational initiative is the No Child Left Behind Act (NCLB), which was signed into law in 2001. Like its predecessors, NCLB calls for stronger accountability in learning and proven, research-based educational methods.

What has been noticeably absent across all these potential reform initiatives are the insights and understandings contained in the psychological research on teaching and learning. It was just such a perspective that led Charles Spielberger, President of the American Psychological Association (APA), in 1990, to charge members of APA to take a larger role in the reform of America's schools. In response to Spielberger and the burgeoning body of federal reform initiatives, APA appointed a task force of experts in psychology and education whose charge was to develop a framework of principles based on the field's understanding of what promotes optimal learning (APA Presidential Task Force on Psychology in Education, 1993). The 12 original principles that emerged from this initial task force were subsequently revised and expanded by another APA task force, major scientific societies, psychological organizations, and professional educational associations (APA, 1995). The final 14 principles represent a synthesis of what is known about learners and optimal learning from a psychological perspective and were conceived as a framework for guiding educational practice.

Prior to discussing the principles and their value for teachers and teaching, it seems imperative to explain the notion of *learner-centered* as conceptualized in the APA document. Intuitively, this term seems to describe a classroom in which activities are focused around the needs of the learner and in which the teacher plays the role of facilitator. Such an understanding is reminiscent of child- or student-centered philosophies associated with preschool and early-childhood education (Lambert & McCombs, 1998). However, as Lambert and McCombs suggested, the *learner-centered principles* extend far beyond the artificial boundaries of formal schooling: "The principles apply to all of us, cradle to grave, from students in the classroom to teachers, administrators, parents, and others influenced by the process of schooling" (p. 9). An extremely comprehensive definition of learner-centered has been offered by McCombs and Whisler (1997). Specifically, learner-centered refers to the following:

> The perspective that couples a focus on individual learners (their heredity, experiences, perspectives, backgrounds, talents, interests, capacities, and needs) with a focus on learning (the best available knowledge about learning and how it occurs and about teaching practices that are most effective in promoting the highest levels of motivation, learning, and achievement for all learners). This dual focus, then, informs and drives educational decision making. (McCombs & Whisler, 1997, p. 9)

As such, the overarching value of the learner-centered principles for teachers and teaching is that they focus both on the individual student (e.g., background experiences, culture, and needs) and on what psychological research reveals about optimal learning (Murphy & Alexander, 2006). Since the principles are deeply rooted in psychological research, they provide educators with a valid mechanism for understanding students and the processes that undergird educational change. As a result, the principles have been promoted for contributing to meaningful and enduring school reform. Because of their precise attention to the nature of learning from both an individual and collective perspective, we believe that a thorough knowledge of the principles can be an effective catalyst for systemic change. We believe such rooted reform will be far more likely to improve schools than the rather trendy and sometimes questionable reforms of the past (Alexander et al., 1996).

Furthermore, given their broad and comprehensive scope, these learner-centered principles can be beneficial to teachers, teaching, and schools for other reasons. For instance, the principles can foster professional development (see Valli & Hawley, this volume). Specifically, learner-centered principles offer teachers a psychological portrait of students and the processes that stimulate or stifle their learning. Teachers can then compare their own personal knowledge and competencies against this psychological framework. Subsequent professional development activities can then be planned to meet the needs of the individual or the collective. Regrettably however, many preservice and inservice teachers receive very little formal training in such psychological dimensions of learners and learning (Alexander, Murphy, & Woods, 1997), suggesting a great need for professional development in these areas.

We have chosen to focus on five extremely important themes contained in these principles rather than to discuss each of the 14 individual items specified in the APA document. Specifically, pared down to their fundamental roots, we hold that the learner-centered principles relate to five essential dimensions of meaningful learning (Murphy & Alexander, 2006). These five dimensions, extensively investigated in psychology and related disciplines, fall under the following headings: (1) the knowledge base, (2) motivation and affect, (3) strategic processing or executive control, (4) development and individual differences, and (5) situation or context. For each of these areas, we consider key findings from the educational research ("What We Know"), along with implications for teachers and teaching ("What It Means"). A summary of these research findings and educational implications appears in Table 2.1.

THE KNOWLEDGE BASE

One's existing knowledge serves as the foundation of all future learning by guiding organizations and representations, by serving as a basis of association with new information, and by coloring and filtering all new experiences.[1]

What We Know

One of the most powerful and consistent findings to emerge from cognitive research over the past several decades pertains to the power

Table 2.1   Research Underlying the Various Dimensions of the Learner-Centered Principles and Their Implications for Teachers and Teaching

Research Findings	Educational Implications
The knowledge base	
Prior knowledge predicts future learning.	It is important to have a firm grasp of what students know and believe and to use that knowledge as an instructional bridge.
Knowledge is multifaceted and multidimensional.	Structure learning tasks so that students understand what, how, and when.
Knowledge misconceptions can deter or interfere with future growth.	It is best to provide experiences that enable students to correct or modify their misunderstandings prior to teaching new content.
Motivation and affect	
Intrinsic motivation and personal interest lead to greater achievement.	It is important to structure activities that will tap students' deep-seated interests.
Learning is enhanced when students' goals are focused on learning and mastery of content, rather than performance.	When choice and a sense of agency in learning tasks are permitted them, students will likely perform better on learning tasks.
Students' beliefs about their abilities to complete a task are at least as important as their actual abilities.	Structure incremental activities that allow students to build their abilities as well as their beliefs about how well they can perform.
Strategic processing or executive control	
Learning is enhanced when students use cognitive and metacognitive strategies.	Students must be taught how to think reflectively about their learning and performance.
Strategic processing and executive control are influenced by the novelty of the task or situation.	Training in strategic processing should be regularly linked to new tasks and new situations.
Strategic processing is by definition both purposeful and effortful.	Create an environment that rewards and encourages strategic processing.

(Continued)

Table 2.1 (Continued)

Research Findings	Educational Implications
Development and individual differences	
There are predictable and defined global patterns in human development.	Not every child in a particular classroom should be expected to be at the same developmental level.
Individuals retain their uniqueness.	Embrace individual differences and help students use their
Individual learner differences can both help and hinder the learning process.	individual differences to enhance individuality in learning.
Both heredity and environment influence development and individual differences.	Recognize that both a student's heredity and experiential factors contribute to who that student is as a learner.
Situation or context	
The social context is an influential factor in learning.	Classrooms should encourage both individual and social learning and growth.
All learning is filtered through one's sociocultural context and knowledge.	Consider activities that explore and challenge the context through which students view learning.
Teachers are vital components in facilitating and guiding the social exchanges that take place in classrooms.	Provide direct and individual assistance in student learning.

of the *knowledge base* (i.e., the total of all an individual knows or believes) on learning (Alexander, Schallert, & Hare, 1991). That is, the knowledge base is an extremely strong force that directs students' attention, colors their judgments about what is relevant or important, impacts their comprehension and memory, and shapes the way they perceive their world (e.g., Reynolds & Shirey, 1988). A student's prior experiences, beliefs, and knowledge serve as the scaffold that supports the construction of future knowledge (Alexander, 2005). From this perspective, knowledge has come to be viewed as a multi-faceted construct that encompasses many interactive dimensions (e.g., sociocultural knowledge, domain knowledge, and personal beliefs). For example, Lipson (1983) examined how students' religious orientations influenced the way they comprehended and recalled passages about religious practices. Similarly, Chambliss and Garner (1996) investigated how adults' views on logging practices in the Western United States altered their reading of persuasive texts. Knowledge is also multidimensional, in that there are several states (i.e., declarative, procedural, and conditional) and multiple forms of knowledge (e.g., in-school knowledge and out-of-school knowledge). By *declarative knowledge*, we mean the more factual understanding or "knowing what" or "knowing that." *Procedural knowledge*, by comparison, refers to "knowing how" to do something (Alexander et al., 1991). *Conditional knowledge* pertains to understanding when or where to apply one's knowledge. In addition, students' knowledge can sometimes remain buried in memory or be seriously flawed or misleading (e.g., Chinn & Brewer, 1993). Therefore, although knowledge is generally a positive force in learning, there are times when this is not the case. Specifically, when learners operate on incomplete and inaccurate knowledge, their existing misconceptions can actually deter or interfere with future growth.

What It Means

Each student constructs knowledge in accordance with his or her past experiences. Thus, it is extremely important that teachers use various forms of formal and informal assessments to gauge what students know or believe to be true. This understanding can then be used as a scaffold for future lessons and learning tasks. For example, a teacher might use students' current understandings about the rising and setting of the sun as a beginning point for a lesson on the earth's rotation. In addition, educators should strive to structure activities so that the various states or forms of knowledge are explored. For example, a biology teacher teaching the parts of the cell may have students play the role of individual components in the cell. In doing so, the student would also learn both the "whats" and "hows" of cell functioning. One benefit of such hands-on instruction in the sciences is its promotion of multiple forms of knowing (e.g., Gardner, 1993). Finally, teachers must be aware of the naive understandings or misconceptions that students may hold in an area of study. Armed with this knowledge, teachers can confront their students' underdeveloped or malformed notions within the context of instruction (Mason, 1996).

In many cases, students base their conceptions of scientific processes on their out-of-school experiences. As a case in point, many students think that watering the lawn keeps the lawn green, when, in fact, photosynthesis is the scientific process that makes grass and other plants green. Instead of just teaching about photo-synthesis, teachers might have the students conduct an experiment that would counter their naive understandings. By doing so, teachers can help students construct a richer and more accurate knowledge base that will enable future learning.

MOTIVATION AND AFFECT

Motivational or affective factors, such as intrinsic motivation, personal goals, attributions for learning, and self-efficacy, along with the motivational characteristics of learning tasks, play a significant role in the learning process.

What We Know

As is evident to most teachers, learning is altered by motivational and affective factors within the learner and in the learning environment (Pintrich & Schunk, 2001). Indeed, the research on motivation and affect has documented that personal interest, intrinsic motivation, and internal commitment contribute to greater learning (e.g., Ames & Ames, 1989). That is, topics or areas of study for which students possess deep-seated interest or are internally motivated to pursue will likely relate to higher achievement. Similarly, learners who have goals of pursuing understanding (i.e., mastery or learning goals) rather than performing for external rewards or recognition are more apt to achieve in schools (e.g., Murphy & Alexander, 2000). In particular, when students set their sights on learning for its own sake rather than to gain acclaim or rewards, they are more apt to achieve competence (Alexander, 1997).

Finally, students with strong self-efficacy beliefs (i.e., beliefs that one can achieve a particular task outcome) are more likely to succeed in schools (e.g., Bandura, 1986; Pietsch, Walker, & Chapman, 2003). That is, research suggests that a student's belief about his or her ability to achieve some goal or execute some task-related activity is at least as influential in learning outcomes as his or her actual ability. At the same time, learners are apt to show higher levels of motivation (e.g., interest or involvement) for some fields of study compared with others, and for certain tasks but not for others (e.g., Alexander, Kulikowich, & Schulze, 1994). In sum, it would seem that the application of the literatures in motivation and affect to the reshaping and reformation of the educational system will need to consider not only learners' general needs, desires, self-perceptions, and emotional states or orientations but also their specific interests, goals, and desires.

What It Means

Essentially, students are driven or motivated by their deep-seated interests. When tasks or learning outcomes parallel those interests, students achieve. As such, the classroom environment in which students operate plays a significant role in learning. Therefore, teachers should acknowledge students' goals and interests and cultivate an academic climate that is supportive and encouraging of students' individual interests and goals, to the extent that students' goals further the desired instructional goals (Ryan & Deci, 2000; Wentzel, 1996).

Student choice and self-determination can also enhance motivation. For example, a teacher instructing students on ecosystems might allow each individual to choose the type of ecosystem he or she would like to study. Then, the teacher can draw similarities across the various ecosystems studied by the students. One caveat about motivation, however, is that no student is equally motivated in all areas of study (Pintrich & Schunk, 2001). That is, teachers should understand that no student is highly and consistently engaged in academic pursuits. Although there are a number of reasons for students' lack of motivation, teachers should recognize that students are often unmotivated about tasks or subjects for which they believe they will not succeed. To overcome such beliefs, teachers can structure incremental activities that allow students to build their abilities, and these small successes will enable students to believe in their ability to achieve.

STRATEGIC PROCESSING OR EXECUTIVE CONTROL

The ability to reflect upon and regulate one's thoughts and behaviors is essential to learning and development.

What We Know

Effective learners not only possess a body of organized and relevant knowledge but also have the ability and willingness to direct, reflect on, and oversee their own mental functioning and to assess their own performance (McCombs, 1998). Studies have consistently demonstrated that learning is enhanced when individuals have knowledge of and apply appropriate cognitive and metacognitive or self-regulatory strategies during the learning process (e.g., Garner & Alexander, 1989). Essentially, those who reflect on their own thinking and learning performance and use that self-knowledge to alter their processing are more likely to manifest significant academic growth than those who do not (Winne, 1995). Students' use of self-monitoring strategies, however, is highly dependent on the educational situation or context (Garner, 1990). For example, successful students may choose to monitor tasks they perceive as difficult, whereas less successful students may choose to do very little monitoring or regulating on the same tasks. Indeed, the reflection and strategic efforts must, almost by definition, vary as the demands of the task or the nature of the context changes (e.g., Lave, 1988; Resnick, 1991).

To assume that one can simply have students memorize and routinely execute a set of strategies is to misconceive the nature of strategic processing or executive control. Such rote applications of these procedures represent, in essence, a nonstrategic approach to strategic processing. It has become increasingly clear, as well, that strategic processing or executive control is not only a purposeful undertaking but also an effortful one (Borkowski, Carr, & Pressley, 1987). This means that it is difficult to bring about changes in students' strategic processing without addressing issues of motivation, interest, and self-regulation (Alexander, 1997).

What It Means

Students rarely come to school with a repertoire of strategies for performing school-based tasks. Thus, students must be taught how to monitor their own mental processing. Furthermore, students should be shown how particular strategies are most effectively applied to particular activities. In addition, teachers should realize that training in strategic processing must be broad in scope and extended over time if there is to be any hope that those strategic processes will transfer to new tasks or situations (Pressley, 1995). To aid in this transfer, teachers will want to apply new strategies to routine tasks and routine strategies to novel tasks. Moreover, because strategic thinking takes time and energy, teachers must build into their plans sufficient time for reflection and the use of appropriate incentives (Garner, 1990). By creating an environment that rewards and encourages strategic processing under varying conditions, teachers can help students see that the time and effort required for strategic behavior is justified. Teachers who make strategic processing an explicit and valued component in instruction and who orchestrate and maintain such a challenging but supportive learning environment can expect their efforts to translate into greater learning gains for their students.

DEVELOPMENT AND INDIVIDUAL DIFFERENCES

Learning, while ultimately a unique adventure for all, progresses through various common stages of development influenced by both inherited and experiential/ environmental factors.

What We Know

An important transition in research on human development and individual differences is the recognition that learning is characterized by the continual interplay between the *nomothetic* (generalizable) and *idiographic* (individualistic) components of human development. In other words, human learning and growth is a continuous interchange between (a) the generalizable patterns that give human thoughts and actions their predictability and (b) the individualistic characteristics and behaviors that are inevitable. Indeed, whether the focus is on cognitive, socioemotional, or moral domains, educators must be knowledgeable of common benchmarks of human development (e.g., Case, 1993; Kohlberg, 1981). However, because every individual enters the world with a different genetic or biological history, a particular psychological makeup, and idiosyncratic preferences and because individuals develop within varied sociocultural environments (e.g., Ogbu, 1974), their ultimate constructions are unique.

To be sure, the typical and unique patterns of human development are complementary, not contradictory or even separate. Our own teaching and research have made this relationship apparent. For instance, we have seen educators make instructional and research decisions seemingly based solely on broad notions of cognitive development, missing strong signs of mental capability evident in the learning environment (e.g., Alexander, Willson, White, & Fuqua, 1987). In contrast, we have witnessed instructional difficulties that emerge when teachers entered the classroom without an understanding of the global developmental patterns that learners of particular ages, experiences, or backgrounds are likely to exhibit (Alexander & Knight, 1993; Murphy & Alexander, 2006). In essence, optimal learning results when educators understand and appreciate the fluid and complex nature of human change.

But what are the sources of development? Are growth and change in learners the consequences of inheritance or experience? Human growth is influenced by both inherited and experiential factors. It remains debatable and empirically testable as to which of these powerful forces exerts the most influence on learners' growth. Depending on the specific aspects being examined, at times it may appear that changes in human thinking, feeling, or actions are more reflective of one's inherent abilities, capabilities, conditions, or predispositions (e.g., Berk, 1999; Chomsky, 1986; Scarr, 1992). At other times, however, the research would seem to support the position that development is more a reflection of one's life experiences and the context in which one learns and grows (e.g., Bronfrenbrenner, 1986; Ogbu, 1974). By strategically acknowledging the potency of both heredity and environment, educators avoid entering this continuing debate.

What It Means

When teachers peer over the students in their classrooms, they should be able to identify patterns of cognitive, socioemotional, and moral development. Although not all of these patterns are age specific, teachers should be knowledgeable about the typical developmental levels expected for a particular age or grade. By knowing and understanding these various patterns, teachers can then plan developmentally appropriate activities and tasks that challenge students and enhance learning. However, teachers must not be blind to the fact that no two developmental paths are identical. The typical patterns of development are also accented by individual learner differences that can serve to both help and hinder the process of learning.

Rather than ignoring either of these patterns, we encourage teachers to address both the typical patterns and individual differences in their lesson planning. By allowing freedom of choice and agency in developmentally appropriate tasks, teachers will encourage the positive aspects of both typical patterns and individual differences. Finally, teachers should understand that students' heredity and environment contribute to who they are as learners. While teachers cannot change a student's heredity, they can orchestrate learning environments that match a student's general and individualistic needs and goals.

SITUATION OR CONTEXT

Learning is as much a socially shared undertaking as it is an individually constructed enterprise.

What We Know

The recognition that learning is continuously and markedly shaped by the social context in which it occurs is one of the most powerful observations to emerge in recent psychological literature (e.g., Lave, 1988; Rogoff, 1990). Researchers who investigate the social nature of learning have explored various aspects of this phenomena, including socially shared cognition (Resnick, Levine, & Teasley, 1991), distributed intelligence (Pea, 1989), shared expertise (Brown & Palincsar, 1989), guided participation (Rogoff, 1990), and anchored instruction (Cognition and Technology Group at Vanderbilt, 1990).

In many ways, the biological structure that separates the individual mind from the sociocultural context in which the mind functions can be thought of as a highly permeable fabric through which thoughts, feelings, and impressions move freely. Furthermore, with each passage through this permeable fabric, these thoughts, feelings, and impressions are filtered and transformed, often without a conscious awareness on the part of the learner or those within the situation or context. While some filtering may be productive, students may filter out information that does not conform to their preconceived notions (Buehl, Alexander, Murphy, & Sperl, 2001). This is due in part to the fact that schools are, after all, social institutions in which groups of individuals are brought together to share the educational experience. Students are in constant contact with peers and other adults during the course of instruction, which may encourage them to maintain or change their previous understandings (Murphy & Edwards, 2005).

One outcome of this growing body of research is the understanding that the context in which learning occurs in certainly nontrivial (Bereiter & Scardamalia, 1989). It is also apparent that the role of the teacher as the facilitator and guide of these social exchanges is vital (Radziszewska & Rogoff, 1988); in essence, when learners were able to benefit from the guidance of a knowledgeable adult (e.g., teacher) who promoted their exploration and interchange, performance was enhanced. Corresponding with Vygotsky's (1934/1986) concept of a *zone of proximal development*, it has also been suggested that the guidance provided by the more knowledgeable and skilled adult or peer should correspond to the knowledge and skills of the learner. Thus, as the learner develops in an area or in relation to a given task, the level of assistance provided by the teacher should decrease proportionately (e.g., Brown & Palincsar, 1989). This lessening of external direction and support from a teacher or adult should theoretically contribute to more independent functioning on the part of the student and, likewise, enhance the possibility of transfer that the acquired knowledge or skill will occur both in and out of class.

What It Means

Although educators likely perceive that the situation or context plays a role in the learning process, they may not understand the depth to which it can help or hinder learning. Indeed, the situation and context influence every aspect of individual and social learning. We encourage teachers to attend to both individual and social dimensions of learning. In addition, teachers should provide activities (e.g., readings or experiments) that challenge students' views of the world (Wilkinson, Murphy, & Soter, 2005). We are not suggesting that a teacher should reject students' perceptions.

However, the teacher should facilitate student exploration of alternative viewpoints (Buehl, Manning, Cox, & Fives, 2005).

One side effect of the socially shared learning movements has been a diminished regard of direct or individual instruction (Alexander & Murphy, 1998). Instead of routinely structuring learning as an independent or collective enterprise, teachers should make grouping decisions thoughtfully and purposefully, with consideration of learning goals and student needs. Moreover, even when lessons are more focused on group processes, there will likely be times that the teacher will need to intercede and directly teach skills or strategies that enhance the learning process.

CONCLUDING REMARKS

Even though we have explored five psychological dimensions as separate factors in this discussion, they actually work in concert to promote optimal learning. As researchers, we can theoretically and empirically extract cognition from affect, knowledge from strategic processing, or sociocultural background from development, but these dimensions, along with the others addressed in the principles, remain inextricably intertwined in the real world. For example, the knowledge base is both an aspect of development (e.g., Chi, 1985) and a part of motivation (e.g., Schiefele, 1991). Similarly, development is integrated with individual differences and sociocultural background (e.g., Ogbu, 1974; Scarr, 1992), just as strategic processing is correlated with one's motivational or affective state (e.g., Hidi & Anderson, 1992).

In light of the interdependence of these dimensions, educators have a greater chance to make significant and long-term changes by approaching learning in a systemic fashion (Salomon, 1991). In his analysis of human behavior and the experiences from which it arises, Dewey (1930) expressed this precept with these words: "No act can be understood apart from the series to which it belongs" (p. 412). We could not agree more. Moreover, as our analysis demonstrates, extensive research upholds the important roles that the knowledge base, strategic processing or executive control, motivation and affect, development and individual differences, and situation or context play in student learning. Embracing and applying the psychological research base encompassed in APA's learner-centered principles can have positive and far-reaching consequences for both teachers and students as the teaching profession progresses into the 21st century.

NOTE

1. These brief section summaries are adapted from Alexander and Murphy (1998) and Murphy and Alexander (2006).

REFERENCES

Alexander, P. A. (1997). Mapping the multidimensional nature of domain learning: The interplay of cognitive, motivational, and strategic forces. In M. L. Maehr & P. R. Pintrich (Eds.), *Advances in motivation and achievement* (Vol. 10, pp. 213–250). Greenwich, CT: JAI Press.

Alexander, P. A. (2005). *Psychology in learning and instruction.* Upper Saddle River, NJ: Prentice Hall.

Alexander, P. A., & Knight, S. L. (1993). Dimensions of the interplay between learning and teaching. *Educational Forum, 57,* 232–245.

Alexander, P. A., Kulikowich, J. M., & Schulze, S. K. (1994). How subject-matter knowledge affects recall and interest on the comprehension of scientific exposition. *American Educational Research Journal, 31,* 313–337.

Alexander, P. A., & Murphy, P. K. (1998). The research base for APA's learner-centered psychological principles. In N. Lambert & B. McCombs (Eds.), *Issues in school reform: A sampler of psychological perspectives on learner-centered schools* (pp. 33–60). Washington, DC: American Psychological Association.

Alexander, P. A., Murphy, P. K., & Woods, B. S. (1996). Of squalls and fathoms: Navigating the seas of educational innovation. *Educational Researcher, 25*(3), 31–36, 39.

Alexander, P. A., Murphy, P. K., & Woods, B. S. (1997). Unearthing academic roots: Educators' perceptions of the interrelationship of philosophy, psychology, and education. *Educational Forum, 61,* 172–186.

Alexander, P. A., Schallert, D. L., & Hare, V. C. (1991). Coming to terms: How researchers in learning and literacy talk about knowledge. *Review of Educational Research, 61,* 315–343.

Alexander, P. A., Willson, V. L., White, C. S., & Fuqua, J. D. (1987). Analogical reasoning in young children. *Journal of Educational Psychology, 79,* 401–408.

American Psychological Association Board of Educational Affairs. (1995, December). *Learner-centered psychological principles: A framework for school redesign and reform.* Washington, DC: American Psychological Association.

American Psychological Association Presidential Task Force on Psychology in Education. (1993, January). *Learner-centered psychological principles: Guidelines for school redesign and reform.* Washington, DC: American Psychological Association/Mid-Continent Regional Educational Laboratory.

Ames, C., & Ames, R. (Eds.). (1989). *Research on motivation in education: The classroom milieu* (Vol. 3). San Diego: Academic Press.

Bandura, A. (1986). *Social foundations of thought and action: A social cognitive theory.* Englewood Cliffs, NJ: Prentice Hall.

Bereiter, C., & Scardamalia, M. (1989). Intentional learning as a goal of instruction. In L. B. Resnick (Ed.), *Knowing, learning, and instruction: Essays in honor of Robert Glaser* (pp. 361–392). Hillsdale, NJ: Erlbaum.

Berk, L. E. (1999). *Infants and children: Prenatal through middle childhood* (3rd ed.). Boston: Allyn & Bacon.

Borkowski, J. G., Carr, M., & Pressley, M. (1987). "Spontaneous" strategy use: Perspectives from metacognitive theory. *Intelligence, 11,* 61–75.

Bronfrenbrenner, U. (1986). Ecology of the family as a context for human development: Research perspectives. *Developmental Psychology, 22,* 723–742.

Brown, A. L., & Palincsar, A. S. (1989). Guided, cooperative learning and individual knowledge acquisition. In L. B. Resnick (Ed.), *Knowing, learning, and instruction: Essays in honor of Robert Glaser* (pp. 393–451). Hillsdale, NJ: Erlbaum.

Buehl, M. M., Alexander, P. A., Murphy, P. K., & Sperl, C. T. (2001). Profiling persuasion: The role of beliefs, knowledge, and interest in the processing of persuasive texts that varied by argument structure. *Journal of Literacy Research, 33,* 269–301.

Buehl, M. M., Manning, D. K., Cox, K., & Fives, H. (2005, August). Exploring pre-service teachers' initial and informed reactions to teaching as persuasion. In H. Fives (Chair), *Teaching as persuasion: Is the metaphor viable?* Symposium presented at the Annual Meeting of the American Psychological Association, Washington, DC.

Case, R. (1993). Theories of learning and theories of development. *Educational Psychologist, 28,* 219–233.

Chambliss, M. J., & Garner, R. (1996). Do adults change their minds after reading persuasive text? *Written Communication, 13*(3), 291–313.

Chi, M.T.H. (1985). Interactive roles of knowledge and strategies in the development of organized sorting and recall. In S. F. Chipman, J. W. Segal, & R. Glaser (Eds.), *Thinking and learning skills: Research and open questions* (Vol. 2, pp. 457–483). Hillsdale, NJ: Lawrence Erlbaum.

Chinn, C. A., & Brewer, W. F. (1993). The role of anomalous data in knowledge acquisition: A theoretical framework and implications for science instruction. *Review of Educational Research, 63,* 1–49.

Chomsky, N. (1986). *Knowledge of language: Its nature, origin, and use.* New York: Praeger.

Cognition and Technology Group at Vanderbilt. (1990). Anchored instruction and its relationship to situated cognition. *Educational Researcher, 19*(6), 2–10.

Dewey, J. (1930). Conduct and experience. In C. Murchism (Ed.), *Psychologies of 1930* (pp. 410–429). Worcester, MA: Clark University Press.

Gardner, H. (1993). *Creating minds.* New York: Basic Books.

Garner, R. (1990). When children and adults do not use learning strategies: Toward a theory of settings. *Review of Educational Research, 60,* 517–529.

Garner, R., & Alexander, P. A. (1989). Metacognition: Answered and unanswered questions. *Educational Psychologist, 24,* 143–148.

Goals 2000: Educate America Act, Pub. L. No. 103-227, 108 Stat. 125 (1994).

Hidi, S., & Anderson, V. (1992). Situational interest and its impact on reading and expository writing. In K. A. Renninger, S. Hidi, & A. Krapp (Eds.), *The role of interest in learning and development* (pp. 215–238). Hillsdale, NJ: Erlbaum.

Kohlberg, L. (1981). *The philosophy of moral development.* New York: Harper & Row.

Lambert, N. M., & McCombs, B. L. (Eds.). (1998). *How students learn: Reforming schools through learner-centered education.* Washington, DC: American Psychological Association.

Lave, J. (1988). *Cognition in practice.* Cambridge, UK: Cambridge University Press.

Lipson, M. Y. (1983). The influence of religious affiliation on children's memory for text information. *Reading Research Quarterly, 18,* 448–457.

Mason, L. (1996). An analysis of children's construction of new knowledge through their use of reasoning and arguing in classroom discussions. *International Journal of Qualitative Studies in Education, 9*(3), 411–433.

McCombs, B. L. (1998). Integrating metacognition, affect, and motivation in improving teacher education. In N. Lambert & B. L. McCombs (Eds.), *Issues in school reform: A sampler of psychological perspectives on learner-centered schools* (pp. 379–408). Washington, DC: American Psychological Association.

McCombs, B. L., & Whisler, P. T. (1997). *The learner-centered classroom and school: Strategies for enhancing student motivation and achievement.* San Francisco: Jossey-Bass.

Murphy, P. K., & Alexander, P. A. (2000). A motivated exploration of motivation terminology. *Contemporary Educational Psychology, 25,* 3–53.

Murphy, P. K., & Alexander, P. A. (2006). *Promoting academic excellence: Research-based principles for teaching and learning.* Thousand Oaks, CA: Corwin.

Murphy, P. K., & Edwards, M. N. (2005, April). What the studies tell us: A meta-analysis of discussion approaches. In I. Wilkinson (Chair), *Making sense of group discussions designed to promote high-level comprehension of texts.* Symposium presented at the annual meeting of the American Educational Research Association, Montreal, Canada.

Murphy, P. K., & Mason, L. (in press). Changing knowledge and changing beliefs. In P. A. Alexander & P. Winne (Eds.), *Handbook of educational psychology* (2nd ed.). New York: Lawrence Erlbaum.

National Commission on Excellence in Education. (1983). *A nation at risk: The imperative for educational reform.* Washington, DC: U.S. Government Printing Office.

No Child Left Behind Act of 2001, Pub. L. No. 107-110, 115 State 425 (2002).

Ogbu, J. U. (1974). *The next generation: An ethnography of education in an urban neighborhood.* New York: Academic Press.

Palincsar, A. S., & Brown, A. L. (1984). Reciprocal teaching of comprehension-fostering and monitoring activities. *Cognition and Instruction, 1,* 117–175.

Pea, R. D. (1989). Socializing the knowledge transfer problem. *International Journal of Educational Research, 2,* 639–663.

Pietsch, J., Walker, R., & Chapman, E. (2003). The relationship among self-concept, self-efficacy, and performance in mathematics during secondary school. *Journal of Educational Psychology, 95,* 589–603.

Pintrich, P. R., & Schunk, D. H. (2001). *Motivation in education: Theory, research, and applications* (2nd ed.). Englewood Cliffs, NJ: Prentice Hall.

Pressley, M. (1995). More about the development of self-regulation: Complex, long-term, and thoroughly social. *Educational Psychologist, 30,* 207–212.

Radziszewska, B., & Rogoff, B. (1988). Influence of adult and peer collaboration on children's planning skills. *Developmental Psychology, 24,* 840–848.

Resnick, L. B. (1991). Shared cognition. In L. B. Resnick, J. M. Levine, & S. D. Teasley (Eds.), *Perspectives on socially shared cognition* (pp. 1–20). Washington, DC: American Psychological Association.

Resnick, L. B., Levine, J. M., & Teasley, S. D. (1991). *Perspectives on socially shared cognition.* Washington, DC: American Psychological Association.

Reynolds, R. E., & Shirey, L. L. (1988). The role of attention in studying and learning. In C. E. Weinstein, E. T. Goetz, & P. A. Alexander (Eds.), *Learning and study strategies: Issues in assessment, instruction, and evaluation* (pp. 77–100). San Diego: Academic Press.

Rogoff, B. (1990). *Apprenticeship in thinking: Cognitive development in social context.* New York: Oxford University Press.

Ryan, R. M., & Deci, E. L. (2000). Intrinsic and extrinsic motivations: Classic definitions and new directions. *Contemporary Educational Psychology, 25,* 54–67.

Salomon, G. (1991). Transcending the qualitative-quantitative debate: The analytic and systemic approach to educational research. *Educational Psychologist, 20*(6), 10–18.

Scarr, S. (1992). Developmental theories for the 1990's: Development and individual differences. *Child Development, 63,* 1–19.

Schiefele, U. (1991). Interest, learning, and motivation. *Educational Psychologist, 26,* 229–323.

Vygotsky, L. (1986). *Thought and language* (A. Kozulin, Trans.). Cambridge: MIT Press. (Original work published 1934)

Wentzel, K. R. (1996). Social and academic motivation in middle school: Concurrent and long-term relations in academic effort. *Journal of Early Adolescence, 16,* 390–406.

Wilkinson, I. A. G., Murphy, P. K., & Soter, A. O. (2005, August). *Group discussions as learning environments for promoting high-level comprehension of texts.* Paper presented at the 11th biennial meeting of the European Association for Research on Learning and Instruction, Nicosia, Cyprus.

Winne, P. H. (1995). Inherent details in self-regulated learning. *Educational Psychologist, 30,* 173–187.

CHAPTER THREE

Improving Achievement for All Students

The Meaning of Staff-Shared Understanding and Commitment

Fred M. Newmann

- Schools enhance student performance and minimize disparities in student achievement when their teachers demonstrate shared understanding of and commitment to a common, specific intellectual mission.
- A common intellectual mission is most effective when teachers attend to three criteria for intellectual quality: selection of significant curriculum content, accuracy and precision, and teaching for in-depth understanding.
- The common intellectual mission serves as a foundation for strong professional community, which improves instruction and thereby improves student achievement.
- To establish high expectations for all students, effective schools use common standards, but also different instructional approaches that respond to students' unique backgrounds and interests.

- Building and sustaining the school culture reflected above requires strong leadership by the principal and by teacher leaders to focus staff energy on instruction, reflective teacher dialogue, trust, and internal accountability within the school.

The goal of improving student achievement is rarely questioned, but how to measure it and how to define indicators of success are problematic. Measured most frequently through conventional standardized tests that call mainly for recall of information and basic literacy and computation skills, achievement can also be measured through tests that call for complex intellectual work involving in-depth understanding, analysis, and elaborated forms of communication. This chapter synthesizes research using both approaches to measuring student achievement. Schools maximize the likelihood of improving student achievement, measured either way, when the school staff shares an understanding of and commitment to a common, specific intellectual mission. The synthesis of research in this chapter is intended to clarify the meaning of shared understanding and commitment and conditions in schools that promote it.[1]

COMMON SPECIFIC INTELLECTUAL MISSION

As teachers talk with one another and with students about the kind of achievement they expect, they use a common language that communicates a specific intellectual mission for the school, a mission that goes beyond vague slogans such as "All students can learn" or "Improve our test scores." To build a school mission focused on improved student achievement, the staff must craft general language to identify intellectual outcomes that teachers from all the grade levels and subject areas in the school can endorse. Particular grade levels and subject areas can then add more precision to the general standards by specifying the substantive content to be taught.

An example of a common specific intellectual mission is a school that emphasized five "habits of mind," such as identifying the perspective of an author and assessing the quality of evidence presented. Another school, which emphasized complex thinking and problem solving connected to real-world issues, summarized its mission as "applied learning." Some schools focus on a list of competencies that all students are expected to master in order to graduate to the next level of schooling. Other schools establish a common agenda for learning by requiring all students to take a specific set of classes, each being taught according to criteria for intellectual quality such as those discussed below.

Some schools forge missions that may enjoy shared understanding and consensus, but concentrate more on the logistics of techniques and procedures than on the intellectual quality of student work. Certain approaches to teaching literacy, use of manipulatives in mathematics instruction, cooperative learning, hands-on laboratory work, advanced technology, portfolio assessment, or community-based learning are examples of procedures or techniques that may serve as missions without emphasizing specific intellectual goals for students. In more effective schools, however, the intellectual goals remain so paramount that before adopting proposed new teaching techniques or practices, the staff scrutinizes them to make sure they are likely to lead to specific intellectual outcomes. In effective schools, teachers exercise individual discretion over their teaching and use unique classroom styles, but their discretion is guided by and subjected to shared understanding of and commitment to the intellectual mission.

INTELLECTUAL QUALITY

Even with diverse intellectual missions, schools that are effective in boosting student achievement give primary attention to the intellectual quality of student work. Educators pay close attention to three criteria: teaching significant curriculum content, accuracy and precision in teaching and student performance, and in-depth understanding in teaching and student performance.

Significant Curriculum Content

The development of standards for curriculum and assessment in the United States is an effort to ensure that all students have an opportunity to learn significant curriculum content. Because the modern knowledge explosion makes it impossible to teach everything worth knowing and because of diverse cultural perspectives on what knowledge is of most worth, reaching consensus on standards within schools, districts, states, and the nation is highly controversial.

Teachers are continuously pressured to teach massive amounts of information and skills. Effective schools, nevertheless, devote serious effort to deciding what knowledge and skills are most important, authoritative, and up-to-date within legitimate fields of knowledge and most likely to be useful to their students in further education and life. Teachers in these schools don't teach material simply because it appears in a text or is required on a test. They think about and consciously decide which content and skills are substantively worthwhile and backed by the authority of respectable research. To help with these decisions, teachers and administrators have used outlines of significant, challenging curriculum developed by national professional organizations and curriculum projects of districts and states. But regardless of the specific sources of content, educators in effective schools make a special effort to avoid trivial curriculum or busywork. Instead, they try to ensure that the curriculum offers legitimate intellectual substance at all grades to all students.

Accuracy/Precision

In effective schools, when teachers help students learn facts, concepts, theories, algorithms, and conventions for written and oral communication, they emphasize and celebrate "getting it right." Assignments may call for more than one "right answer," but even when the solution is ambiguous or when more than one response can be considered well-grounded, teachers insist that students' statements be consistent with authoritative knowledge in the relevant discipline or area of expertise. Communicating clearly and precisely is also important. Teachers help students pay scrupulous attention to style and detail so that students will learn to avoid misrepresentation and say exactly what they mean so that it is properly understood. This concern for accuracy and precision extends to teachers' evaluations of the materials they use, to the discussions they hold with one another, and to their own teaching behavior.

In-Depth Understanding

Significant curriculum content and accuracy/precision in representing it are important to boosting student achievement, especially on conventional tests. But if students are to demonstrate high-level intellectual work, they must be able to go beyond recitation of isolated facts and definitions and beyond superficial awareness of a large body of information and proper use of basic skills—to organizing, synthesizing, and interpreting this knowledge. High-level intellectual performance illustrates construction of knowledge aimed at in-depth understanding of what is studied. To achieve in-depth understanding, teachers in effective schools limit the scope of curriculum so they can spend more time exploring the complexities and nuances of fewer topics. And they help students to see how real-life issues that challenge the intellect can be illuminated and often resolved through application of academic learning.

Effective schools that aim primarily toward conventional measures of student achievement may put less emphasis on in-depth understanding, with greater attention to accuracy and precision in learning significant content. Effective schools that pursue more authentic intellectual work put high priority on in-depth understanding.

Ideally, most teachers would agree with these criteria for intellectual quality, yet educators often perceive a conflict between teaching the multitude of basic facts and skills required by standardized tests and teaching to higher-level outcomes. Research indicates, however, that teaching to higher-level outcomes does not jeopardize student scores on standardized tests. In fact, studies indicate that teaching to higher-level outcomes tends to boost student scores on standardized tests.[2] The most effective teachers probably do not try to "cover everything," but decide what aspects of a subject or skill are really most important. They teach these topics in depth to promote high levels of understanding and competence. Deep knowledge and high mastery in the essential areas then transfer to assist students in figuring out answers to many questions or problems that have not been explicitly studied.

Educators within schools differ enormously in the intellectual resources they offer and in the intellectual rigor they expect from students. Apart from teacher differences within schools, some schools succeed far more than others in improving student achievement on conventional tests and on tests demanding more complex intellectual work. These successful schools often have strong professional communities.

PROFESSIONAL COMMUNITY

Teachers in effective schools have a common understanding of their main intellectual goals, but unanimity on intellectual mission does not entail mechanical, uniform compliance with a "party line," routinized teaching, or static, rigid curriculum. To the contrary, shared understanding of and collective commitment to central goals often stimulates lively faculty debate on how best to achieve the goals. Staff discussion often entails a continuous loop of asking how to improve, trying new approaches and evaluating them, and redesigning curriculum, assessment, and teaching. Reflective dialogue of this sort requires trust among teachers and administrators, time, and the opportunity to collaborate in teams. Honest, critical discussion occurs within a culture of collective responsibility that reinforces shared understanding and schoolwide consensus.

In effective schools, student success becomes a collective responsibility of the staff. Teachers work to enhance not only their own students' learning, but other students' as well, for example, by helping to enforce standards of intellect and conduct throughout the school, even when it may involve possible conflict with colleagues. This norm—that all teachers are responsible for all students—helps to sustain each teacher's commitment. It puts peer pressure to be more accountable on those staff members who may not have carried their fair share. And collective responsibility offers support to those teachers who may previously have worked alone and beyond the call of duty, yet still felt unable to help some students.

Collective responsibility is demonstrated by teachers working long hours to improve their practice and to support students. Teachers in effective schools have confidence in their students' potential even when the students' lives beyond school present enormous challenges to physical, social, and emotional development. When students face conditions that deprive them of opportunities to engage in concentrated study and undermine their will to achieve, these teachers do not give up on students. They insist that it is the teachers' and students' responsibility to beat the odds and to overcome possible failures of the past in school and beyond.

To hold all students to high intellectual standards, teachers offer special help and support, not only through individualized teaching and tutoring but also by establishing important norms of confidence, respect, and caring. These teachers convey confidence that students will earn success through hard work on academic tasks; they reinforce student peers for careful listening, responding seriously to one another's concerns and helping one another with schoolwork; and they provide a "safe" environment in which students have the opportunity to make mistakes and to try again without being judged as "stupid."

In some schools, a significant number of teachers may be burned out, just coasting toward retirement, or for other reasons not interested in collaborating to build shared understanding of and commitment to high-level outcomes. How can schools develop a professional community when many teachers don't want to cooperate?

Different strategies are needed, depending upon whether teachers seem to be resisting because of reasonable or unreasonable concerns. Reasonable concerns could include any of the following: (a) "Since we have tried many reforms in the past that were either abandoned very quickly or showed no signs of success, why should I have any confidence that this reform effort will succeed?" (b) "Collaboration to reach some common standards sounds like a good idea, but this will take lots of time and effort, and I'm already working 50 hours a week"; and (c) "The prospect of collaborating is scary, because I'm not sure how to handle criticism of my teaching and not sure I can give helpful feedback to others." These concerns need to be addressed by showing faculty the research on effective schools, by offering sufficient administrative support to give teachers time to develop their missions, and by providing opportunities for productive sharing in an intellectually honest but personally supportive and trusting environment.

Teachers who resist because of unreasonable concerns include those who believe so strongly that educationally disadvantaged students will never succeed in school that they refuse to discuss the issue, those who insist that they must be left alone in their classrooms as professionals to do whatever they think best, and those who don't care whether their students succeed or fail, but just show up on the job to collect a paycheck. The administration must move such teachers out of the school or isolate them sufficiently to minimize their negative effects on the collective effort.

HELPING DIVERSE STUDENTS ACHIEVE: COMMONALITY AND DIFFERENTIATION

Perhaps the greatest challenge for teachers, especially with increased emphasis on common standards and high-stakes tests, is how to cope with student diversity. Students come to class with different levels of competence and academic preparation, different degrees of motivation to succeed in schoolwork, different cultural backgrounds, different intellectual interests, and different social skills and levels of maturity. The persisting dilemma is how to respect and address individual differences and at the same time maximize success for ambitious academic standards. In effective schools, teachers walk a tightrope between two prominent approaches in the handling of student diversity.

One approach insists that all students must study a common curriculum and be required to meet the same specific high standards for success. Advocates of "common" student experiences point to the dangers of catering excessively to student differences through special programs and curriculum tracking that have persistently delivered lower-quality education to students of lower socioeconomic status, students of color, and students with histories of school failure. Since highly differentiated programs have led to blatant educational inequities, advocates of common experiences want all students to enroll in a common, high-quality program and to pass common tests. The common approach may minimize the inequities of excessive differentiation, but it also poses a danger: curriculum, teaching, and assessment offered only in a single, standard form can make it difficult for students from unique backgrounds to succeed in mastering the material and to succeed; without any flexibility in response to their unique needs, these students may lose interest, fail, and drop out.

The second approach is to take students' diverse backgrounds more prominently into account and design special curricula, classes, and programs to address these directly. The intent is not to relax intellectual standards, but to use different avenues to develop the intellect rather than expecting all students to conform to a single, common path. Some students may be assigned to remedial programs to boost basic competencies enough so that they can eventually participate in a mainstream college prep curriculum. Other students may enroll in different career cluster programs to help them channel their efforts toward economically productive pursuits that may not require 4 years of college. The differentiation of student programs avoids trying to fit all students into one mold, but it also involves a big risk: Some programs tend to perpetuate much lower intellectual standards than others.

Effective schools usually use both commonality and differentiation in curriculum, teaching, and assessment, while deliberately attempting to exploit the advantages and guard against the abuses of each. For example, when common curriculum and assessments are required of all students, special efforts are made to help students who may be ill-prepared, perhaps through additional remedial and tutorial work and tailoring daily assignments to students' different topical interests or in effective elementary school reading programs that group students into achievement levels and design instruction accordingly. In contrast, when students are grouped into different programs, such as English as a second language or bilingual, gifted and talented, college prep, or vocational, special efforts are made to ensure that the highest expectations for intellectual work permeate every class; for example, many high schools have aimed for common high standards of academic achievement by enriching the curricula of vocational/technical programs.[3] In short, effective schools take deliberate steps to ensure that differentiation in curricula and instruction maximizes student progress toward high-level outcomes instead of discriminating against some students through long-term lower expectations, which is more often the result of tracking.

Theoretically, both commonality and differentiation have the potential to boost student achievement. But since each harbors the possibility of major disservice to less educationally advanced students, the key is to fashion a creative combination. Research has not identified a specific mix of common and differentiated experiences that works for the teaching of all subjects to all students.

MAKING IT HAPPEN

Research describes what it means for schools to have shared understanding of and commitment to improving achievement for all students and documents the effectiveness of such schools. Research is less conclusive on how to increase shared understanding of and commitment to higher achievement for all in less effective schools, but guidance as to where to focus reform activity has emerged.

Concentrate on Instruction to Improve Achievement

Schools often address issues that divert attention from instruction to maximize achievement. Providing a safe, orderly environment; socializing students to behave responsibly; attending to students' physical and emotional well-being; offering extracurricular activities; or managing shared governance are all legitimate functions for schooling, but to the extent that these issues dominate faculties' and administrators' time and energy, they drain resources from instruction that improves intellectual outcomes. Even efforts to implement specific pedagogical practices, such as cooperative learning, portfolios, or case studies, may not enhance student achievement unless they are aligned with the school's intellectual mission. The more successful reform initiatives of districts and schools have increasingly focused professional development, faculty committee work, collection, and dissemination of information.

Mindful of the importance of parent support for student achievement, more successful educators take steps to explain to parents what it means to teach toward high levels of achievement and why this is important for their children's success, to show that teachers are concerned about and competent to teach their children, to help parents feel comfortable talking with teachers, and to celebrate with parents their children's production of high-quality work. To build this kind of support with parents requires careful planning, often in collaborative partnership between schools and community organizations to work on specific school improvement goals.[4]

Teacher Reflective Dialogue

Shared understanding and commitment cannot be imposed top-down from principals, superintendents, or state education agencies. Teacher buy-in, understanding of and commitment to an intellectual mission, and the success of collaborative work depend on teachers having opportunities to discuss, question, argue, and reflect upon the justification and feasibility of particular student achievement goals. Understanding and commitment is generated as teachers share points of view, examine evidence and arguments, and work toward agreements that they believe are grounded in honest professional inquiry. In more successful schools, administrators provide time, teacher work group experiences, and facilitative leadership, often through instructional coaches, that sets norms for reflective dialogue about the central intellectual goals, appropriate curriculum, effective instruction, and evaluation of success with students.

Trust

Honest reflective dialogue occurs only within an environment of trust among teachers and between teachers and administrators. Trust involves perceiving other education professionals as having good intentions in working with students and staff, keeping one's word, being competent to do the work at hand, and being willing to listen openly. Teacher leaders and administrators who recognize the importance of trust will demonstrate their own trustworthiness to staff, support occasions in which staff can demonstrate and develop trust with one another, and confront relationships among staff in cases in which trust needs to be improved.

Accountability

High-stakes testing by districts, states, and the federal government is intended to motivate teachers and administrators, and setting district or state curriculum standards is meant to build shared understanding of the goals for student achievement. But a number of studies have shown that external accountability alone is insufficient. Shared understanding and commitment to improved achievement are more likely to be reinforced by strong internal accountability within a school (or an academic department within a high school). Strong internal accountability includes teachers within a school setting clear goals for their students' achievement; teachers examining teaching, curriculum, assessment, and student work and test scores; staff using this information to guide improvement activities; and celebrating success within grade levels, subject areas, and the school as a whole. When local administrators hold teachers accountable for achievement results, this is most likely to increase shared understanding, commitment, and student achievement when the accountability is reciprocal, that is, when administrators are accountable to teachers for providing the resources teachers need, such as professional development, help from coaches, planning time, and instructional materials, to achieve the desired results.

Effective schools promote shared understanding and commitment not only by hiring personnel committed to the norms discussed above but also by creating structures for teacher teaming, teaching, and professional development that permit teachers and students to spend significant amounts of time together. As they spend more time together, they get to know one another better, which offers more opportunity to develop mutual respect and trust. Examples of the structures include teachers instructing the same group of students for several hours a day and/or for 2 or more years, teachers in a grade level having several hours per week of common planning time, teachers or coaches observing teaching and conferring about their observations, and the full staff spending several days a year in staff development sessions working on a common schoolwide issue. These structural supports, combined with selective hiring, norms of high expectations, and allocation of technical resources aimed toward conditions discussed above should maximize shared understanding of and commitment to improving high levels of student achievement for all.

NOTES

1. This chapter is a synthesis of sources of evidence and analysis of school effectiveness listed in the "References and Resources" section. A useful definition for an *effective school* is one with a record of high student achievement on either conventional tests or on more authentic assessments and in which disparities in achievement between students of different socioeconomic, racial/ethnic, and gender groups are minimal.

While the research listed shows connections between staff-shared understanding and commitment to improving student achievement and strong connections between organizational features of schools and staff understanding and commitment, the research generally shows only correlation, but not causation. To demonstrate causation in the rigorous sense, it would be necessary to conduct experimental studies in which students are randomly assigned to teachers and schools with differing degrees of shared understanding of and commitment to improved achievement and differing organizational supports for such understanding and commitment. However, since it is usually neither feasible nor ethical to conduct such studies in education, research rarely verifies true causal relationships.

2. These studies include research on the teaching of mathematics, reading, and writing to disadvantaged students (Knapp, Shields, & Turnbull, 1992; Lee, Smith, & Newmann, 2001; Newmann, Bryk, & Nagaoka, 2001); teaching mathematics in Grades 1, 2, and 8 (Carpenter, Fennema, Peterson, Chiang, & Loef, 1989; Cobb, et al., 1991; Silver & Lane, 1995); teaching reading in Grades 1, 2, and 3 (Tharp, 1982); teaching mathematics and science in high school (Lee, Smith, & Croninger, 1997); and teaching social studies in high school (Levin, Newmann, & Oliver, 1969).

3. Success for All is an example of the approach to achievement grouping in reading (http://www.successforall.net), and High Schools that Work is a program that works toward common high-level outcomes for both college prep and vocational programs (http://www.sreb.org/programs/hstw/HSTWindex.asp).

4. For more information and assistance in developing comprehensive programs of school, family, and community partnerships that support school goals for student success, contact the National Network of Partnership Schools at Johns Hopkins by visiting the Web site: http://www.csos.jhu.edu/p2000/sixtypes.htm. Also see the following sources:

Epstein, J. L., Coates, L., Salinas, K. C., Sanders, M. G., & Simon, B. S. (1997). *School, family, and community partnerships: Your handbook for action.* Thousand Oaks, CA: Corwin Press.

Lueder, D. (1998). *Creating partnerships with parents.* Lancaster, PA: Technomic Publishing.

National PTA. (2000). *Building successful partnerships.* Bloomington, IN: National Educational Service.

REFERENCES AND RESOURCES

References are coded to indicate which of five issues in this chapter the reference addresses most directly. A reference may address more than one issue, but it is categorized only according to the issue most relevant to this article.

1 = Review or synthesis of research on school effectiveness, usually using conventional achievement measures

2 = Study of the meaning and importance of shared understanding and commitment to student achievement measured either through standardized tests or tests of higher-level intellectual work

3 = Study of the issue of commonality and differentiation in instruction

4 = Study of organizational conditions such as professional community, trust, and accountability that promote shared understanding and commitment to improving student achievement measured either through standardized tests or tests of higher-level intellectual work

5 = Study of effects of teaching for higher-level intellectual outcomes on conventional achievement test scores

2   Ancess, J. (2003). *Beating the odds: High schools as communities of commitment.* New York: Teachers College Press.

1   Bliss, J. R., Firestone, W. A., & Richards, C. E. (1991). *Rethinking effective schools: Research and practice.* Englewood Cliffs, NJ: Prentice Hall.

2   Bryk, A. S., & Driscoll, M. E. (1988). *The high school as community: Contextual influences, and consequences for students and teachers.* Madison: University of Wisconsin-Madison, National Center on Effective Secondary Schools.

2   Bryk, A. S., Lee, V. E., & Holland, P. B. (1993). *Catholic schools and the common good.* Cambridge, MA: Harvard University Press.

4   Bryk, A. A., & Schneider, B. (2002). *Trust in schools: A core resource for improvement.* New York: Russell Sage Foundation.

5   Carpenter, T. P., Fennema, E., Peterson, P. L., Chiang, C., & Loef, M. (1989). Using knowledge of children's mathematics thinking in classroom teaching: An experimental study. *American Educational Research Journal, 26*(4), 499–531.

5   Cobb, P., Wood, T., Yackel, E., Nicholls J., Wheatley, G., Trigatti, B., & Perlwitz, M. (1991). Assessment of a problem-centered second-grade mathematics project. *Journal for Research in Mathematics Education, 22*(1), 2–29.

2   Coleman, J. S., & Hoffer, T. (1987). *Public and private high schools: The impact of communities.* New York: Basic Books.

2   Darling-Hammond, L., Hightower, A., Husbands, J. L., LaFors, J. R., Young, V. M., & Christopher, C. (2003). *Building instructional quality: "Inside out" and " outside in" perspectives on San Diego's school reform.* Seattle: Center for the Study of Teaching and Policy, University of Washington.

2   Edmonds, R. R., & Frederiksen, J. R. (1979). *The search for effective schools: The identification and analysis of city schools that are instructionally effective for poor children.* Washington, DC: ERIC Document Reproduction Service No. ED 170 396.

4   Elmore, R. F. (2002). *Bridging the gap between standards and achievement: The imperative for professional development in education.* Washington, DC: Albert Shanker Institute.

4   Goddard, R. D., Tschannen-Moran, M., & Hoy, W. K. (2001). A multilevel examination of the distribution and effects of teacher trust in students and parents in urban elementary schools. *Elementary School Journal, 102*(1), 3–17.

5   Knapp, M. S., Shields, P. M., & Turnbull, B. J. (1992). *Academic challenge for the children of poverty: Summary report.* Washington, DC: Office of Policy and Planning, U.S. Department of Education.

1   Kyle, R. M. J., & White, E. H. (Eds.). (1985). *Reaching for excellence: An effective schools sourcebook.* Washington, DC: National Institute of Education.

1   Lee, V., Bryk, A., & Smith, J. (1993). The organization of effective secondary schools. *Review of Research in Education, 19,* 171–267.

4   Lee, V. E., & Smith, J. (1995). Effects of high school restructuring and size on gains in achievement and engagement for early secondary school students. *Sociology of Education, 68*(4), 241–270.

5   Lee, V. E., Smith, J., & Newmann, F. M. (2001). *Instruction and achievement in Chicago elementary schools.* Chicago: Consortium on Chicago School Research.

5   Lee, V. E., Smith, J. B., & Croninger, R. G. (1997, April). How high school organization influences the equitable distribution of learning in mathematics and science. *Sociology of Education, 70,* pp. 128–150.

2   Lee, V. E., Smith, J. B., Perry, T. E., & Smylie, M. A. (1999). *Social support, academic press, and student achievement.* Chicago: Consortium on Chicago School Research.

4   Leithwood, K., Seashore Louis, K., Anderson, S., & Wahlstrom, K. (2004). *How leadership influences student learning.* New York: Wallace Foundation.

5   Levin, M., Newmann, F. M., & Oliver, D. W. (1969). *A law and social studies curriculum based on the analysis of public issues: A final report.* Washington, DC: Office of Education, Bureau of Research, U.S. Department of Health, Education, and Welfare.

4   Little, J. W. (1982). Norms of collegiality and experimentation: Workplace conditions of school success. *American Educational Research Journal, 19*(3), 325–340.

4   Little, J. W., & McLaughlin, M. W. (Eds.). (1993). *Teachers' work: Individuals, colleagues, and contexts.* New York: Teachers College Press.

2   Louis, K. S., Kruse, S. D., & Marks, H. M. (1996). Schoolwide professional community. In F. M. Newmann & Associates (Eds.), *Authentic achievement: Restructuring schools for intellectual quality* (pp. 179–203). San Francisco: Jossey-Bass.

4   Marks, H. M., Doane, K. B., & Secada, W. G. (1996). Support for student achievement. In F. M. Newmann & Associates (Eds.), *Authentic achievement: Restructuring schools for intellectual quality* (pp. 209–227). San Francisco: Jossey-Bass.

4   McLaughlin, M. W., & Talbert, J. E. (2001). *Professional communities and the work of high school teaching.* Chicago: University of Chicago Press.

4   Mohr, N., & Dichter, A. (2003). *Stages of team development: Lessons from the struggle of site-based management.* Providence, RI: Annenberg Institute for School Reform.

4   Newmann, F. M., & Associates. (1996). *Authentic achievement: Restructuring schools for intellectual quality.* San Francisco: Jossey-Bass.

5   Newmann, F. M., Bryk, A. S., & Nagaoka, J. (2001). *Authentic intellectual work and standardized tests: Conflict or coexistence.* Chicago: Consortium on Chicago School Research.

4   Newmann, F. M., Smith, B., & Allensworth, E. (2001). *School reform with focus: Benefits and challenges of instructional program coherence.* Chicago: Consortium on Chicago School Research.

4   Newmann, F. M., & Wehlage, G. G. (1995). *Successful school restructuring: A report to the public and educators.* Madison: Center on Organization and Restructuring of Schools, Wisconsin Center for Education Research, University of Wisconsin.

3   Oakes, J., Gamoran, A., & Page, R. N. (1992). Curriculum differentiation: Opportunities, outcomes, and meanings. In P. W. Jackson (Ed.), *Handbook of research on curriculum: A project of the American Educational Research Association* (pp. 570–608). New York: Macmillan.

4   Popkewitz, T. S., Tabachnik, B. R., & Wehlage, G. G. (1982). *The myth of educational reform: A study of school responses to a program of change.* Madison: University of Wisconsin Press.

1   Purkey, S. C., & Smith, M. S. (1983). Effective schools: A review. *Elementary School Journal, 83*(4), 427–452.

2   Rutter, M., Maughan, B., Mortimore, P., & Ouston, J. (1979). *Fifteen thousand hours: Secondary schools and their effects on children.* Cambridge, MA: Harvard University Press.

3   Secada, W. G., Gamoran, D., & Weinstein, M. G. (1996). Pathways to equity. In F. M. Newmann & Associates (Eds.), *Authentic achievement: Restructuring schools for intellectual* quality (pp. 228–244). San Francisco: Jossey-Bass.

5   Silver, E., & Lane, S. (1995). Can instructional reform in urban middle schools help students narrow the mathematics performance gap? *Research in Middle Level Education, 18*(2), 49–70.

4   Siskin, L. S. (2003, Spring). Colleagues and "yutzes": Accountability inside schools. *Voices in Urban Education,* p. 1.

3   Slavin, R. E. (1987). Ability grouping and achievement in elementary schools: A best-evidence synthesis. *Review of Educational Research, 57*(3), 293–336.

3   Slavin, R. E. (1990). Achievement effects of ability grouping in secondary schools: A best-evidence synthesis. *Review of Educational Research, 60*(3), 471–499.

4   Smylie, M. A., Allensworth, E., Greenberg, R., Harris, R., & Luppescu, S. (2001). *Teacher professional development in Chicago: Supporting effective practice.* Chicago: Consortium on Chicago School Research.

4   Spillane, J. P. (2004). *Standards deviation: How schools misunderstand education policy.* Cambridge, MA: Harvard University Press.

5   Tharp, R. G. (1982). The effects instruction of comprehension: Results and description of the Kamehameha Early Education Program. *Reading Research Quarterly, 17*(4), 503–527.

4   Waters, J. T., Marzano, R. J., Waters, T., & McNulty, B. A. (2005). *School leadership that works: From research to results.* Alexandria, VA: Association for Supervision and Curriculum Development; Aurora, CO: Mid-Continent Research for Education and Learning.

CHAPTER FOUR

Professional Communication and Collaboration

Judith Warren Little

Central to the vigor and success of a school is the strength of its teacher workforce. This discussion focuses on one source of strength: the fabric of teachers' professional relationships. Drawing from the past two decades of research on teachers' work and experience in school improvement, my aim is to supply schools with a way of thinking about their roles in contributing to the professional relationships experienced by teachers. I have concentrated my attention on teachers, but the same arguments could reasonably be made for administrators, counselors, paraprofessionals, and other specialists.

STRONG OR WEAK TIES AMONG TEACHERS: WHAT DOES THE SCHOOL PROMOTE?

Consider what kind of "communication maps" might be generated by shadowing several individual teachers for a week. The likely scenarios vary widely. At one extreme, we would expect to find teachers who spend entire days without more than a few words to another teacher and whose professional interactions are sporadic at best. Such teachers embody the enduring image of the isolated teacher behind the closed classroom door: Nodes in the communication net are few and widely spaced, having minimal significance for the teacher's life and work. At the other extreme, we would find teachers whose week is crowded with professional encounters both inside and outside the school. In this scenario, the classroom walls are more permeable, and the communication net is more densely and colorfully woven; teachers see themselves as members of one or more professional communities that may range from small, intimate partnerships to far-flung networks. Between these extremes, the possibilities multiply.

The variety in these "communication maps" derives in part from the qualities or circumstances of individual teachers. Aspects of personality, attitudes toward teaching, teaching workload, or family obligations all may shape teachers' dispositions to forge close ties with their colleagues. Acknowledging these individual differences, it nonetheless remains evident that the school itself influences the nature and extent of teachers' professional communication and collaboration. Despite some individual teacher variation, schools have been shown to vary in the professional cultures they support and thus in the typical configuration of communication one finds among teachers. It follows that schools might more deliberately promote and organize the kinds of professional exchange that benefit teaching and learning.

Research and experience enable schools to assess the kinds of professional communication they foster and the ways in which that communication influences teachers' knowledge, beliefs, practice, and commitment. Is a given school an "isolating" place to work? A place that breeds cliques and factions? A place that fosters innovation by creative individualists? An environment that cultivates close collaboration? All in all, what kinds of professional contacts and ties are valued and supported, and which are disparaged or deemed unimportant?[1]

Schools That Isolate

On the whole, both the traditions of teaching and the architecture of the school reinforce privacy and independence, making truly vigorous colleagueship both rare and relatively unstable. An isolating school does little to mediate the "cellular" structure of separate classrooms joined mainly by a common parking lot. Indeed, a school may intensify isolation by the way it organizes time, space, responsibilities, or resources and by permitting a culture of protective individualism.

The communication maps characteristic of isolating schools would show exchanges to be infrequent, short, and dominated by personal (nonteaching) topics. Beginning teachers would struggle on their own, reporting no offers of help. Teachers would profess little knowledge of one another's teaching or little familiarity with students outside their own classes. Time available outside the classroom would be limited and would be devoted to individual pursuits—planning, grading papers, calling parents, taking a break—but not to collaborative work related to teaching. Teachers would find it difficult to secure resources for out-of-school professional activity (conferences, school visits, and the like). The overall atmosphere might range from congenial to toxic but, in any event, would rarely engage teachers on matters of teaching.

Schools That Support the "Independent Artisan"

Many teachers would find the portrait of extreme isolation to be overdrawn. Although working primarily on their own classroom pursuits, they would deny being isolated from the company of colleagues or from new ideas, methods, or materials. Their portrait would coincide well with what Michael Huberman (1993) termed the "independent artisan." Huberman maintained that the image of the independent artisan, creatively tinkering with new ideas and materials within the privacy of the classroom, is compatible with the organizational realities of teachers' work: the structural separation of the classroom, the immediate and specific demands of classroom life, and the egalitarian traditions of teaching. This model receives additional support from other researchers who have shown that teachers may have good and pressing reasons to preserve their independence and innovate on their own.

In a school that fosters the independent artisan, communication maps would show teachers pursuing periodic contacts with colleagues (often outside the school) that expand their resources for the classroom. Teachers would respond readily to requests for help, share materials on occasion, and have access to resources for occasional professional development.

In one scenario, the "independent artisan" model might result in a school that takes pride in being a collection of highly individual but capable innovating teachers and in supplying teachers with incentives and resources for the independent innovations they undertake. Missing from that scenario, however, is any provision for moving collectively on schoolwide priorities and problems or any mechanism for ensuring that all that independent "tinkering" serves students well. In an alternative scenario portrayed by Talbert and McLaughlin (2002), artisanship in teaching would derive its inspiration and support from rich, collaborative cultures with shared commitments to student success.

Schools That Foster Collaborative Cultures

Research confirms the power of professional community to heighten teachers' effectiveness and strengthen the overall capacity of a school to pursue improvements in teaching and learning. Increasingly, we find evidence that some aspects of a school's professional culture, especially a collective responsibility for student success, are associated with student achievement. Yet this body of research also illustrates the complexities of teacher community. The work that teachers undertake together may be ambitious or superficial; the relationships they establish may be harmonious or conflict ridden; tightly knit groups may unite or balkanize a school. Furthermore, recent investigations have uncovered a number of endemic tensions in collaboration: the underestimated potential for conflict among teachers working closely together, the difficult balance between collaborative endeavors and individual interests, and the sheer demand that collaboration places on time and energy.

One of the central accomplishments of recent research has been to more clearly illuminate the kinds of professional solidarity or community that benefit schools and students. McLaughlin and Talbert (2001) distinguished between two kinds of strong teacher community: "traditional" community and what they termed "teacher learning community." Teachers in traditional communities share well-defined views regarding the content they teach and what students should learn, but they display little inclination to question those views even in the face of student difficulty or failure. Teacher learning communities, in contrast, are united by their commitment to student learning and a corresponding inclination to inquire deeply into matters of teaching and learning. As used by McLaughlin and Talbert, the term "teacher learning community" refers to "teachers' joint efforts to generate new knowledge of practice and their mutual support of each others' professional growth" (p. 75).

Such teacher learning communities thus have a distinctive character. They question and challenge teaching practices when students experience difficulty in learning, and they routinely investigate new possibilities for teaching and learning. Such groups maintain an open curiosity about their own practices, and they manage difference and conflict in generative ways. They embrace a shared obligation to promote student success and well-being, and they develop collective expertise by employing problem solving, critique, reflection, and debate. Similarly, in *An Emerging Framework for Analyzing School-Based Professional Community*, Kruse, Louis, and Bryk (1995) identified shared values focused on student learning, reflective dialogue, collaboration, and "deprivatization" of practice as characteristics of professional community. Those characteristics, Kruse et al. argued, are, in turn, supported by certain structural conditions of time, space, responsibility, communication, and decision-making autonomy and by cultural or human resource conditions that include openness to improvement, access to expertise, trust and respect, supportive leadership, and socialization of new members.

Consistent with the emerging portrait of the teacher learning community, communication maps in "collaborative" schools would show a higher density of communication focused specifically on teaching and learning. Teachers would more often communicate about the progress of students, develop curriculum or assessments together, and spend time in one another's classrooms. Their week would incorporate regularly scheduled time for consultation and collaboration in addition to personal planning time. One might expect to find experienced teachers routinely observing and coplanning with beginning teachers, or teachers at a grade level comparing examples of student writing, or members of an interdisciplinary group trying to determine authentic links between subjects. Links to outside sources of ideas and support would be common, with school resources subsidizing teachers' participation in networks, special projects, professional development activity, teacher research, and reform partnership arrangements.

The larger the school, the more likely it is that all three of these portraits—isolation, independent experimentation, and close collaboration—apply in some degree. Overall, the prospects for school improvement grow as schools take deliberate steps to reduce the isolation of teachers and to build professional communication that is both intensive and extensive. Along the path from isolation to community are several possibilities worth cultivating: steady support for individual explorations, reason and opportunity for small collaborations, and a schoolwide environment conducive to teacher learning.

EXTENDING COMMUNICATION AND COLLABORATION

From the wider array of structural and cultural supports for collaboration and professional community, I have distilled three for close attention. These conditions lend themselves in part to formal decision making at the school level but also require concerted leadership and consistent culture building.

Shared Interests and Purposes

Meaningful collaboration arises out of genuine interests or purposes held in common. Professionals are more likely to collaborate when they have a problem that can't be solved, a goal that can't be achieved, or an interest that can't be satisfied by individuals working on their own. Teachers may find reason to work together or to learn from one another because they teach similar subjects, grade levels, or students or because they teach in similar circumstances. For example, one elementary school committed itself to a goal that students would read fluently and confidently by the end of third grade. To ensure that the responsibility did not fall solely on the third-grade teachers, teachers in all the primary grades began meeting regularly to look at samples of student work, talk about what it means to "read fluently and confidently," examine instructional alternatives, and develop solutions to problems. They considered new options for teaching the primary grades, such as remaining with a single cohort of students from first to third grade, turning to each other for materials and ideas for each grade level.

> *Questions:* What shared problems, goals, or interests bring teachers together? Where do teachers find colleagues whose interests most closely intersect with their own, understanding that they may be in other schools? What do teachers stand to accomplish together or learn from and with one another?

Opportunity

Schools create opportunity for professional exchange principally by expanding the amount of discretionary (out-of-classroom) time available to teachers. Schools differ, sometimes dramatically, in the amount and concentration of out-of-class time available during the salaried week and year. In principle, American communities would do well to invest in a more favorable ratio of out-of-class to in-class time. Yet without altering the number of paid teacher days or lengthening the official duty day, many schools have reorganized time to enable teachers to collaborate on a daily or weekly basis. Elementary schools have "banked" time on 4 days to gain a minimum release day once a week. Secondary schools have organized prep times to join teachers who have reason to work together and have reallocated blocks of faculty meeting time to ensure that subject departments or cross-subject teams have the time needed for substantive work together.

Making good use of common meeting times proves difficult unless teachers have both reason and time to meet frequently. Out-of-classroom time has a large appetite, and there is much in the everyday experience of schools to feed it. Among the five restructured schools profiled by Louis and Kruse and their colleagues (1995), only two organized time in ways that promoted professional community. Although the examples tend to be few, they show how teachers may benefit from collaboration opportunities constructed at multiple levels: at the school level; within a grade level, department, or team; as members of informal study groups; or as participants in networks outside the school. Stokes (2001) described one innovative elementary school that organized multiple opportunities of precisely these different types, with school-level collaboration focused on schoolwide issues and problems and other activities facilitating collaboration within specific grade levels or among voluntary teacher inquiry groups. Each form of inquiry worked well to enable some kinds of learning or to tackle some kinds of problems, while being less well suited to others. To develop this constellation of activities required that the staff develop both *normative capacity*, "values that support self-study as an important kind of learning," and *technical capacity*, "the structures, processes, knowledge, and activities by which the school staff does the actual work of inquiring into their practices" (Stokes, 2001, pp. 150–151).

> *Questions:* How are time and space configured to support frequent and focused communication among teachers and to permit periods of extended collaboration? What other opportunities do teachers have to communicate and consult with colleagues and others outside school, to be in each other's presence informally, or to see each other at work with students?

Resources

With greater frequency, teachers enjoy access to technology that facilitates communication (from telephones to the Internet) and to appropriate meeting or workspace. Beyond these rudimentary supports for communication, however, professional exchange requires and thrives on access to appropriate material resources and to diverse and valued sources of expertise. Successful collaborative groups tend to be adept at exploiting new information, seeking out alternative ideas and solutions, and inviting productive criticism. In one example described by Horn (2005), a group of high school mathematics teachers dramatically boosted student achievement by working together on a weekly basis to develop or modify ambitious curricular materials and help one another with instructional problems. Their success was substantially aided by the ways they developed for talking with one another about issues of teaching and learning and by their use of a common set of materials and instructional practices. They were further aided by the relationships the group formed with reform-oriented mathematics networks and with researchers and teacher educators from neighboring universities. What becomes evident in this and other case study research is the importance of resources of knowledge and skill in addition to material resources and structural opportunity (time and space). Overall, collaboration is more likely to yield benefits when it is informed by knowledge of three sorts: *substantive* knowledge that improves the quality of ideas, plans, and solutions; *process* knowledge, skill and norms that make a group effective as a group; and *political* and other contextual knowledge that makes the group effective in its larger environment. From a school and district perspective, teachers' access to all the relevant resources arguably constitutes an important investment in the quality of teaching.

> *Questions:* What resources do teachers have readily available to add to their stock of knowledge and ideas? What preparation and support do teachers receive for making good use of professional development, networking opportunities, or new technologies?

THE TROUBLES THAT COLLEAGUES ENCOUNTER

Even granted the conditions outlined above, teachers might anticipate certain challenges. Here are two such challenges that implicate policy, practice, and leadership conditions at the school level. The first centers on the difficulty of developing collaboration that is sufficiently robust and enduring to yield real benefits for teaching and learning. The second challenge centers on the potential for teacher overload and on organizational policies and practices that plausibly support increased communication and collaboration among teachers without generating stress and burnout.

Coping Productively With Difference, Disagreement, and Conflict

For all the appealing imagery associated with collaboration, teachers' stories abound with tales of difficulty and disappointment. A few common problems stand out in failed collaborations: disagreements over basic issues of teaching and learning, the balance between collaboration and autonomy, the tricky divide between "making a suggestion" and "telling someone what to do," jealousies and resentments regarding specific decisions (the devil really is in the details), and inadequate knowledge and confidence needed to make working with colleagues at least as effective as working alone.

In recent years, researchers have devoted more attention to how productive teacher collaborations develop over time and what goes on inside collaborative groups that fosters teacher learning and instructional improvement. The resulting research documents a growing realization that the most productive teacher groups find ways to uncover and wrestle with issues of difference and disagreement. Close collaborations bring fundamental beliefs and preferences to the surface (often unexpectedly) and may reveal points of deep disagreement. Personal and professional relationships suffer strain when teachers must wrestle with competing beliefs and practices. We find teachers who espouse a wish to collaborate nonetheless "backing off" when they uncover deeply felt differences regarding curriculum priorities, standards for student work, or instructional preferences. For example, one group of English teachers discovered that they held very different views about how much choice students should be able to exercise in selecting independent reading material as part of a new ninth-grade course on which they were collaborating. The unanticipated conflict produced an awkward and difficult exchange, after which members of the group quickly agreed to defer to individual preferences. Although the group continued to work together on the course, a pattern was established: In the face of conflict, collective agreement would give way to individual autonomy. (This example is described in more detail in Little, 2003; see also Achinstein, 2002a and 2002b.)

Pamela Grossman and colleagues in *Toward a Theory of Teacher Community* (Grossman, Wineburg, & Woolworth, 2001), echoed the difficulty that teachers experience when differences become public. The researchers described a shift from "pseudo-community" to "authentic community" as an interdisciplinary group of high school teachers gradually came to grips with difference and conflict over an 18-month period. As the authors summed up the challenge,

The work of school-based community demands new forms of social participation from its members. In a profession constructed around norms of privacy, taking responsibility for the learning of other adults is a radical departure from business as usual. Pressing colleagues for clarification in a public setting requires not only a particular intellectual stance, but enormous social skill and careful negotiation to prevent hurt feelings and possible shutdown. Learning to argue productively about ideas that cut to the core of personal and professional identity involves the skillful orchestration of multiple social and intellectual capacities. (Grossman, Wineburg, & Woolworth, p. 980)

For teachers to seriously engage in professional communication with their colleagues, they must be able to initiate open and critical discussions of instruction and student learning. Mentoring and advising must constitute an accepted and valued aspect of school life. Staff must be able to put forward new ideas and critically evaluate ideas as they are tried out in practice—but also live with one another through the messiness of discovery. In doing so, they must find factors other than personality differences to explain the difficulties they are having and must also contend with well-documented reluctance to offer advice, openly express concerns, or examine the roots of disagreement.[2]

Work Overload Problems, or Too Much of a Good Thing

Teachers in small, teacher-controlled partnerships manage to sort out their workload commitments: how much collaboration they will undertake and how much in-school and out-of-school time it will consume. However, in most ambitious and productive collaborations, those time commitments tend to be substantial. Teachers speak with pride of their accomplishments, while also complaining of exhaustion. Ambitious collaboration brings a sense of professional renewal but also intensifies the risk of stress and burnout.

In addition, expectations for communication and formal collaboration tend to increase in a school with the onset of shared decision making or other schoolwide improvement initiatives.

Teachers may be provided time and resources to collaborate, but for purposes and tasks defined by others, a problem Hargreaves (1991) labeled "contrived collegiality." Teachers may thus feel that they are losing control of the focus and scope of collaboration— and that they are being "meeting'd to death." Administrators or colleagues who witness teachers' efforts to regain control over their time may interpret such efforts as "resistance," but the teachers view them as necessary efforts to restore order in their priorities.

To reduce the possibility of burnout (or the necessity of resistance) requires in part that teachers be relieved of overload and supported in concentrating collaboration where it counts most. In one analysis of collaborative time commitments and career stress, Bartlett (2004) showed how schools vary in the steps they take to moderate work overload when teachers collaborate—and the costs to schools and teachers when such steps are inadequate. Fostering and adequately supporting meaningful collaboration thus emerges as a crucial task of school leadership.

CONCLUSION

At the very least, one must imagine schools in which teachers are in frequent conversation with each other about their work, have easy and necessary access to each other's classrooms, take it for granted that they should comment on each other's work, and have the time to develop common standards for student work. (Meier, 1992, p. 602)

In these words, Deborah Meier envisioned the school environment conducive to "reinventing teaching," and it is demonstrably a collaborative one. This chapter presents a condensed framework for examining the professional relationships characteristic of a school and for assessing the conditions that foster or impede collaboration. The framework encompasses shared purposes focused on teaching and learning; adequate opportunity; and material, social, and intellectual resources. Missing, of course, are the specific histories and contexts that give nuance to each school workplace and shape the possibilities and limitations of change. This framework may help teachers and administrators to make the possibilities visible; to pursue them fully will require curiosity, tenacity, and inventiveness, but begins with talk about teaching.

NOTES

1. In the descriptions that follow, the isolating school is most widely associated with Lortie's (1975) analysis of teaching conditions. The "independent artisan" model is based most directly on Huberman's (1993) use of that term and his argument about structural impediments to schoolwide professional community. To characterize schools that foster a "collaborative culture" or "teacher learning community," I have drawn on my own research and a wide range of other contributors whose work appears in the list of "References and Resources."

2. Group problem-solving strategies include diagnosing the sources of apparent group failure (problems with the nature of the task, the group's authority, competing interests, available knowledge and skill, and the like). Ambivalence about advice and helping, or about public dissent, is not unique to teaching. There is an extensive body of social-psychological research on this matter. I have summarized parts of it elsewhere (Little, 1990a) to explain some of the difficulties encountered by formal mentoring programs.

REFERENCES AND RESOURCES

The following readings provide the basis for the arguments summarized in this brief overview. Only a few have been directly cited in the text. I have tried to keep the list concise and to concentrate on published sources available to American educators.

Achinstein, B. (2002a). *Community, diversity, and conflict among school-teachers: The ties that blind.* New York: Teachers College Press.

Achinstein, B. (2002b). Conflict amid community: The micropolitics of teacher collaboration. *Teachers College Record, 104*(3), 421–455.

Ball, S. J. (1987). *The micro-politics of the school: Towards a theory of school organization.* London: Methuen.

Bartlett, L. (2004). Expanding teacher work roles: A resource for retention or a recipe for overwork? *Journal of Education Policy, 19,* 565–582.

Blase, J. (Ed.). (1991). *The politics of life in schools: Power, conflict, and cooperation.* Newbury Park, CA: Sage.

Clark, C. M. (Ed.). (2001). *Talking shop: Authentic conversation and teacher learning.* New York: Teachers College Press.

Darling-Hammond, L. (1997). *The right to learn: A blueprint for creating schools that work.* San Francisco: Jossey-Bass.

DiPardo, A. (1999). *Teaching in common: Challenges to joint work in classrooms and schools.* New York: Teachers College Press.

Feiman-Nemser, S., & Floden, R. (1986). The cultures of teaching. In M. Wittrock (Ed.), *Handbook of research on teaching* (3rd ed., pp. 505–526). New York: Macmillan.

Grossman, P., Wineburg, S., & Woolworth, S. (2001). Toward a theory of teacher community. *Teachers College Record, 103*(6), 942–1012.

Hargreaves, A. (1991). Contrived collegiality: The micropolitics of teacher collaboration. In J. Blase (Ed.), *The politics of life in schools: Power, conflict, and cooperation.* Newbury Park, CA: Sage.

Hargreaves, A. (1993). Individualism and individuality: Reinterpreting the teacher culture. In J. W. Little & M. W. McLaughlin (Eds.), *Teachers' work: Individuals, colleagues, and contexts* (pp. 51–76). New York: Teachers College Press.

Hill, D. (1995). The strong department: Building the department as learning community. In L. S. Siskin & J. W. Little (Eds.), *The subjects in question: Departmental organization and the high school* (pp. 123–140). New York: Teachers College Press.

Horn, I. S. (2005). Learning on the job: A situated account of teacher learning in high school mathematics departments. *Cognition & Instruction, 23*(2), 207–236.

Huberman, M. (1993). The model of the independent artisan in teachers' professional relations. In J. W. Little & M. W. McLaughlin (Eds.), *Teachers work: Individuals, colleagues, and contexts* (pp. 11–50). New York: Teachers College Press.

Johnson, S. M., & Kardos, S. (2004). Professional culture and the promise of colleagues. In S. M. Johnson & The Project on the Next Generation of Teachers, *Finders and keepers: Helping new teachers survive and thrive in our schools* (pp. 139–166). San Francisco: Jossey-Bass.

Kruse, S. D., Louis, K. S., & Bryk, A. S. (1995). An emerging framework for analyzing school-based professional community. In K. S. Louis, S. D. Kruse, & Associates (Eds.), *Professionalism and community: Perspectives on reforming urban schools* (pp. 23–42). Thousand Oaks, CA: Corwin Press.

Lee, V. E., & Smith, J. (1996). Collective responsibility for learning and its effects on gains in achievement and engagement for early secondary school students. *American Journal of Education, 104*(2), 103–147.

Lieberman, A. (Ed.). (1988). *Building a professional culture in schools.* New York: Teachers College Press.

Lieberman, A., & McLaughlin, M. W. (1992). Networks for educational change: Powerful and problematic. *Phi Delta Kappan, 73*(9), 673–677.

Little, J. W. (1990a). The mentor phenomenon and the social organization of teaching. *Review of Research in Education, 16,* 297–351.

Little, J. W. (1990b). The persistence of privacy: Autonomy and initiative in teachers' professional relations. *Teachers College Record, 91*(4), 509–536.

Little, J. W. (1999). Organizing schools for teacher learning. In L. Darling-Hammond & G. Sykes (Eds.), *Teaching as the learning profession: Handbook of teaching and policy* (pp. 233–262). San Francisco: Jossey Bass.

Little, J. W. (2003). Inside teacher community: Representations of classroom practice. *Teachers College Record, 105*(6), 913–945.

Little, J. W., Gearhart, M., Curry, M., & Kafka, J. (2003). "Looking at student work" for teacher learning, teacher community, and school reform. *Phi Delta Kappan, 83*(5), 184–192.

Lortie, D. (1975). *Schoolteacher.* Chicago: University of Chicago Press.

Louis, K. S., Kruse, S. D., & Associates. (Eds.). (1995). *Professionalism and community: Perspectives on reforming urban schools.* Thousand Oaks, CA: Corwin Press.

McLaughlin, M. W., & Talbert, J. E. (2001). *Professional communities and the work of high school teaching.* Chicago: University of Chicago Press.

Meier, D. (1992). Reinventing teaching. *Teachers College Record, 93*(4), 594–609.

Rosenholtz, S. (1989). *Teachers' workplace.* New York: Longman.

Scribner, J. P., Cockrell, K. S., Cockrell, D. H., & Valentine, J. W. (1999). Creating professional communities in schools through organizational learning: An evaluation of a school improvement process. *Educational Administration Quarterly, 35*(1), 130–160.

Siskin, L. S. (1994). *Realms of knowledge: Academic departments in secondary schools.* London: Falmer Press.

Stokes, L. (2001). Lessons from an inquiring school: Forms of inquiry and conditions for teacher learning. In A. Lieberman & L. Miller (Eds.), *Teachers caught in the action: Professional development that matters* (pp. 141–158). New York: Teachers College Press.

Talbert, J. E., & McLaughlin, M. W. (2002). Professional communities and the artisan model of teaching. *Teachers and Teaching: Theory and Practice, 8*(3/4), 325–343.

Westheimer, J. (1998). *Among schoolteachers: Community, autonomy and ideology in teachers' work.* New York: Teachers College Press.

CHAPTER FIVE

Teacher Use of Formal Assessment in the Classroom

Eva L. Baker

HIGH-STAKES ACCOUNTABILITY AND THE ASSESSMENT OF STUDENT LEARNING

Teachers have always made judgments about the progress of their students. These judgments have been based on methods as diverse as student recitation, review of homework, evaluation of classroom discussion, observation of behavior, test performance, and analyses of student projects. The purpose of these objectives has been to monitor progress, provide feedback to the students, and create a record of performance for the teacher to use in planning instruction and as a basis for giving an end-of-course grade. Giving grades has been a key method to reinforce teachers' status and authority in classrooms. Although the dramatic rise in

AUTHOR'S NOTE: The work reported herein was supported under the Educational Research and Development Centers Program, PR/Award Number R305B960002 and Award Number R305A050004, as administered by the Institute of Education Sciences, U.S. Department of Education. The findings and opinions expressed in this report do not reflect the positions or policies of the National Center for Education Research, the Institute of Education Sciences, or the U.S. Department of Education.

accountability in recent years has sought to substitute external criteria for the judgments teachers make internal to their courses, grade point average—that is, the summary measure of classroom assessments—still holds an important place in the measure of student performance and an important role in determining students' future options. Grade point averages are a common way of making distinctions about students' academic qualifications.

So what are the newer accountability provisions, and how do they affect internal classroom testing practice? The No Child Left Behind Act of 2001 (NCLB, 2002) and the Improving American Schools Act (1994) represented serious procedural moves under the aegis of Title I to reform all school practices in the name of raising standards for all children and closing the gap between lower-performing students, lower-performing institutions, and the goal of proficiency for all students by 2014. The increase in external assessment and measurement, with relatively short-term sanctions for poor performance, has highlighted new challenges in teacher classroom assessment, including new sorts of curriculum and teacher preparation, and the desire to anticipate performance that will determine how many schools have not met the targets (adequate yearly progress goals) set by each state. A renewed emphasis on teacher use of assessment in the classroom is intended to support the progress of school performance. What it may have done simultaneously is to shift the principal authority for learning to external sources. Part of this chapter examines this transfer of power, and part addresses what can be done internally through technical and professional development to strengthen the classroom assessment process.

In the policy arena, a key impetus for concern about teachers' use of test information is the prevailing belief about the competitiveness of U.S. students in comparative, international studies of achievement. U.S. students continue to underperform in these comparisons (Gonzales et al., 2004; Lemke et al., 2004; McGaw, 2005). On the national level, studies of student performance in the National Assessment of Educational Progress report that most students are failing to achieve proficiency, although some improvement has been seen in math (Perie, Grigg, & Dion, 2005; Perie, Grigg, & Donahue, 2005). The NCLB conception of adequate yearly progress (AYP), a metric that may need technical improvement, sends the message that all is not well with U.S.

student performance and, in particular, but not exclusively, that there are difficulties with students from poor economic environments. Although there are statistical artifacts in the AYP calculations, the findings are troubling. Many schools are being identified as low performing or failing.

There is conflicting information about gaps being closed. Are gaps being closed because the emphasis is on bringing underperforming students up while letting the growth of higher performing students flatten out? In other words, if differences in performance between higher performing and traditionally underperforming students are coming closer, is it because our most proficient students are not making similar strides? Additional troubling evidence comes from higher education, where colleges and universities report enrolling ever-increasing numbers of underprepared students who have met admission standards but do not have the skills to succeed in entry-level mathematics or writing courses. Business and industry leaders continue to complain that they must mount expensive training programs to prepare new hires for entry-level positions. Before the attacks on America on September 11, 2001, businesses sought to hire immigrant professionals and are now, because of market changes, increasing their reliance on international outsourcing for entry-level jobs.

Despite numerous counterexamples that argue that students today are performing as well as ever, we are in an era of rising expectations regarding content knowledge, skill levels, and school completion occurring at the time of an influx of diverse students. Nonetheless, the consistency of information and of beliefs about inadequate student achievement from a wide variety of sources has given rise to educational reforms on the local, state, and national levels. If NCLB is viewed as a set of goals rather than mechanical procedures to ensure success, most people would support the intended outcomes of the legislation. And what inferences might be drawn about teacher classroom performance?

One obvious question is whether teachers have similarly detected poor performance in their own classrooms. Teachers' summative judgments, corresponding to external tests such as state assessments, are encapsulated in the grades they give students. Judging from general reports of grade inflation, the answer seems to be that inadequate student performance is not completely reflected in teachers' grading practices. Without getting sidetracked by a discussion of the utility of grades for motivation or alternatives to conventional grading practices, let us turn to the practical matter of external examinations and recent changes in their uses.

It is clear that external examinations, such as state assessments, now occupy a place in the public's mind that has exaggerated their value. These tests are seen to be equivalent to the desired learning of students, rather than a sample of a range of knowledge and skills that the test items or tasks actually represent. At the policy level, then, distinctions between testing and learning are not made, nor is the quality challenged of the tests that are claimed to measure the state standards. Sadly, the inadequacy of this perspective can be seen by any analysis of the correspondence or "alignment" of desired outcomes (state curriculum or content standards), the subareas actually tested, and the curriculum (and attendant professional development) available to teachers. Flowing from the acceptance of end-of-year external test scores as the gold standard of performance and in light of sanctions for schools, a major shift has occurred in the role of in-class assessment practices. The dominant argument had been that classroom assessment was to have a diagnostic function and that a skilled teacher with sufficient subject matter expertise could examine student performance, help determine where and why students were having difficulty, and provide careful, supportive feedback for the learners. Black and Wiliam (1998), among others (Baker, 2003; Haertel & Herman, 2005), have argued for assessments that expand and deepen the understanding of students and teachers about desired learning and measured outcomes. Earlier arguments were made that teacher-designed classroom assessments were to fill in the gaps in areas that could not be well treated in broad-spectrum, large-scale state tests. Performance on these measures would be summarized in students' grade point average, and along with the external measures, some sort of balanced curriculum would be crafted. A common concern, however, was that the enacted curriculum varied by school, the teachers' choices of assessment were widely different, and teacher standards, even independent of the students taught, were similarly nonuniform.

How should we address the diversity of teacher assessments of student performance? One direct response of policymakers has been to seek to assist teachers to be more effective in the judgments they make about students. One strategy is to improve the way teachers design and use tests and test results (Baker, 2003; Black & Wiliam, 1998; Stiggins, 2002).

These remedies in testing practices target core principles of learning: fairness, effectiveness, and efficiency. In the case of fairness, the desire is to increase consistency of meaning of grades from classroom to classroom and from school to school. When the population of students was similar from school to school, no one was much concerned about variations between stricter or more lenient grading by teachers; any differences were expected to average out. Now that many urban schools deal almost exclusively with disadvantaged students, it is important to document that grading standards are fair, with no particular group of students getting special advantage. This assumption of fairness is needed to ensure the meaningfulness of high school diplomas and for making comparative judgments based on students' grades, for example, in college admissions procedures.

The effectiveness and efficiency arguments relating to teacher testing practices have far less to do with grading and what is called *summative evaluation* of a unit or a course and much more to do with helping all students attain their maximum levels of performance during the course of instruction. *Formative evaluation,* or, more fashionably, *formative assessment,* is the technical term that describes the use of test results to improve teaching practice and student learning. The purpose of such tests, for instance, those given weekly or monthly, is to identify areas needing additional attention or effort as well as to provide evidence of progress and accomplishments. The use of test results in this case is intended to improve the learning of students who were tested by involving (a) students in reflecting on their work, (b) parents for appropriate assistance, and (c) teachers who would need to undertake additional approaches to help students reach academic goals. Considering instructional improvement in longer cycles, it is reasonable for an instructional team to look at the performance of fourth-grade students for 2006 to 2007 and take into account their areas of weaknesses when planning for the 2007 to 2008 school year. This type of formative evaluation provides information to the teaching staff. Undermining the utility of this approach is that some teachers may not see student performance as subject to improvement and may substantially attribute the poor performance to factors outside the instructional setting.

Consequently, teachers may be more likely to accept results as the best that could have been achieved—instead of analyzing findings and making changes in instructional practices that might contribute to some improvement.

These analyses are not presented as an assertion of their truth, but rather to offer an explanation for the attention given to test data in general and teachers' use of test results in particular. If U.S. students were performing well in international comparisons and other external tests and all teachers were highly respected as professionals, such discussions would be markedly less likely.

IMPROVING THE USE OF CLASSROOM TESTS

To improve classroom use of tests, five basic properties of the assessment should be considered: (1) The assessment must be valid; (2) it must be fair; (3) it must be credible; (4) it must be practical; and (5) it must generate useful results. Let us briefly consider each of these properties.

Validity is a concept that means the test measures the aspect (or construct) of student performance of interest. For example, if a good writer can get a high score on a history essay knowing very little history, the test would not be a valid measure of the student's understanding of history. The wrong inference would be drawn from the data. If a student who can do complex mathematics fails a math test because the word problems are written in an unfamiliar language, the test would not be a valid measure of mathematics for that student. Validity also has to do with test content, particularly whether the test includes or excludes content that it would be expected to measure. For example, a test involving literary devices that excluded similes would have its validity challenged by English teachers who believe that similes represent an essential component of that content area. Validity most generally has to do with the purpose of the test. Certain tests may be very good for identifying the best or worst students in a class but not very good for providing diagnostic information. When tests are discussed or proposed, it is always a good idea to raise a question about how the validity of the test has been investigated, for what types of students, and for what particular purposes or uses. In tests used to make judgments about the quality of instruction offered in a class or a school, it would be desirable to show that the test itself is sensitive to variations in instruction (other than simple presentation) and not solely measuring a student's background or other input variables. A simple strategy would be to look at whether classroom instruction can interrupt correlations of pretest to posttest. In an effective system, strong posttest performance should wipe out the predictability of preassessment when instruction has been effective.

Fairness, our second major element, undergirds much of American values and is an extremely important part of testing practice. Most simply, the precept of fairness means that students should receive examination scores that reflect their particular levels of expertise and are free of influences based on group membership, such as gender, language group, or cultural background. Of course, the concept of fairness also implies that the "rules" for preparing, administering, and scoring a test were followed and that scores were not influenced by cheating, inappropriate practice, or unacceptable hints, for instance. Scores should not be influenced by students' backgrounds, their differential familiarity with the method of testing, or the use of scoring practices that favor one type of student over another. Because fairness is so important, it is a primary justification for using tests that can be scored objectively.

The third important attribute of tests is their credibility to relevant parties. *Credibility* means the extent to which a test is perceived to be worthwhile and its results trusted. If tests are not credible to teachers, they will not be administered or, if mandated, their results will not be taken seriously. If tests have low credibility with students, many may not try hard and their results will not be good measures of the real levels of their accomplishments. If tests are not credible to parents and the public, their results will be dismissed as meaningless and efforts will be made to change the tests to be more in line with public expectations. Right now, there is a conflict in the credibility of measures, with many teachers doubting the appropriateness of state examinations, in contrast to most policymakers and some parents.

The fourth property of a test, *practicality,* refers to the ease of its use in regular classroom settings. If a test is discretionary and also not practical, it will not be used at all or not be used for long. If a test is required and not practical, in that, for example, it takes too much time or requires special materials not easily available or managed, unforeseen and different adjustments in administration procedures in classrooms will occur that could well invalidate the results.

Finally, classroom tests need to generate results that are *useful*. Tests that give teachers an overall estimate—that students do well or poorly—are less desirable than tests that give guidance about specific topics or skills that need improvement. But more detail is not always better. The level of detail must match the ability of the teacher to make use of the information. For instance, teachers are unlikely to be able to make use of highly refined test results in situations where limited instructional materials are available. For teachers to make very detailed test results useful in planning for each student in a class, there must be deep resources in teachers' personal repertoires or school curriculum and teaching assets. Unfortunately, teachers may become "deskilled" in expanded repertoires to use when students have difficulties. The influx of scripted curricula and time management constraints provide disincentives for teachers to go beyond the requirements. Furthermore, the "pacing" plans of some curricula make finding the occasion to interweave needed instruction far more difficult.

Two approaches will be described that are intended to help teachers to use student results in more effective ways. Standards-based reform has resulted in the development by almost every state of a set of *standards* to guide instruction and testing. One kind of standards focuses on the identification of important goals in content to be achieved at various grade levels or age ranges. Some states and districts have identified standards to be met for every grade, whereas others have chosen important points in student development (e.g., at the end of primary education, at the end of elementary school, at the beginning of high school, and at high school graduation). In most cases, these standards bear remarkable resemblance to what used to be called *curriculum goals, curriculum guidelines,* or *frameworks* and are intended to describe what students should be expected to accomplish. They are often phrased in a general way, for example, "Students should apply linear and geometric measurement principles to real-life problems," and then may be augmented by more explicit content specifications, for instance, types of included polygons, to provide further guidance. For the most part, states and districts have reviewed model content standards prepared by national groups focused in particular subject matters, such as those of the National Council of Teachers of Mathematics or the National Science Foundation.

These standards are intended to provide guidance for determining both the kinds of learning students should be encouraged to experience and the types of examinations that should be given to students. In the purest form, standards-based assessments would provide a coherent framework for teaching and learning. What is particularly interesting about this cycle of educational reform is its emphasis on high standards for all students. Not since the *Sputnik* era, when, again, international competition was a major impetus for reform, have experts in subject matter provided "challenging" goals for students and educational systems.

The second development in this round of reform is the emphasis on *assessments* that map to standards. Many of the standards require students to complete tasks that involve multiple days, multiple steps, and collaboration. The type of assessment most appropriate to measure many of these more complex standards is *performance-based assessment.* Performance-based assessment is an important initiative because in addition to assessing statements of standards, it is based on the idea that assessment must be like student learning. This simple idea turns on its head the more familiar idea of *alignment,* that student learning needs to match the methods used in testing. Because of performance-based assessment's deep dependence on learning as psychologists and researchers have come to understand it, performance assessments have certain characteristics. Students are expected to construct their answers, because research in learning suggests such constructions are the way students acquire meaning. Students may be asked to perform tasks that have multiple steps, acquiring knowledge or determining the next operation based on the results of a prior activity or prior knowledge. Students may occasionally work in groups, because collaboration has been shown to be an important approach for many learners. The consequences of these attributes are performance assessments that take considerable time (no more 2-minute test items), that require judgments or raters to determine level of performance (no more answer key), and that use language as the basis for explaining how and why problems were solved rather than simply inspecting solutions. The time these performance assessments take inevitably limits the number that can be administered in any one subject area, in interdisciplinary topics, or to any one student. The cost of ratings by judges also limits the number of performance assessments that can be administered. Consequently, it is not feasible for the educational system to assess the attainment of all of the standards it seeks to achieve. So it may be desirable that teachers will use their own classroom examinations or other methods to assess many of the standards. But will it happen in the current policy and practice environment?

HOW CAN TEACHERS USE STANDARDS-BASED PERFORMANCE ASSESSMENTS IN THEIR CLASSROOMS?

In this section, I will discuss an idea about the improvement of classroom assessment practices. Classroom assessment should focus on an intellectual model of learning that can help teachers teach. Our model of learning uses knowledge from cognition and learning research as the bases for assessment design. It adds subject content into the mix by emphasizing coherences across topics and within topics, by mapping the detailed relationships in content knowledge, for example, in mathematics or history (Chung, Delacruz, & Bewley, 2004; Chung, Delacruz, Dionne, & Bewley, 2003; Chung, de Vries, Cheak, Stevens, & Bewley, 2002; Niemi, Chung, & Bewley, 2003; Vendlinski et al., 2004). This model takes cost into account by relying on reusable designs and scoring schemes, and, best of all, it has been tried repeatedly and found to perform as advertised (Brown, in press; Goldschmidt & Martinez-Fernandez, in press; Martinez-Fernandez & Goldschmidt, in press; Niemi, Baker, & Sylvester, in press; Niemi, Wang, Steinberg, Baker, & Wang, in press; Wang, Niemi, & Wang, in press).

We have discovered that there are two compatible approaches to bringing learning-based assessment to classrooms. The first way, emphasizing *teacher professional development*, places substantial burden on the intellectual resources of the teacher. The second way explores the creation and use of *classroom assessments*, which we call POWERSOURCE©, as the focus of a long-term experimental study supported by the Institute of Education Sciences (IES).

The teacher professional development approach will help teachers organize the way they go about their assessment jobs, and our research has shown that it takes considerable time, energy, and knowledge of subject matter to do a good job with performance assessments. Skeleton guidance for current professional development uses a simple set of guidelines to get people under way:

1. Determine which standards are being measured by external means, through the use of district or state assessments, commercially available tests, and so on.

2. Seek to acquire whatever is available that specifies the content to be assessed (expanded content standards) or the type of measures and student expectations in the assessments to be administered (performance standards).

3. See to it that one source of classroom examinations is based on components or comparable measures that will be used externally to evaluate the students and the school. (For example, if students are expected to use particular procedures in solving mathematics problems, such as a number line, a classroom assessment should be developed that in part uses the same general procedures.)

4. Determine which standards have been articulated that are impractical for the education system to measure formally and decide which of these standards can be examined by using one's own personal examination procedures.

As the basis for both improved teacher professional development and our alternative POWERSOURCE© approach (to be discussed later), *model-based assessment,* the learning-based model of classroom assessment developed at the National Center for Research on Evaluation, Standards, and Student Testing (CRESST), generates specifications for each type of learning to be measured and then uses the same general approach in different subject matters. Figure 5.1 shows the five key types of learning CRESST has identified (content understanding, problem solving, collaboration, communication, and self-regulation). Most goals (and relevant assessments) in schools are made up of a combination of these learning types, in the same way an individual's DNA is made up of different combinations of genes.

Figure 5.1   CRESST Model of Learning-Based Assessment

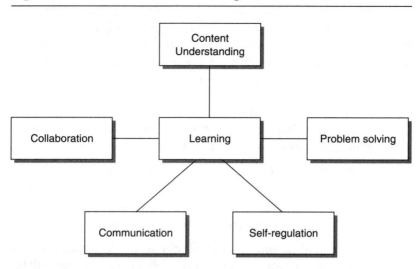

For each of these areas, at least one set of specifications has been developed for guiding the design, use, and scoring of performance assessments. These specifications include the types of materials provided to students, the administration procedures, and the scoring criteria or rubric. For example, in the area of problem solving, the specifications provide a number of choices for the assessment team. They might choose to focus on problems that have multiple right answers or single right answers. The goals of interest might emphasize problems that are clearly formulated. As a comparison, the assessment could focus on problems that are complicated and need further clarification. Other choices are whether students are provided with all the information necessary to solve the problem, are expected to have already acquired the information, or are provided opportunity to seek relevant information (e.g., in their books, in the library, or on the Internet). Performance in problem solving can use criteria related to problem identification, strategy selection, use of prior knowledge, and fluency. It should be clear that such components in scoring criteria not only encompass important attributes of problem solving (documented in the research literature) but also provide areas that teachers can address in both initial and any continuing instruction to assist students in acquiring competence.

What is most important about the problem-solving model as it has been formulated is that its structure can be applied to different subject matter areas, for instance, social studies, mathematics, and science. Thus, a teacher or assessment team needs only to learn the specifications well (or create their own) and apply them to multiple subjects taught in the classroom or school. Specifications have also been widely used in the area of content understanding, in which students are presented with source materials that include relevant content information. Primary source materials are used in history and geography, for example, speeches, letters, films, and maps. In language arts, literature or literary analyses or audiotapes can be used. In science, descriptions, write-ups, graphs, or videos of experiments may be provided. In mathematics, problems are provided, and alternative strategies or solutions may be given. The students then prepare analyses and explanations of the source materials. We have obtained these explanations in two ways: The first is the preparation of a written explanation, in which the student explains the key principles involved to a friend or relative and explains why the material is important. These explanations are scored using a well-researched approach involving an overall judgment of the student's content understanding and use of principles, prior knowledge, and argument appropriate to the subject matter. These essays are often scored for English writing conventions as well. The second method of explanation, a knowledge map, uses the same set of specifications and the same stimulus materials, but student responses are provided through graphical depictions of the relationships among key principles and ideas in the form of a knowledge map. These maps, when completed on a computer, are immediately scored in terms of their fidelity to maps made by an expert or teacher. The benefit of using a model-based approach to learning and assessment is its general applicability to multiple subject matters and the relief it provides from reinventing assessment approaches time after time. There is also some evidence that teaching toward one assessment (e.g., in a topic in history) helps students apply the appropriate analytical process to an assessment on a different topic, or what is called "transfer."

Without doubt, creating one's own performance assessments is a task involving great commitment. But to do so when standards-based reform is under way provides a unique opportunity to integrate two aspects of assessment that have been largely separated from each other: external or accountability-focused assessment and teacher-designed classroom assessment intended to provide feedback and improve learning. If both sorts of assessment can be generated from conceptions of learning that also guide instruction, there is a real opportunity to improve the performance of our students in a coherent, sensible way. Integrity of the educational system will ultimately depend on the coincidence of goals, learning, teaching, and assessment. Approaches that attract these elements rather than set them in opposition to one another are essential to the success of our schools.

Our first approach depends on teachers' use of our model and their knowledge to create assessments. We recognize that there are some practical difficulties here. We are exploring a second approach, ES POWERSOURCE©, that differs in four major ways. First, it provides teachers with some professional development and continuing Web-based support and gives them the formative assessments that are to be used in the course of 3 years of pre-algebra and algebra study, along with scoring support and rubrics. This reduces the test development burden on them. The second new feature is that the assessments themselves are selected to simultaneously measure major ideas that recur within and over the course sequence, opening up the possibility to provide more coherent measurement and learning for students, as they are confronted with examples in interim tests in the good-old-fashioned "spiral" way of meeting and reencountering skills at a higher level of complexity. A third new feature is the explicit use of a "map" or representation of the content skill relationships for both assessment design and instruction. The content map allows teachers and students to know where they are at any one time as they progress on goals.

Fourth, a new template for assessment has been gleaned from the work of Mayer (personal communication, November 2005), Sweller (personal communication, November 2005), Chi (2000), and Merrill (2002). This template illustrates what a worked example looks like and has been supported in the literature as resulting in better acquisition, recall, and transfer to new situations. In addition, we intend to continue the emphasis on student explanation of procedural or problem-solving tasks. Students will be asked to show their work and to provide a brief, reasoned statement about why they attempted to solve their problems (pre-algebra or algebra) in the way they have. Thus, the worked example applies both to the problem and to the characteristics of a good explanation.

As a small addendum, we are also experimenting with narrative templates for our series of periodic test items, similar to the consistent cast of characters or avatars in games, and adding gamelike suspense. We expect these measures to be given somewhere between 12 to 20 times a year, and we believe we need to work in a relatively inexpensive suspense story, the narrative of which is revealed as problems are solved. Naturally, we need to focus on distractibility, keeping the language appropriate for the students, and the value-added aspect of this approach. In addition, we are creating performance aids for teachers and students to help them stay on target. Developing performance aids for teachers has become a challenging task, in the light of varied curricula in different classrooms and districts. Because of the rigidity of some instructional pacing plans, we are trying to be innovative, using the computer to offer shorter, high-density, instructional "vitamins" in the form of small, online, instructional parcels. These are intended to help the student (and perhaps refresh the teacher) with an on-the-spot method of teaching what is needed, and they are related to a consistent misunderstanding or perhaps the lack of prior knowledge. They may be available during class, in afterschool programs, in homerooms, or on a home computer. We are also conducting studies of targeted feedback and the development of additional instructional options for teachers.

Our POWERSOURCE© approach, in which we provide assessments, maps, performance aids, and computer support, implements all of the goals of our first 20 years of model-based assessment, but it acknowledges a set of sometimes harsh realities. Teachers may not be vitally interested in classroom assessment of students as a means to improve instruction. They may very well be focused on "teaching to the external tests" they are given. This new approach, POWERSOURCE©, builds in the coherence from the subject matter as well as the complex cognition. We believe that both attributes should show up in the third year of the study on the longitudinal performance of students and on their demonstrated transfer. We are also stepping firmly into familiar ground: the linking of classroom assessment with learning for teachers and students. We expect an encouraging report on POWERSOURCE© findings for two reasons: first, because of the careful work we have done integrating what we have learned and the major contributions of others and, second, because we are using a "gold standard" research design, randomly involving every student in approximately 20 experimental schools for 3 years. Our findings will point the way to integrating classroom assessment and sustained and important student learning.

REFERENCES

Baker, E. L. (2003, Summer). Multiple measures: Toward tiered systems. *Educational Measurement: Issues & Practice, 22*, pp. 13–17.

Black, P., & Wiliam, D. (1998). Assessment and classroom learning. *Assessment in Education, 5*, 7–74.

Brown, R. S. (in press). Using latent class analysis to set academic performance standards. *Educational Assessment.*

Chi, M. T. H. (2000). Self-explaining: The dual processes of generating inference and repairing mental models. In R. Glaser (Ed.), *Advances in instruction psychology* (Vol. 5, pp. 161–238). Mahwah, NJ: Erlbaum.

Chung, G. K. W. K., Delacruz, G. C., & Bewley, W. L. (2004). Performance assessment models and tools for complex tasks. *International Test and Evaluation Association (ITEA) Journal, 25*(1), 47–52.

Chung, G. K. W. K., Delacruz, G. C., Dionne, G. B., & Bewley, W. L. (2003). Linking assessment and instruction using ontologies. *Proceedings of the I/ITSEC, 25*, 1811–1822.

Chung, G. K. W. K., de Vries, L. F., Cheak, A. M., Stevens, R. H., & Bewley, W. L. (2002). Cognitive process validation of an online problem solving assessment. *Computers in Human Behavior, 18*, 669–684.

Goldschmidt, P., & Martinez-Fernandez, J-F. (in press). The relationship among measures as empirical evidence of validity: Performance assignments, SAT-9, and high school exit exam performance incorporating effects of school context. *Educational Assessment.*

Gonzales, P., Guzmán, J. C., Partelow, L., Pahlke, E., Jocelyn, L., Kastberg, D., & Williams, T. (2004). *Highlights from the trends in international mathematics and science study (TIMSS) 2003* (NCES 2005-005). U.S. Department of Education, National Center for Education Statistics. Washington, DC: U.S. Government Printing Office. Retrieved January 10, 2006, from http://nces.ed.gov/pubs2005/2005005 .pdf

Haertel, E. H., & Herman, J. L. (2005). A historical perspective on validity arguments for accountability testing. In J. L. Herman & E. H. Haertel (Eds.), *Uses and misuses of data for educational accountability and improvement* (pp. 1–34). *National Society for the Study of Education Yearbook* (Vol. 104, Pt. 2). Chicago: National Society for the Study of Education. Distributed by Blackwell Publishing.

Improving America's Schools Act of 1994, Pub. L. No. 103-382, 108 Stat. 3518 (1994).

Lemke, M., Sen, A., Pahlke, E., Partelow, L., Miller, D., Williams, T., Kastberg, D., et al. (2004). *International outcomes of learning in mathematics literacy and problem solving: PISA 2003 Results from the U.S. perspective* (NCES 2005-003). Washington, DC: U.S. Department of Education, National Center for Education Statistics. Retrieved January 10, 2006, from http://nces.ed.gov/pubs2005/2005003.pdf

Martinez-Fernandez, J-F., & Goldschmidt, P. (in press). Comparing student and teacher reports on opportunity to learn and their relationship to student achievement. *Educational Assessment.*

McGaw, B. (2005, September). *A century of testing: Ideas on solving enduring accountability and assessment problems.* Paper presented at The 2005 CRESST Conference: Celebrating 20 Years of Research on Educational Measurement, University of California, Los Angeles.

Merrill, M. D. (2002). Knowledge objects and mental models. In D. A. Wiley (Ed.), *The instructional use of learning objects* (pp. 261–280). Washington DC: Agency for Instructional Technology & Association for Education Communications and Technology.

Niemi, D., Baker, E. L., & Sylvester, R. M. (in press). Scaling up, scaling down: Seven years of performance assessment development in the nation's second largest school district. *Educational Assessment.*

Niemi, D., Chung, G. K. W. K., & Bewley, W. L. (2003, April). *Assessment design using ontologies: Linking assessment, content, and cognitive demands.* Paper presented at the annual meeting of the American Educational Research Association, Chicago.

Niemi, D., Wang, J., Steinberg, D. H., Baker, E. L., & Wang, H. (in press). Instructional sensitivity of a language arts performance assessment. *Educational Assessment.*

No Child Left Behind Act of 2001, Pub. L. No. 107-110, 115 Stat. 1425 (2002).

Perie, M., Grigg, W., & Dion, G. (2005). *The nation's report card: Mathematics 2005* (NCES 2006-453). U.S. Department of Education, National Center for Education Statistics. Washington, DC: U.S. Government Printing Office. Retrieved January 11, 2006, from http://nces.ed.gov/nationsreportcard/pdf/main2005/ 2006453.pdf

Perie, M., Grigg, W., & Donahue, P. (2005). *The nation's report card: Reading 2005* (NCES 2006-451). U.S. Department of Education, National Center for Education Statistics. Washington, DC: U.S. Government Printing Office. Retrieved January 11, 2006, from http://nces.ed.gov/nationsreportcard/pdf/main2005/2006451.pdf

Stiggins, R. J. (2002). Assessment crisis: The absence of assessment for learning. *Phi Delta Kappan, 83,* 758–765.

Vendlinski, T. P. J. F., Munro, A., Pizzini, Q. A., Bewley, W. L., Chung, G. K. W. K., Stuart, G., & Delacruz, G. C. (2004). Learning complex cognitive skills with an interactive job aid. *Proceedings of the I/ITSEC, 26,* 761–772.

Wang, J., Niemi, D., & Wang, H. (in press). Predictive validity and fairness of a language arts performance assessment. *Educational Assessment.*

CHAPTER SIX

Assessment as Learning

Lorna M. Earl

THE TIMES THEY ARE A-CHANGIN'

Education has been at the forefront of politics and policy for several decades, with many governors, presidents, prime ministers, and premiers being labeled the "education leader." As Hargreaves (1994) told us, "Few people want to do much about the economy, but everyone—politicians, the media, and the public alike—wants to do something about education" (p. 15). The role of education is being hotly debated in board rooms, living rooms, and staff rooms, and teachers are caught in the middle of what often appear to be conflicting and countervailing demands, struggling to maintain their balance. Nevertheless, teachers are the ones who are responsible for the daily work of implementing reforms in their classrooms, making decisions about what to teach, how to teach, and how to assess.

Whatever else, it is likely that the next century will continue to be chaotic and the success of the culture will rely heavily on having citizens with a host of new literacies—computer, scientific, civic, and cultural. To function productively, all students, not just a few, will need to attain the foundation skills of language and mathematics and a whole range of "new basics," such as accessing, interpreting, and applying information; critical thinking and analysis; solving novel problems; making informed judgments; working independently and in groups; and discerning an appropriate course of action in ambiguous situations.

Traditionally, many students have left school to become part of an uneducated or undereducated lower class. In the world of the future, society cannot afford to squander or waste this human potential. We are entering an era in which the goal of schooling is to educate all children well, rather than selecting a "talented tenth" to be prepared for knowledge work (Darling-Hammond, 1994). It is no longer sufficient for schools to sort their students and cull out the ones who don't fit the school's recipe for learning. Instead, learning (of all kinds, for all futures) is becoming the fundamental purpose of schooling. This is a dramatic change in the assumptions underlying education, and it requires a different view of schools, schooling, teachers, teaching, and, particularly, assessment. In this conception, *schools* have the responsibility for preparing all students for tomorrow's world; *teachers* have the wherewithal to guide all students to high levels of learning; and *assessment*, first and foremost, is part of student learning. Assessment, viewed this way, is both individual and collective. It is the key to more targeted teaching and schoolwide improvement.

CLASSROOM ASSESSMENT: SERIOUS STUFF

This chapter is about classroom assessment, the kind of assessment that teachers do in classrooms. Certainly, large-scale district or state assessment has a place; but massive cultural, social, economic, political, environmental, and technological changes have meant that every facet of schooling, including classroom assessment, has been subjected to investigation and rethinking. Throughout most of the 20th century, classroom assessment was considered a mechanism for providing an index of learning, and it followed a predictable pattern: Teachers taught, tested students' knowledge of the material, made judgments about students' achievement based on the testing, and then moved onto the next unit of work. Historically, tests, quizzes, and projects have occurred at or near the end of instruction, as the bases for reporting to parents and making selection or placement decisions. Assessments differentiated or sorted students into groups and, in the process, set or confirmed their future schooling, their likely employment, and the course of their lives. This process worked well enough for most students and went largely unchallenged, as long as there were plenty of places for the majority of students to lead productive and worthwhile lives, many of which did not depend directly on passing or failing in school (e.g., agriculture, manufacturing, trades). As the world has changed, this approach is proving to be inadequate. High school graduation is a minimum prerequisite for almost all jobs; and students and their parents are refusing to accept the judgment of educators as fair, especially when the criteria for judgment are vague or kept secret and the result is that some receive status, opportunity, and are valued, while others are excluded or their opportunities diminished.

So, this approach to assessment has come into question as societal expectations for schooling have changed, cognitive science has provided new insights into the nature of learning, and the traditional role of assessment in motivating student learning has been challenged.

Classroom assessment has been shown to be one of the most powerful levers for enhancing student learning. Black and Wiliam (1998) synthesized over 250 studies linking assessment and learning and found that the intentional use of assessment in the classroom to promote learning improves student achievement. Merely increasing the amount of time on assessment, however, does not necessarily enhance learning. Rather, when teachers use classroom assessment to become aware of the knowledge, skills, and beliefs that their students bring to a learning task, use this knowledge as a starting point for new instruction, and monitor students' changing perceptions as instruction proceeds, classroom assessment promotes learning.

When learning is the goal, teachers and students collaborate and use ongoing assessment and pertinent feedback to move learning forward. When classroom assessment is frequent and varied, teachers can learn a great deal about their students. They can gain an understanding of students' existing beliefs and knowledge and can identify incomplete understandings, false beliefs, and naive interpretations of concepts that may influence or distort learning. Teachers can observe and probe students' thinking over time and can identify links between prior knowledge and new learning. Learning is also enhanced when students are encouraged to think about their own learning and to review their experiences of learning. Assessment provides the feedback loop for this process.

DIFFERENTIATING ASSESSMENT PURPOSES

If classroom assessment is such a powerful contributor to learning, what is it that teachers can do to maximize its impact? First, they need to attend to theories about how people learn. The human mind is a fascinating but mysterious organ. So much about how it works is still unknown. Teachers, as the guides of the mind, have a responsibility to remain ever vigilant to new knowledge about learning and to continually rethink their approaches to teaching and their assessment practices in relation to learning theory. Perhaps the most accessible and influential document about learning is called *How People Learn: Bridging Research and Practice,* published by the National Research Council (Donovan, Brandsford, & Pellegrino, 1999). It details three insights about learning:

- People come to learning with preconceptions about how the world works. If their initial understanding is not engaged, they may fail to grasp the new concepts and information or may learn them superficially and revert to their preconceptions in real situations.
- To develop competence in an area of inquiry, people must have a deep foundation of factual knowledge, understand facts and ideas in the context of a conceptual framework, and organize knowledge in ways that facilitate retrieval and application.
- A "metacognitive" approach to instruction can help people learn to take control of their own learning by defining learning goals and monitoring their own progress in achieving them.

These conceptions of learning suggest a very different conception of assessment, one that is both modern and ancient, rooted in the far past but establishing assessment as an inextricable part of learning in the present. It is ironic that the word *assessment* is derived form the Latin word *assidere,* "to sit with" (Wiggins, 1993).

Its very origin implies more than marks, percentiles, grade point averages, and cut scores. It also suggests a perspective that eschews efficiency and economy as assessment hallmarks. The word conjures up images of teachers observing students, talking and working with them to unravel their understandings and mis-understandings, making assessment an integral part of learning that offers detailed feedback to the teacher and the student (Earl & LeMahieu, 1997).

These notions of *assessment for learning* and *assessment as learning* reflect a view that learning is a process of taking in information, interpreting it, connecting it to existing knowledge or beliefs, and, if necessary, reorganizing understanding to accommodate the new information (Shepard, 1991). If people learn by establishing their own understanding from their experiences, assessment is not only part of learning, it is the critical component that allows learners and teachers to check their understanding against the views of others and against the collective wisdom of the culture as it has been recorded in the knowledge, theories, models, formulas, solutions, and stories that make up the curriculum and the disciplines. The notion that assessment is inextricably tied to learning challenges the very core of many educational practices and raises the specter for teachers of fundamentally changing much of what they do. This challenge is daunting but seductive, especially for teachers who see teaching as a moral enterprise and the moral purpose of teacher as enhancing or enriching the lives of their students (Fullan, 1993, 1999). There is no "one right way" to assess students; rather, there are different purposes for assessment. Teachers need to recognize the various purposes and differentiate them so that they can utilize their assessment practices to give themselves and their students routine information about how students are thinking and making sense of the material, as a basis for next steps in teaching and in learning.

Classroom assessment has always been used for a variety of purposes, but the purposes are becoming more differentiated and complex. As classroom assessment purposes become more complex, it is not easy to use one assessment process for the many different purposes. Assessment activities work best when the purpose is clear and explicit and the assessments are designed to fit that purpose.

MOVING TO ASSESSMENT FOR LEARNING AND ASSESSMENT AS LEARNING

Typically, teachers use three intertwined but distinct assessment purposes: assessment of learning, assessment for learning, and assessment as learning.[1]

Assessment of Learning

Assessment of learning is assessment used to confirm what students know, to demonstrate whether or not they have met the standards, and to show how they are placed in relation to others. In assessment of learning, teachers use assessment to provide statements of proficiency or competence for students. Its purpose is summative, intended to certify learning and report to parents and students about their progress in school, usually by signaling students' relative positions compared to other students. Assessment of learning in classrooms is typically done at the end of something (e.g., a unit, a course, a grade, a key stage, a program) and takes the form of tests or exams that include questions drawn from the material studied during that time. There is a strong emphasis on comparing students, and feedback to students comes in the form of marks or grades, with little direction or advice for improvement. These kinds of testing events indicate which students are doing best and which ones are doing poorly.

Assessment for Learning

Assessment for learning is designed to give teachers information to modify the teaching and learning activities in which students are engaged in order to differentiate and focus on how individual students approach learning. It suggests that students are all learning in individual and idiosyncratic ways, while recognizing that there are predictable patterns and pathways that many students go through. The emphasis is on teachers using the information from carefully designed assessments to determine not only what students know but also to gain insights into how, when, and whether students use what they know, so that they can streamline and target instruction and resources. Assessment for learning shifts the emphasis from summative to formative assessment and from making judgments to creating descriptions that can be used in the service of the next stage of learning. In assessment for learning, teachers collect a wide range of data so that they can modify the learning work for their students. They craft assessment tasks that open a window on what students know and can already do and use the insights that come from the process to design next steps in instruction. To do this, teachers use observation, worksheets, questioning in class, student-teacher conferences, or whatever mechanism is likely to give them information that will be useful for their planning and teaching. Marking is not designed to make comparative judgments among the students, but to highlight each student's strengths and weaknesses and provide students with feedback that will further their learning.

Clearly, teachers are the central characters in assessment for learning as well, but their role is quite different than in the assessment-of-learning approach. In assessment for learning, teachers use their personal knowledge of the students and their understanding of the context of the assessment and the curriculum targets to identify particular learning needs. Assessment for learning happens in the middle of learning (often more than once), not at the end. It is interactive, with teachers providing assistance as part of the assessment. It helps teachers provide the feedback to scaffold next steps. And it depends on teachers' diagnostic skills to make it work. Before teachers can plan for targeted teaching and classroom activities, they need to have a sense of what it is that students are thinking. *What is it that they believe to be true?* This process involves much more than asking, "Do they have the right or wrong answer?" It means making students' thinking visible and understanding the images and patterns that they have constructed in order to make sense of the world, from their own perspectives.

Record keeping in this approach may include a grade book, but teachers also rely on records such as checklists of student progress against expectations, artifacts, portfolios of student work over time, and worksheets to trace the progression of students along the learning continuum.

Assessment as Learning

Assessment as learning is a particular case of assessment for learning, but it is so important that it deserves special attention by teachers. Assessment as learning emphasizes using assessment as a process of developing and supporting metacognition for students. Assessment as learning focuses on the role of the student as the critical connector between assessment and learning. Students, as active, engaged, and critical assessors, make sense of information, relate it to prior knowledge, and use it for new learning. This is the regulatory process in metacognition. It occurs when students personally monitor what they are learning and use the feedback from this monitoring to make adjustments, adaptations, and even major changes in what they understand. When teachers focus on assessment as learning, they use classroom assessment as the vehicle for helping students develop, practice, and become comfortable with reflection and critical analysis of their own learning.

LINKS TO WHOLE-SCHOOL IMPROVEMENT

So, how does changing classroom assessment connect with whole-school change? Well, schools change when people change—in their hearts and in their minds. This kind of deep change happens only when teachers individually and collectively recognize that there is a reason to change and feel strongly enough about it to learn new approaches and do things differently. Teacher learning is a very potent vehicle for improving schools, and classroom assessment is something that teachers want to learn about. The bonus is that it is also positively related to increases in student learning. Classroom assessment is a "high-leverage" focus to engage the staff in thinking about what and how they might behave differently for the sake of student learning.

When individual teachers use more effective instructional practices, some students benefit, but this usually does not have any major effect on the rest of a school. However, when even one teacher changes his of her assessment practices, especially in the dramatic way described in this chapter, it will inevitably cause dissonance and even irresolvable tension for the teacher and the school. Changing classroom assessment is not something that individual teachers can do on their own. The process is closely tied to the organization and accountability mechanisms that exist in schools and to teachers' beliefs about the role of schools and the nature of learning. At the same time, classroom assessment can be a powerful force in establishing a solid base for a school to prepare its students for coping with an uncertain future.

Changing classroom assessment involves more than just tinkering around the edges. It requires that a school faculty seriously consider their beliefs about the very foundations of learning and teaching. As teachers start small to develop more understanding of assessment and its potential in schools, they gradually slip into the territory of thinking big as they become a professional community. Teachers working in schools that are professional communities believe they can make a difference; they take risks and work together to redefine their roles; they insist on continuous growth and perpetual learning; and they see themselves as responsible, on a daily basis, for their own and their colleagues' development (Stoll & Fink, 1996). As Hargreaves and Fullan (1991) stated, "They [teachers in professional communities] never stop learning and they are always looking to improve their practice" (p. 85). Most important, they see themselves as a team that collectively can move far beyond their individual accomplishments.

Assessment has the potential to be one of the most powerful levers for school renewal. Not only does improving assessment have serious implications for improving student learning, it also provides a legitimate and tangible focus for teachers to work collectively to explore their own beliefs, expectations, and requirements for their students as they learn and engage in different and more focused practices in all classrooms.

GETTING THERE

It won't be a simple task to change assessment in schools. In fact, there will be many vocal opponents to the views described in this chapter. But opposition is not a sufficient reason for refusing to try. The suggestions in this section arise from schools in which changing assessment has been proposed, tried, and adapted by teachers working together in all kinds of schools, at all grade levels, and in a variety of places around the world. They are offered as starting points for some schools and touchstones for others. They can be used for discussion and for action as educators venture along or continue on the pathway of assessment as learning.

Use Assessment to Transform Your School

The educational change literature is full of references and studies that describe collaboration among teachers as a characteristic of effective schools. Researchers who focus on improving classroom assessment have found the same thing (Darling-Hammond, Ancess, & Falk, 1995). When teachers engage in discussions about students' work, they share ideas about evidence for learning and build a mutual expertise that no one else possesses and that no one from outside the group could give them. These discussions are not abstract musings about what student work might look like. Teachers need to look at actual student work and discuss its quality. As they consider the work of a large number of students and talk about why they have made certain judgments, they are able to compare the work of their students to the work of students from other classes (and even other schools), and they make their assumptions, standards, and beliefs about learning explicit. In the process, they must either defend their beliefs or change them. It is always amazing to watch groups of teachers become aware of the diversity that exists in the expectations they hold. But the real excitement begins when they struggle to clarify, to explain, to understand, and ultimately to establish some agreement about what constitutes high-quality student work, so that the phrase *high standards* is connected to actual performance, not abstract ideals. They not only describe the experience as professionally rewarding and enlightening but also begin to feel more confident about their roles as assessors.

Work Together

Teacher *moderation,* as the collaborative process of teachers doing joint or group assessment of student work has come to be called, has proven to be a very powerful focus for school planning that creates a sense of solidarity for staff as they move forward. It also provides direct and immediate "payoff" by establishing and maintaining consistency and accuracy in classroom assessment and reducing teachers' insecurity about their assessment practices. Teachers often worry about their assessment and evaluation decisions. They are plagued by questions: How sure am I that I'm right? Is this really an accurate and fair picture of this student's learning? These questions become particularly important when teachers' judgments carry serious consequences for students. In measurement terms, these are issues of *reliability* and *validity.* Teachers don't need to know the nuances of these concepts, but they do need to be able to ensure that their assessments are both reliable and valid. When teachers work together to establish criteria for judging their students' work, set standards, locate examples of quality work, and make group decisions, the collaboration has many spin-offs. At the very least, it gives teachers some confidence in their decisions, because they did not come to them in isolation.

In the long run, teachers develop agreement about the nature and quality of their assessments and of students' work. By sharing the decisions about how to assess, there are fewer discrepancies in student assessment standards and procedures between grades and classes; teachers develop a deeper understanding of curriculum and of individual students; and they engage in the intense discussions about standards and evidence that lead to a shared understanding of expectations for students, more refined language about children and learning, and consistent procedures for making and communicating judgments.

Declare the Purpose and Spread the Word

If assessment addresses learning, parents and students deserve to be on the inside, working toward the same ends as teachers. Assessment is where the "rubber hits the road." It is the visible declaration of what counts in school and of how well students and schools are doing. Teachers in a school need a united message, and they need to broadcast this message to students and the parents by showing them in actions and words that learning and assessment are exercises of self-discovery for students and that teachers are their guides, their mentors, and their mirrors. Make students participants in their own learning. Provide them with many opportunities to use assessment as a process to challenge their own knowledge and beliefs, not by waiting for "right answers," but by comparing their understanding with the current wisdom that appears in books, in other media, via technology, and, not least, in the expertise of teachers. And most of all, make them discriminating and questioning consumers.

When students and parents understand what is expected of them and the expectations don't shift with each new teacher, they have a much better chance of meeting the expectations. Faculty should develop learning targets that are clear and select a whole range of descriptions and examples of good work for teachers, students, and parents to see, discuss, and adjust. Reporting to students and parents should not be static, symbolic accounting, but continuous, reciprocal conversations about progress and about learning. Judgments should not arrive suddenly, by surprise, when the time for action is far past, but as shared decisions heralding next steps in learning in a somewhat predictable environment. Everyone gains when he or she is part of the process and of the solution.

Make Connections

The essence of assessment as learning for teachers is akin to that of talented conductors holding the complete musical score in their heads, with a flair for improvisation. They must hear the nuances of each instrument, intuit the emotions of the players, allow them the freedom to experiment, and subtly guide and extend the talent and virtuosity of each of them in personal ways, by providing feedback and encouragement on a moment-by-moment basis. What better focus for professional development than teachers, working together and becoming virtuoso conductors of student learning, who know the targets, can see and hear the performances, and provide the guidance for students to get better and better.

Self-Assessment Should Be the Ultimate Goal

Stiggins (1993) said it all: If you want to appear accountable, test your students. If you want to improve schools, teach teachers to assess their students. If you want to maximize learning, teach students to assess themselves. Students need to become their own best assessors. A participatory democracy depends on citizens who can make informed and defensible decisions. If students are to become critical thinkers and problem solvers who can bring their talents and knowledge to bear on unanticipated problems, they must develop high-level skills of self-assessment and self-adjustment. It is not likely that students will become competent, realistic self-evaluators on their own. They need to be taught skills of self-evaluation and have routine and challenging opportunities to practice and validate their own judgments (Earl & Cousins,

1995). Broadfoot (1994) described a study in Britain in which teachers came to realize that the things that really made a difference in students' motivation and the quality of their learning were (a) sharing and discussing curriculum goals with students; (b) encouraging students to set their own learning targets and make "learning plans"; (c) involving students in assessing their own work so that they were more willing to, more responsible for, and more able to monitor their own learning; and (d) reviewing progress together with students and revising "learning plans," based on information from classroom assessments. Effective assessment empowers teachers and students to ask reflective questions and consider many strategies

Classroom assessment matters for students, for teachers, and for schools of the future. One can imagine a time when assessment is not viewed with foreboding and terror, not separated from teaching and learning, not used to punish or prohibit access to important information, and not seen as a private, mystical ceremony. Instead, assessment and teaching/learning will be reciprocal, each contributing to the other in ways that enhance both. Teachers in schools will be talented conductors who can draw the best from their students and make their learning obvious to the world outside schools. As Haney (1991) observed,

> Once teachers begin such efforts, the difficulties fall away and their work becomes, in a sense, easier. They become thoughtful observers, documenters and organizers of evaluation. In the end, these fresh directions are not as complex as they appear. They call upon us to ask, in relation to purpose, what would cause us to say that our students are thinkers, readers, writers and comprehenders of knowledge, and to then work out systematic processes to follow up such questions. In doing so, we make assessment a more powerful educational tool and return credibility to school practice. Most important, though, we improve the quality of student learning. (p. 166)

NOTE

1. Some authors use *assessment for learning* to encapsulate the ideas described here in two categories, *assessment for learning* and *assessment as learning*.

REFERENCES

Black, P., & Wiliam, D. (1998). Inside the black box: Raising standards through classroom assessment. *Phi Delta Kappan, 80*(20), 139–148.

Broadfoot, P. (1994, October, 8). *Assessment and evaluation: To measure or to learn?* Invited address at the International Conference on Evaluation, Toronto, Canada.

Darling-Hammond, L. (1994). Performance-based assessment and educational equity. *Harvard Educational Review, 64*(1), 5–30.

Darling-Hammond, L., Ancess J., & Falk, B. (1995). *Authentic assessment in action.* New York: Teachers College Press.

Donovan, M. S., Brandsford, J., & Pellegrino, J. (Eds.). (1999). *How people learn: Bringing research and practice.* Washington, DC: National Academy Press.

Earl, L., & Cousins, B. (1995). *Classroom assessment: Changing the face, facing the change.* Toronto, Canada: Ontario Public School Teachers' Federation.

Earl, L., & LeMahieu, P. (1997). Rethinking assessment and accountability. In A. Hargreaves (Ed.), *Rethinking educational change with heart and mind* (pp. 149-168). Alexandria, VA: ASCD.

Fullan, M. (1993). *Change forces: Probing the depths of educational reform.* London: Falmer Press.

Fullan, M. (1999). *Change forces: The sequel.* London: Falmer Press.

Hargreaves, A. (1994). *Changing teachers, changing times.* Toronto, Canada: OISE Press.

Hargreaves, A., & Fullan, M. (1991). *What's worth fighting for in your school.* Toronto, Canada: Ontario Public School Teachers' Federation.

Haney, W. (1991). We must take care: Fitting assessments to function. In V. Perrone (Ed.), *Expanding student assessment* (pp. 142–163). Alexandria, VA: ASCD.

Shepard, L. (1991). Psychometricians beliefs about learning. *Educational Research, 36*(2), 179–192.

Stiggins, R. (1993, April 23). Classroom assessment: Train-the-trainer workshop, Toronto, Canada.

Stoll, L., & Fink, D. (1996). *Changing our schools.* London: Open University Press.

Wiggins, G. (1993). *Assessing student performance.* San Francisco: Jossey-Bass.

C H A P T E R   S E V E N

Transforming Professional Development

Understanding and Organizing Learning Communities

Ann Lieberman and Lynne Miller

The need for continuous professional development of teachers may be one of the few areas in which policymakers, researchers, professional associations, the public, and school personnel all agree. However, this agreement seems to evaporate when we ask these questions: What counts as professional development? What matters most to teachers? How can professional development be organized, supported, and sustained to ensure long-term commitment to student learning goals? There are many reasons these kinds of questions provoke disagreement. Districts and states often look toward expediency. It is easy to hire consultants and to give workshops, invite speakers, and create courses that teach district and school personnel how to enhance their repertoires. Such an approach may work when the content is packaged in a way that lends itself to adaptation in order to address teachers' classroom practices, but it does not lead to the transformation of teaching that the times demand.

We argue here that the kinds of changes that schools need to embrace require invention, adaptation, and a new sense of community that have heretofore not been a part of the culture of most schools (Little, 1996; McLaughlin & Talbert, 1993). It is necessary to focus on creating professional learning strategies that are long-term and collaborative and are supported by enabling policies shaped by the constituencies who are involved in the routines of schools and have an investment in their renewal. Such strategies, while more difficult to mount than traditional approaches, lead to authentic changes in teaching practice and improved student learning. It follows that if professional development is to be effective, it needs to be reconceived as the linchpin of school reform (Darling-Hammond, 1993; Elmore, 1996; Little et al., 1987) and not as a set of activities that are decontextualized from teachers and their classrooms; it has to focus on the relationships that occur between principals, teachers, and their peers, as well as between teachers and their students and the content that is taught. As Elmore (1996) found in his research, professional development is not "taking back" something to the school; rather, it permeates the work of the school. New practices are created or learned in the school. They are not a fixed menu.

How is this to happen? And what does research have to offer? Three bodies of research and practice help us understand the purposes and practices that are involved in thinking about and organizing for a conception of professional development that is rooted in school renewal and the everyday practices of teachers: (1) adult and teacher development and change, (2) school organization to support ongoing learning communities, and (3) educational reform networks that support teacher learning.

ADULT AND TEACHER DEVELOPMENT AND CHANGE

Teachers function as both individuals and as members of a school community. Like the children they teach, they are a diverse group. They vary in age, life conditions, happenstance of birth and experience, and how they respond to change. Too often, planning for professional learning loses sight of the differences among teachers and emphasizes organizational roles and responsibilities at the expense of individual concerns and needs. Developmental perspectives on adulthood and teacher development provide insight into the needs of teachers as they live their personal and professional lives. The research on how teachers change offers additional understanding about how teachers make meaning of the new challenges and demands they face. Every staff is a collection of individuals, each with his or her life and career story. One size does not fit all; this is as true for teachers as it is for the students they teach.

Perspectives on Adult and Teacher Development

One way to view adults and teacher development is as a linear sequence of stages that are linked with particular ages or years of service. Early researchers in adult development, such as Erikson (1963) and Levinson (1978), supported this view, that adults pass through relatively fixed stages of development. For Erikson, the stages were tied to psychosexual development; for Levinson, they were connected to age-related life tasks. For both, the stages chart a predictable movement along a continuum from early to middle to late adulthood. Huberman (1995) viewed the teaching career in the same way. He chronicled five distinct stages, each of which is linked to years of practice: survival and discovery in the first 3 years, developing a sense of instructional mastery in years 4 to 6, moving toward either increased commitment and enthusiasm or frustration and doubt in years 7 through 18, and culminating in an exit marked by either serenity or bitterness. The Academy for Educational Development (1985) defined a progression of stages in terms of pedagogy: from an early focus on the day-to-day problems of managing discipline and instruction, to the development of a personal survival kit, to, at midcareer, attaining a plateau of generalized pedagogy (providing the best instruction for the most students). Only a small number of teachers progress to the stage of differentiated pedagogy, in which they discover fresh routes to effectiveness and consistently adapt instruction and the curriculum to the needs, interest, and abilities of all students.

Fessler and Christensen (1992), building on the work of these sequential theorists, offered a more complex, layered, and dynamic view of teacher development, seeing the teaching career as being influenced by three interdependent spheres. The first two spheres represent the stages of adult and teacher development in constant interaction with each other. A third sphere of external influences (such as unions, regulations, management style, public trust, societal expectations, and professional organizations) affects the other two. Taken together, the three spheres interact in such a way that no two teachers develop in the same way or react to the same life and career events in a predictable fashion.

The unpredictability of adult and teacher development has been taken up by more recent researchers and theorists. Wrightsman (1994), McAdams & de St. Aubin (1998), and Settersten & Hagestad (1996) introduced the idea of the social clock and located life stages within the context of specific cultures and populations rather than viewing them as a universal progression. Feminist theorists have portrayed adult development as a continuous reworking of issues of relationship and identity (Jordan, 1997), comparing women's development to "an ever changing web of connectedness" (Merriam & Caffarella, 1999, p. 110), in which empathy, and not individual progress and accomplishment, is the goal. Other researchers consider cultural and historical events to be major influences on how a person's life is shaped. These events, though interpreted differently by the people who are impacted, often define a cohort of people as a generation (Merriam & Caffarella, 1999). The idea of generational identification with specific events and time periods was taken one step further by Howe, Strauss, and Matson (2000). In this view, the "baby boom generation," those born between 1943 and 1960, are being succeeded by "Generation X," born 1961 to 1981. "Boomers" are marked by idealism, ideological inflexibility, and institutional commitments, while "Generation X-ers" are characterized by mistrust of ideologies and of idealism; they value pragmatism, free agency, and entrepreneurship and place little stock in institutional loyalty.

Susan Moore Johnson and her research group have described how these generational differences manifest themselves in schools. They found that Boomer teachers tend to value autonomy over teamwork and remain loyal to one school and one career for a lifetime; they oppose differential payments that encourage competition among peers and show little interest in career advancement. The new generation of teachers privilege teamwork over autonomy and entrepreneurship over institutional loyalty. They want jobs that provide variety and opportunities for risk taking, and they do not approach teaching as a calling or as a lifetime commitment. Johnson and her team believe that this new generation will exhibit different career cycles and patterns of development and will force a reconceptualization of the teaching career and a new kind of professional development (Johnson, 2004; Peske, Liu, Johnson, Kauffman, & Kardos, 2001). Among Moore's recommendations are a comprehensive induction program, continuous interaction and collaborative work with experienced teachers, curriculum that aligns with standards, and more attention to special education needs.

Perspectives on Teacher Change

Loucks-Horsley and Stiegelbauer (1991), drawing on over two decades of research about the personal concerns of teachers undergoing a change, cautioned that "change is a process, not an event" and that teachers must adapt to change personally and developmentally. The seven levels of concern Loucks-Horsley and Stiegelbauer identified are *awareness* (I am not concerned about it); *information* (I would like to know more about it); *personal* (How will using this affect me?); *management* (I seem to be spending all of my time getting materials ready); *consequence* (How is my use affecting the students? How can I refine it to have more impact?); *collaboration* (How can I relate what I am doing to what others are doing?); and *refocusing* (I have some ideas about something that would work even better).

Showers, Joyce, and Bennett (1987) offered another view. They concluded that teachers need to first understand the theory or reason behind any change, must see demonstrations of the new practice in a real classroom, must have time to practice the new behaviors associated in an supportive environment, and, finally, need opportunities for feedback and coaching from colleagues and supervisors. If any of these conditions is not present, the authors argue, teacher change will not take hold and teachers will retreat to old and familiar practices.

Guskey (1986) presented yet another perspective, questioning the conventional wisdom that a change in teacher beliefs and attitudes must precede any changes in teacher practice. Guskey's research supported just the opposite relationship. He argued that substantial change in teacher attitudes and beliefs occurs only after teachers have changed their practices and they see the results of these changes in student outcomes. This chain of events is explained by the intense relationships teachers have with their students and the connections they make between what they believe and what they see working in their own classrooms.

Finally, Rob Evans (1996) offered a more psychological account of individual change, challenging the usefulness of the social science models. He began with the assumption that people seek "patterns, stability, and meaning" (p. 41) in both their personal and professional lives. He then argued that a change effort, if it is to be successful, has to "accept the realities of human nature" (p. 51) and that any other approach is naive and ineffective. Furthermore, he focused on the personal meaning that teachers make when they are asked to change their practices. These meanings include experiencing change as loss; as a threat to competence; as a source of stress, uncertainty, and confusion; and as leading to conflict and the opening of old wounds. Change, then, has to be undertaken in such a way that it reduces fear and moves people from loss to commitment, from old to new competence, from confusion to coherence, and from conflict to consensus.

ORGANIZING SCHOOLS TO SUPPORT ONGOING LEARNING COMMUNITIES

Although teachers are individuals, their professional development takes place in groups, within particular settings, with particular cultures, and in particular contexts. Little (1993) argued that the dominant "training" model of professional development, which focuses on expanding the skills in a teacher's individual repertoire, is important but may not fit the ambitious visions of reform in teaching and learning. She urged that this model give way to new reform requirements, which place teachers at the helm in school renewal and support them as full partners in improvement and change efforts. Little reminded us that implementation of a new idea does not come simply from a given program; it takes root when a professional community of teachers talk about it, debate it, try it out, and invent new solutions within the context of their own departments, grade levels, teaching teams, or schools. The challenges of reform are complex; they include, in part, agreed-upon standards of achievement, new forms of assessment and accountability, new pedagogical practices, developing strategies to promote active student engagement in learning, and differentiating instruction to meet a wide variety of student learning styles. To achieve these ends, schools need to build a long-term agenda with numerous entry points for teachers.

Professional Learning Communities

There is growing evidence that teacher learning is most powerful, long lasting, and continuous when it occurs as a result of being a member of a group of colleagues who struggle together to plan for their students (Lieberman, 1995a; McLaughlin, 1998; Newmann & Wehlage, 1995). Such groups function as professional learning communities, meeting regularly over time for the purpose of increasing their own and their students' learning and development by engaging in joint work, critical reflection, and problem solving. Professional learning communities reverse the isolation of teachers and offer a place for teachers to work together and connect with each other about their own work and the work of their students. Often, professional learning communities are organized by teachers with the facilitation of their administrators. Comprehensive change does not focus so much on specific projects or innovations as it does on the whole school and how curriculum, instruction, and organization impact teaching and learning.

In a 5-year study of 24 restructuring schools, Newmann and Wehlage (1995) found that student learning improves when schools organize to engage teachers in a community in which they share a common purpose for student learning, engage in collaborative activity to achieve those purposes, and take collective responsibility for doing so. Similar findings have been reported by McLaughlin and Talbert (1993) in their study of secondary schools. They found that professional learning communities in secondary schools were necessary for movement from traditional teacher-centered values to student-centered pedagogy. Teachers in learning communities report that they took the following actions:

- Openly discussed their practices with fellow teachers
- Used different and more active methods with students
- Engaged in collegial social relationships
- Blurred the lines of expert and novice, providing a more egalitarian ethos among more experienced and new teachers
- Collectively built a technical culture that enhanced student learning

Similar themes have been reported in elementary and middle schools (Battistich, Solomon, Kim, Watson, & Schaps, 1995; Dasho & Kendzior, 1995; Fullan, 1991; Lieberman, 1995a; Newmann & Wehlage, 1995). These studies document a process of change that involves teachers in working together as a group; having experiences that are new to them in creating caring communities, and talking about them and learning from them; gaining support from administration; and learning how to handle conflict with peers about learning new ways of teaching and learning or confronting conflicting values of pedagogy and practice. New mechanisms to support opportunities for dialogue and keeping the focus on students are often developed. These processes involve teachers in a collective struggle to try different ways of engaging students. Together, teachers gain confidence in themselves and their colleagues and begin to identify their practices, with larger goals for students. Professional learning communities engage in two types of intellectual and practical work: They generate their own knowledge and methods, and they adapt the curricular and reform ideas of others to meet their needs. For example, a group of elementary teachers may discuss their experiences in keeping their students for 2 years rather than 1 year. As they call on their own experiences and observations, they develop new insights about their practices and how to deepen them. Such a rich exchange of ideas and experiences places a community of teachers in charge of their own learning.

Professional learning communities "are built as teachers, unpacking the baggage of years of unexplained attitudes, beliefs, and practices, come to trust one another enough to participate in group discussions" about their own practices in teaching and learning (Lieberman, 1995b, p. 14). They often employ a set of tools, called *protocols*, guided and structured conversations about teacher and student work. McDonald (2001) made a distinction between conventional forms of conversations and those that are driven by protocols:

> Like most conversations, the conversations provoked by these protocols are relatively unbounded in terms of what any party may think to notice or say. This spontaneity is part of their appeal. Unlike most conversations, however, these are highly structured in terms of who may speak and in what fashion . . . Participants in the protocols generally recognize quickly—though usually after an initial period of discomfort— that the discipline makes the process safe. (p. 217)

Protocols can be used to suspend judgment, tune judgment, and extend judgment schoolwide. For example, the "Collaborative Assessment Conference" allows teachers to suspend judgment as they look at samples of student work; the "Tuning Protocol" engages teachers in conversation about improving or tuning their assignments, assessments, and lesson plans; and the "Slice" promotes an extension of conversation to schoolwide concerns though a systematic collection and examination of student work over the course of 1 day. All of the protocols place the focus on student and teacher work, actively involve teachers in powerful learning experiences, and help create and sustain professional communities.

Professional communities within schools serve to enlarge the focus of professional development from a concern for particular techniques and strategies to a broader concern for the school as a whole and how it is experienced by the students and the teachers who work there. But teachers and schools also need outside partners that enlarge their professional communities and their base of support, provide expanded opportunities for learning and leadership, and offer multiple avenues for the development of teacher commitment.

Contemporary Studies of Learning Communities

Three studies add to our growing understanding of what is meant by professional learning communities and how they develop. In the first study, Westheimer (1998) worked with five features of community established by social theorists, examining two middle schools known for having strong communities and comparing their differences in beliefs about education, teacher participation, interdependence, ways of handling dissent, and, finally, concern for meaningful relationships. Brandeis, a middle school in an affluent San Francisco Bay Area community, had a sixth grade in which teachers made up their own community and shared the belief that all teachers had the right to teach in whatever way they wanted. The teachers participated with each other at meetings and in casual conversations, and they showed their interdependence by occasionally planning collaboratively. Interestingly, the way they handled dissent was to let each teacher do what he or she pleased so that congeniality and harmony could be maintained. The community was characterized by an "ethic of individual professionalism" (Westheimer, 1998, p. 63) within a generally harmonious environment.

In contrast, Mills, an urban middle school, had been closed, and it reopened again in 1984 as a new school with a new faculty and a new set of convictions that addressed their beliefs about the diverse student body in their charge. In this ethnically diverse school, the community ethos was one of egalitarian democracy, inclusivity, and participation (Westheimer, 1998, p. 117). Teachers in this school did joint work, interdisciplinary planning, and participated at many levels in the school and community. And their relationships were of a close nature both inside and outside the school. Dissent was open and heard. Westheimer studied the insides of communities and how they differed on these particular characteristics, one school working together yet individual in their practices, the other school working together in teaching, learning, and connecting to the larger community.

In the second study, Cochran-Smith & Lytle (1999) built a framework for considering three contrasting conceptions of teacher learning and how these conceptions are linked to different ways of thinking about professional development. The first conception is knowledge for practice. The second is knowledge in practice. And the third is knowledge of practice. In *knowledge for practice*, an assumption is made that research generates formal knowledge for teacher use. The implications for professional development are that this research can be disseminated and used. In *knowledge in practice*, the assumption is that knowledge is embedded in exemplary practice and reflection. The implications for professional development are that teachers should focus on experience-based projects and "practical knowledge." In *knowledge of practice*, the assumptions are that teachers learn by making teaching, learning, and research problematic and that professional development occurs when there is critical inquiry that takes place in communities. All three conceptions are in use in the educational field, even as knowledge of practice appears to be the only one that takes place in communities. These researchers clarified the operating assumptions about how teachers learn and the subsequent organization of professional development.

In the third study, Grossman, Wineburg, and Woolworth (2001) attempted to develop a professional community by joining two departments, history and English, in a secondary school in the western United States. They actually created a book club in the hopes that both departments would talk with each another, teach each other, and plan together how they could build a more interdisciplinary way of teaching. The researchers found they were embroiled in the complicated task of learning the "social work" involved in building a professional community. In what has now become a classic study, the authors built a model for the formation of a teacher professional community, employing four phases of development: the formation of group identity and norms of interaction, navigating the fault lines, negotiating the essential tension, and communal responsibility for individual growth. The authors described the beginning, evolving, and mature developmental stages. For example, at the start of a community, individuals are interchangeable and expendable. Most people identify with subgroups. Initially, conflict is hidden or covered up, and people deny that there are differences. As the group grows, conflict comes out into the open, and people recognize differences in others and that colleagues can be resources for one's learning. As the group evolves, people come to see that participation is expected, and eventually members see that it is important to commit to the growth of their colleagues, that conflict is inevitable and need not be destructive, and that there can be an understanding and productive use of difference. In the development of theory, one comes to understand that building a professional community is a slow, steady process as teachers come to learn that conflict and difference are strengths, that teacher learning and student learning are intertwined, and that colleagues can be powerful sources of knowledge and support.

EDUCATIONAL REFORM NETWORKS THAT SUPPORT TEACHER LEARNING

There is increasing evidence that schools that are successful in restructuring themselves are also connected to external sources of support (Cushman, 1996; Darling-Hammond & McLaughlin, 1995; Lieberman & Grolnick, 1996; Lieberman & McLaughlin, 1992; Lieberman & Miller, 1990; Little & McLaughlin, 1991; Lord, 1991; McLaughlin & Talbert, 1993; Newmann & Wehlage, 1995). These external supports take many forms; they may be subject matter collaboratives, reform networks, or school-university partnerships. In all cases, they are coming to be recognized as playing a critical role in reshaping professional development. Perhaps the most successful reform network is the National Writing Project, which involves teachers in an intense summer institute that engages them as writers and teachers and deliberately creates a cadre of teacher-leaders who return to their schools and districts to establish local writing networks.

Networks fill the need for teachers to engage in frank discussion among peers, a need that is too often inhibited or discouraged in school organizations. Research on networks, partnerships, and coalitions is beginning to document how these new border-crossing organizations provide a transition or bridge between the current bureaucratic organization of schools and more democratic forms. Networks are, in fact, professional communities on a larger scale. They have an egalitarian ethos that supports learning alternatives for teachers; they help shape new forms of professional development that are in line with what we know about adult and teacher change over time; and they play a mediating role between practice and policy (Lieberman & Grolnick, 1996; McLaughlin, 1998).

Networks as Intentional Learning Communities

When teachers work across districts, or in some cases across states, they find it easier to question, ask for help, or "tell it like it is," because they are less fearful of exposing their lack of expertise to a critical audience. Even though a great deal of reform knowledge needs to be invented by school-based educators, norms that encourage invention are not yet embedded in the ways most schools and districts operate. Communication comes easier and problem posing is more legitimate when teachers join with like-minded people from outside of their school environments who share a common identity as adults who work in and with schools. Because networks are a more flexible organizational form, they offer new ways of operating. They are more accepting of the ambiguity, complexity, and unfinished nature of the teaching and learning process. As a result, they tend to be more in tune with how educational professionals actually live and view their lives. Networks promote an agenda that combines "just in time" learning, focusing on immediate problems of practice, with explorations of problems of greater complexity that require more time and reflection. In addition, networks offer teachers diverse entry points that are in line with their different life and career stages. Whether they are national in scope or local in scale, networks tie reforms in teaching to the larger agenda of the transformation of schooling. They offer teachers membership in a constructive community, where like-minded professionals engage in a common struggle to educate themselves so that they can better educate their students.

Building Commitment Through Flexible and Responsive Activities

Networks change the meaning of adult learning. They replace norms of prescription and compliance with posing, sharing, and solving problems; they promote discussion that concerns actions and consequences; and they enact a culture that encourages continuous inquiry and reflection. Networks differ dramatically from the organizations in which most teachers live and work. While most formal organizations have permanent structures and create activities to fit the structures, networks have the flexibility to organize activities first and then develop the structures needed to support them. Flexibility allows a network to create an activity or structure, use it as long as it serves the membership's needs and purposes, and end it when it is no longer perceived as valuable. The responsiveness of the network provides for a more developmental approach to adult learning and empowers its members to voice their approval or disapproval. It allows members to build a commitment to the network rather than to a given activity and encourages a more personal and professional involvement in their own learning. In the Southern Maine Partnership, for example, ongoing groups involving public school and university educators became a signature of the network. At one point, more than 15 groups met monthly over dinner for conversation. When participation in the groups waned after several years, the Partnership replaced the monthly group meeting with more fluid "dine and discuss," in which educators met over dinner for more focused conversation on particular topics of interest. The "dine and discuss" evenings have been maintained for more than 8 years; many local districts have imitated the practice and established such evenings for their own staffs and made it a part of their own professional development programs.

The best-known, oldest, and arguably the most successful network in the United States is the National Writing Project. This network has existed for 30 years and is still growing, with 185 local networks connected to a national office in Berkeley, California. What accounts for its success? How does the network get teachers to commit to yet another group, to spending time growing the network? Lieberman and Wood (2003) sought to answer these questions when they observed two National Writing Project summer institutes, at UCLA and at Oklahoma State at Clearwater, and then followed six teachers, three at each site, into their classrooms. They found a great deal of evidence that demonstrated how the ideas developed in the summer institute found their way into the teachers' classrooms. Most important, the researchers were able to describe what made this network successful for teachers. They identified a set of social practices that occurred during the 5-week summer institute, which marks the beginning of each cycle of teachers. Taken together, these social practices exemplify what excites teachers and commits them, not only to the network but also to a community of colleagues, often for life. These social practices lead to a local (and national) professional community and include the following:

- Approaching each colleague as a potentially valuable contributor
- Honoring teacher knowledge

- Creating public forums for teacher sharing, dialogue, and critique
- Turning ownership of learning over to learners
- Situating human learning in practice and relationships
- Providing multiple entry points into the learning community
- Guiding reflection on teaching through reflection on learning
- Sharing leadership
- Promoting a stance of inquiry
- Encouraging a reconceptualization of professional identity and linking it to professional community

In reality, these practices are interactive and mutually dependent. Teachers come to the summer institute as individuals but go home as members of a professional community (Lieberman & Wood, 2003, p. 22).

Networks have their challenges as well as successes. To succeed, they must artfully negotiate between organizing compelling activities and linking them to larger purposes. They have to make and remake decisions about how membership is constituted and how staff roles are constructed. They have to create activities that combine the inside knowledge that teachers develop and the outside knowledge they take from reformers, researchers, and the professions. And they have to be ever vigilant and guard against formalizing informal relationships and activities.

By their very nature, networks are developmental, adaptive, improvisational, and responsive to the individual and organizational concerns of their members. We now have enough research evidence to demonstrate how they link comprehensive school reform to the active work of classroom teachers and, in so doing, invent forms of professional development that acknowledge what we know about adult and teacher development, personal and organizational change, and the power of professional learning communities. As a result, they win the support of university, business, and community-based organizations and professional associations and provide vital exemplars of professional development that meets the demands of the current reform era.

There is increasing evidence that learning communities both inside and outside the school provide teachers with the kind of support and knowledge they need to continually improve their practice. These communities, often organized through networks, also allow for the differences among teachers both in their careers and personal lives. The three bodies of knowledge discussed in this chapter are helping us transform our understanding of professional development in ways that can meet the challenges of today's rapidly changing world.

REFERENCES

Academy for Educational Development. (1985). Improving pedagogy: Phases of teacher development. *Teacher development in schools.* New York: Ford Foundation.

Battistich, V., Solomon, D., Kim, D., Watson, M., & Schaps, E. (1995). Schools as communities, poverty levels of student populations, and students' attitudes, motives, and performance: A multilevel analysis. *American Educational Research Journal, 32*(3), 627–658.

Cochran-Smith, M., & Lytle, S. L. (1999). Teacher learning in professional communities: Three knowledge-practice relationships. In P. D. Pearson & A. Iran-Nejad (Eds.), *Review of research in education* (Vol. 24, pp. 251–307). Washington, DC: American Educational Research Association.

Cushman, K. (1996). Networks and essential schools: How trust advances learning. *Horace, 13*(1).

Darling-Hammond, L. (1993). Reframing the school reform agenda: Developing capacity for school transformation. *Phi Delta Kappan, 74*(10), 753–761.

Darling-Hammond, L., & McLaughlin, M. W. (1995). Policies that support professional development in an era of reform. *Phi Delta Kappan, 76*(8), 597–604.

Dasho, S., & Kendzior, S. (1995, April). *Toward a caring community of learning for teachers: Staff development to support the Child Development Project.* Symposium conducted at the meeting of the American Educational Research Association, San Francisco. Oakland, CA: Developmental Studies Center.

Elmore, R. E. (with Burney, D). (1996). *Staff development and instructional improvement in Community District # 2, New York City.* Paper prepared for the National Commission on Teaching and America's Future.

Erikson, E. (1963). *Childhood and society.* New York: Macmillan.

Evans, R. (1996). *The human side of school change.* San Francisco: Jossey-Bass.

Fessler, R., & Christensen, J. (1992, April). *Teacher career cycle model: A framework for viewing teacher growth needs.* Paper presented at the

Annual Meeting of the American Research Association, Montreal, Quebec.

Fullan, M. (1991). *The new meaning of change.* New York: Teachers College Press.

Grossman, P., Wineburg, S., & Woolworth, S. (2001). Toward a theory of community. *Teachers College Record, 103,* 942–1012.

Guskey, T. (1986, May). Staff development and the process of teacher change. *Educational Researcher 7,* pp. 5–12.

Howe, N, Strauss, W., & Matson, R.J. (2000). *Millennials rising: The next generation.* New York: Vintage.

Huberman, M. (1995). Professional careers and professional development: Some intersections. In T. Guskey & M. Huberman (Eds.), *Professional development in education: New paradigms and practices* (pp. 193–224). New York: Teachers College Press.

Johnson, S. M. (2004). *Finders and keepers: Helping new teachers survive and thrive in our schools* (with the Project on the Next Generation of Teachers). San Francisco: Jossey-Bass.

Jordan, J. V. (1997). A relational perspective for understanding women's development. In J. V. Jordan (Ed.), *Women's growth in diversity* (pp. 9–24). New York: Guilford Press.

Levinson, D. (1978). *The seasons of a man's life.* New York: Knopf.

Lieberman, A. (1995a). Practices that support teacher development: Transforming conceptions of professional learning. *Phi Delta Kappan, 76,* 591–596.

Lieberman, A. (1995b). *The work of restructuring the schools: Building from the ground up.* New York: Teachers College Press.

Lieberman, A., & Grolnick, M. (1996). Networks and the reform of American education. *Teachers College Record, 98,* 7–45.

Lieberman, A., & McLaughlin, M. W. (1992). Networks for educational change: Powerful and problematic. *Phi Delta Kappan, 73,* 673–677.

Lieberman, A., & Miller, L. (1990). Restructuring schools: What matters and what works. *Phi Delta Kappan, 71,* 759–764.

Lieberman, A., & Wood, D. (2003). *Inside the National Writing Project: Connecting network learning and classroom teaching.* New York: Teachers College Press.

Little, J. W. (1993). Teachers' professional development in a climate of educational reform. *Educational Evaluation and Policy Analysis, 15*(2), 129–151.

Little, J. W. (1996, January). *Organizing schools for teacher learning.* Paper presented at the Area Conference on Teacher Development and School Reform, Washington, DC.

Little, J. W., Gerritz, W. H., Stem, D. S., Guthrie, J. W., Kirst, M. W, & Marsh, D. D. (1987). *Staff development in California: Public and personal investment, program patterns, and policy choices.* San Francisco: Far West Laboratory for Educational Research and Development.

Little, J. W., & McLaughlin, M. W. (1991). *Urban mathematics collaboratives: As the teachers tell it.* Stanford, CA: Stanford University, Center for Research on the Context of Secondary School Teaching.

Lord, B. (1991, April). *Subject-area collaboratives, teacher professionalism, and staff development.* Paper presented at the annual meeting of the American Educational Research Association, Chicago.

Loucks-Horsley, S., & Stiegelbauer, S. (1991). Using knowledge of change to guide staff development. In A. Lieberman & L. Miller (Eds.), *Staff development for education in the 90's: New demands, new realities, new perspectives* (pp. 15–36). New York: Teachers College Press.

McAdams, D., & de St. Aubin, E. (1998). *Generativity and adult development: How and why we care about the next generation.* Washington, DC: American Psychological Association.

McDonald, J. (2001). Students' work and teachers' learning. In A. Lieberman & L. Miller (Eds.), *Teachers caught in the action: professional development that matters.* New York: Teachers College press.

McLaughlin, M. W. (1998). Listening and learning from the field: Tales of policy implementation and situated practice. In A. Lieberman (Ed.), *The international handbook of educational change: Vol. 1. The roots of educational change* (pp. 70–84). Dordrecht, The Netherlands: Klüwer.

McLaughlin, M. W., & Talbert, J. (1993). *Contexts that matter for teaching and learning.* Stanford, CA: Center for Research on the Context of Secondary School Teaching, Stanford University.

Merriam, S. B., & Caffarella, R. S. (1999). *Learning in adulthood* (2nd ed.). San Francisco: Jossey-Bass.

Newmann, E., & Wehlage, G. (1995). *Successful school restructuring: A report to the public and educators.* Madison: Center on Organization and Restructuring of Schools, Wisconsin Center for Education Research, University of Wisconsin.

Peske, H. G., Liu, E., Johnson, S. M., Kauffman, D., & Kardos, S. M. (2001). The next generation of teachers: Changing conceptions of a career in teaching. *Phi Delta Kappan, 83,* 304–311.

Settersten, R. A. M., & Hagestad, G. (1996). What's the latest? Cultural deadlines for education and work transitions. *Gerontologist, 36,* 602–613.

Showers, B., Joyce, B., & Bennett, B. (1987). Synthesis of research on staff development: A framework for future study and a state-of-the art analysis. *Educational Leadership, 45*(3), 77–87.

Westheimer, J. (1998). *Among school teachers: Community, autonomy and ideology in teachers' work.* New York: Teachers College Press.

Wrightsman, L. S. (1994). *Adult personality development* (Vols. 1 & 2). Thousands Oaks, CA: Sage.

CHAPTER EIGHT

Design Principles for Learner-Centered Professional Development

Willis D. Hawley and Linda Valli

R esearch clearly shows that teacher expertise is the most significant school-based influence on student learning (Darling-Hammond, 2000; Greenwald, Hedges, & Laine, 1996; McCaffrey, Lockwood, Koretz, & Hamilton, 2003; Rice, 2003; Sanders & Horn, 1998). As a result, one would think that investments in enhancing teacher expertise would be a major focus of school improvement efforts. However, while virtually all school improvement proposals assert that professional development is important, the level of investment in teacher learning is seldom substantial. Moreover, it is difficult to find many defenders of the most commonly used strategies for professional development (see National Commission on Teaching & America's Future [NCTAF], 1996).

Investments in professional development have many purposes. This chapter focuses on two of them:

To strengthen the capacity and motivation of teachers to improve student learning in specific ways

To build new capacity within the school or district (such as enhancing the use of technology in instruction)

If these emphases seem obvious, it should be recognized that a substantial amount of the public funds and most of the resources of individual teachers that are invested directly and indirectly in professional development go to enriching the expertise and career opportunities of individual teachers. Such investments include tuition subsidies and pay increases tied to course work from universities or other providers, attendance at conferences, book clubs, and state and national professional enrichment programs for outstanding teachers. While there are ways these experiences might contribute to school improvement, in most cases they do not. This is not to say that these investments are unworthy; the point is that there are ways to use time and money allocated to professional development that are likely to have a greater influence than others on student learning.

PROFESSIONAL DEVELOPMENT OR PROFESSIONAL LEARNING COMMUNITIES?

Prior to the 1990s, most discussions of professional development focused on particular techniques or content. But as understandings of the influence of school cultures and collaborative action on school effectiveness grew, interest in improving individual teacher performance shifted to "professional learning communities." While concern about the design of formal professional development activities is still evident, the literature on teacher learning is now dominated by research that shows that in really good schools, teachers are continually engaged in learning that is integral to and driven by the collaborative analysis of student performance (McLaughlin & Talbert, 2006). In much of the current literature on enhancing teacher expertise, issues of how best to design professional development are overshadowed by discussions of how best to achieve the conditions needed for professional learning communities, such as interpersonal trust, collaborative processes, and access to evidence that is relevant to both student learning and effective practice.

We have, of course, just created a false dichotomy. Well-designed professional development activities and the conditions that support professional learning communities are interdependent and need to be aligned if either is to be productive. Specific strategies for fostering teacher expertise are important not only in themselves but also because they communicate school goals and influence the skills and values teachers need in order to participate effectively in professional learning communities. Where to start: the redesign of professional development practices or the development of professional learning communities? School leaders need to work on both simultaneously and be aware of the interdependencies involved. This chapter deals with the principles that should shape the design and evaluation of professional development practices. It will be readily apparent that acting on these principles will also foster and sustain professional learning communities.

DESIGN PRINCIPLES FOR EFFECTIVE PROFESSIONAL DEVELOPMENT

There is no shortage of ideas about how best to enhance teacher learning and expertise. How would one decide which approach, or which combination of approaches, is likely to be most productive in a given school? Each has its advocates who claim success in improving student achievement and argue that the particular practice is research based. Moreover, the success of any particular approach is a function of what the goals are, how well it is implemented, and situational influences on its efficacy. What works in one setting may not work in another.

This chapter summarizes a rather large body of research and expert opinion on the effectiveness of professional development in the form of 10 "design principles."[1] These principles can be used to develop a comprehensive approach to professional development for teachers and administrators or to evaluate existing programs and specific practices. We call these design principles "learner centered" for two reasons: first, because professional development should be driven by the needs of students and by what teachers need to know and be able to do to address specific learning needs of their students. Second, professional development should reflect what we know about how people learn. This means that the content and delivery of professional development should address learners' beliefs and prior knowledge, motivation, capacity for strategic processing, individual differences, and situation or context (see Murphy & Alexander, this volume).

One could distinguish two types of principles: those that address the *process* of professional learning and those that focus on the *content*. The distinction, however, breaks down because content and process in professional learning are symbiotic. Obviously, the content is the rationale for investments in professional development, but just as obviously, specific content depends on the needs of students to be served. How one decides on the content is directly related to the process of professional development, because professional learning needs should be defined by student learning needs, a critically important point we will discuss further. Moreover, how teachers learn influences what they learn, especially what they learn about teaching and learning.

Whatever the specific topic of professional development (e.g., how to anticipate and respond to reading comprehension problems), the following principles should be reflected in what and how teachers learn to continuously develop their expertise. These principles focus on the enhancement of teachers' expertise, but they apply as well to the professional development of other educators.

Principle 1: Professional development should be based on collaborative analyses of the differences between (a) actual student performance and (b) goals and standards for student learning.

Professional development should be driven by analyses of the differences between (a) goals and standards for student learning and (b) students' classroom performance, not just end-of-year test scores (Miller, Lord, & Dorney, 1994; Pink & Hyde, 1992; Schmoker, 2002). Such analyses will define what educators need, rather than want, to learn; make professional development student centered; and increase public confidence in the use of resources for professional development (Farkas & Friedman,

1995). Educators can then use the analysis of student work to understand why some students are not learning while some are and to explore the usefulness of alternative strategies for student learning and school improvement, paying close attention to the gains made by diverse types of learners.

The importance of this student-centered focus seems self-evident, but it has not been standard practice. Because students have many needs and the process of defining those needs is often less than systematic, the content of professional development is often characterized by breadth rather than depth. Too often, new teaching strategies, curricular approaches, or organizational designs, pursued as goals in and of themselves, have diverted attention from the school's central goal of improving student learning (Loucks-Horsley, 1995; Newmann & Wehlage, 1995; Peterson, McCarthey, & Elmore, 1996).

While individual teachers should be encouraged to base their teaching strategies on their analyses of what students are learning, schoolwide improvement in learning depends on teacher engagement in collaborative problem solving (Fullan, 2001; Garet, Porter, Desimone, Birman, & Yoon, 2001; Guskey, 1995; Knapp, McCaffrey, & Swanson, 2003; Leithwood, this volume; McLaughlin & Talbert, 2006; Southeast Center for Teaching Quality, 2003). Without collaborative problem solving, individual change may be possible, but school change is not. There are many reasons for this, including the fact that different expertise and perspectives aid problem solving and schoolwide improvement requires schoolwide understanding of the needs and opportunities for change and buy-in to new ways of fostering student learning.

Collaborative problem-solving activities can take many forms, including leadership or grade-level teams, interdisciplinary teams, curriculum development and critique groups, collaborative action research, and study groups. In each situation in which teacher effectiveness is enhanced by collaboration, educators are engaged in active learning that addresses the identification of both the causes and the potential solutions to problems (Desimone, Porter, Grant, Yoon, & Birman, 2002).

Although collaborative problem solving can result in potentially irreconcilable positions or merely perpetuate existing practice, it can, when done skillfully, lead to the clarification of learning needs and the sharing of knowledge and expertise. It can break down teacher isolation (Bryk, Rollow, & Pinnell, 1996); collectively empower teachers (Hargreaves, 1995); create an environment of professional respect (Guskey, 1995); foster intellectual communities (Kazemi & Franke, 2003); and develop a shared language and understanding of good practice (Little, this volume; Newmann & Wehlage, 1995; Rosenholtz, 1989).

If collaborative problem solving focused on the analysis of student performance were easy, there would be more of it. One explanation for its common absence from the work of schools is that school-level educators have not had the opportunity to develop and exercise their analytic capacity for continual school improvement. Educators assert that they do not get sufficient training in the use of data and research. But more important than such technical capabilities of educators are barriers to collaboration rooted in the culture of schools and the availability of adequate time and evidence that would facilitate empirical problem solving. Bringing about significant changes in teaching is hard work, requiring time and support from colleagues and school leaders (Grossman, Wineberg, & Woolworth, 2001). Support is most productive when it is grounded in professional discourse around shared concerns that focus on student learning (Richardson & Placier, 2001).

Principle 2: Professional development should be primarily school based and built into the day-to-day work of teaching.

If the content of professional development is to be based on collaborative problem solving, professional development activities should be primarily school based and integral to school operations (Guskey, 1995; Joyce & Showers, 2002; King, Newmann, & Youngs, 2003; Knapp et al., 2003; Louis, Marks, & Kruse, 1996; Smylie, 1995). This does not mean that teachers should not have access to out-of-school learning experiences through professional associations or networks, graduate study, or teacher centers. However, opportunities to learn in powerful ways are most often connected with the recognition of and solution of authentic and immediate problems (Hodges, 1996)

Motivation to learn and to engage in school change efforts increases when these efforts are linked to improving and assessing daily practice. This is often referred to as *job-embedded learning.* As

Loucks-Horsley (1995) claimed, establishing a better connection between learning and doing increases meaning for the teacher and the likelihood of a stronger impact on students. Smylie (1995) described the optimal workplace being one in which learning arises from and feeds back into work experience, in which learning is considered to be part of work.

Effective professional development that is integral to the day-to-day work of educators requires time for collaborative problem solving and related learning. Such time can be built into the school day through flexible and creative scheduling or by extending the school year (for alternative strategies for finding time for professional development, see http://www.NCREL.org).

Principle 3: Professional development should involve teachers in the identification of what they need to learn and in the development of the learning experiences in which they will be involved.

Professional development should involve learners (e.g., teachers) in the identification of what they need to learn and, when possible, in the development of the learning opportunity and the process to be used (Borko & Putnam, 1995; Little, 1993; Miller et al., 1994; Tillema & Imants, 1995; Wisconsin Center for Educational Research [WCER], 2004-2005). This engagement increases educators' motivation and commitment to learn (Hodges, 1996); affirms their strengths and enhances their sense of efficacy (Pink & Hyde, 1992); empowers them to take instructional risks and to assume new roles and responsibilities (Barr, Anderson, & Slaybaugh, 1992; Pink, 1992); increases the likelihood that what is learned will be meaningful and relevant to particular contexts and problems (Pink & Hyde, 1992); improves instruction (Hodges, 1996); and makes the school culture more collaborative and improvement oriented (Pink, 1992).

If teachers are denied input in their professional development, they are likely to become cynical and detached from school improvement efforts and to reject what is experienced as imposition (Guskey, 1995; Hargreaves, 1995). Lack of involvement also reduces the capacity of the school and district to understand and manage school change (Pink & Hyde, 1992).

Principle 3, like others, requires effective leadership at the school level. In a school in which professional learning is integral to the implementation of the core technology—teaching—being a leader would mean being a facilitator of learning. Reform is short-lived if it is led rather than facilitated by top leadership (Barr et al., 1992; Sergiovanni, 2005). While hierarchical authority creates learned conformity, more egalitarian authority relations "increase the likelihood that individuals will feel and be freer to engage in reflective practice and experimental learning" (Smylie, 1995, p. 99).

This teacher involvement principle needs to be implemented in the context of Principle 1, that professional development should be driven by analysis of data on student performance and evidence of best practice in narrowing the gap between student performance and high goals for student learning. School leaders must keep attention focused on what teachers need to learn, as well as want to learn, in order to close the gap between school goals and school performance. For example, teachers are not likely to identify their need for subject matter knowledge or pedagogical content knowledge (Borko & Putnam, 1995). Professional credibility depends on teachers knowing the material they teach. Yet current understandings of mathematics, science, history, and the arts—and how to teach those subjects—have changed radically in recent years. School leaders must create organizational cultures in which everyone feels good about needing to learn. They must, however, protect teachers from unnecessary and unproductive involvement, unreasonable expectations, and burnout (Guskey, 1995).

Principle 4: The content should reflect the best research on the given topic (e.g., how to enhance the literacy of adolescents).

In and of itself, this principle is obvious. But the problem is to know what the best research says. Reports of research findings are not always clear, and some sources of information about research are more authoritative than others. It is almost always problematic simply to use "the latest" study or to rely on a single expert.

The search costs for acquiring reliable knowledge about best practice can be significantly reduced by relying on syntheses of research that involve a national panel of experts, are explicit about selection criteria, are peer reviewed, and prevent funders and those with conflicts of interest from determining conclusions.

Among the sources that fit these characteristics are the National Research Council (for a list of studies, see http://www.nap.edu) and the What Works Clearinghouse (see http://www.w-w-c.org). Syntheses of research found in two journals of the American Educational Research Association, *Review of Educational Research* and *Review of Research in Education,* are not the work of panels but otherwise meet the tests above. Of course, experts from within the school system and elsewhere should be consulted, but it may be difficult to know whether these experts are up-to-date and open to ideas that are different from those in which they have become invested.

Involving teachers in identifying the best thinking on a topic, for example, through teacher study groups, is often productive because it builds expertise within the school that can be called on when issues arise in developing or implementing a particular approach.

Principle 5: The content of professional development should focus on what students are to learn and how to address the different problems students may have in learning that material.

Clearly, the content of professional development is critically important to its effectiveness. Although the focus will vary with the goals of the school or district, professional development should be closely aligned with the specific content students are expected to learn and the instructional strategies best suited to teach that content (Carpenter, Fennema, Peterson, Chiang, & Loef, 1989; Cohen & Hill, 2000; Garet et al., 2001; Kennedy, 1998; WCER, 2004–2005).

Providing teachers with general information about an instructional procedure (e.g., how to use cooperative-learning techniques) or enrichment courses on subject material (e.g., new developments in biology) usually does not result in improved student learning (Kennedy, 1998). Instead, professional development should focus on the specific content that students are expected to learn and problems that students might confront in learning the content, as well as instructional strategies that address anticipated problems or issues.

Although teachers must know substantially more about a subject than their students, higher-level content knowledge should be tied to the particular lessons students are to learn if teachers are to be expected to use this knowledge to enhance students' learning. Teachers also need to learn how to adapt instructional strategies (e.g., differentiated instruction) to variations in student needs and learning contexts. Teaching teachers only one way to teach a lesson can be counterproductive.

Principle 6: Professional development should provide experiential opportunities to gain an understanding of and reflect on the research and theory underlying the knowledge and skills being learned.

Professional development should provide opportunities to engage in developing a theoretical understanding of the knowledge and skills to be learned (Center on English Learning and Achievement, 2002; Corcoran, 1995; Eraut, 1995; Fullan, 2001; Joyce & Showers, 2002; National Center for Research on Teacher Education [NCRTE], 1991; Richardson & Placier, 2001; Tillema & Imants, 1995).

Since teachers' thinking and classroom behavior are influenced by their knowledge and beliefs, an important component of their professional development needs to be the expansion and elaboration of their professional knowledge base. Results of research, in comprehensible forms, need to be made accessible to teachers, who often cite lack of understanding and limited access to relevant guides to action as reasons for not putting research into practice. Broadly speaking, this would include general pedagogical knowledge, subject matter knowledge, and pedagogical content knowledge, which address areas such as classroom management, conceptions of teaching a subject, and students' understandings and potential misunderstandings of subject matter (Borko & Putnam, 1995; Eraut, 1995).

But new knowledge in itself does not effect change in either beliefs about teaching and learning or behavior (NCRTE, 1991; Spillane, Reiser, & Reimer, 2002). Professional development must engage teachers' beliefs, experiences, and habits. Beliefs people hold about things they care about are difficult to change. Since beliefs filter knowledge and guide behavior, significant transformations of teaching practice are unlikely to occur if beliefs are ignored (Bransford, Brown, & Cocking, 1999; Kazemi & Franke, 2003). Creating effective professional development opportunities means helping teachers (re)consider both their formal and their practical teaching knowledge (Bransford et al., 1999; Joyce & Showers, 2002). For example, Borko and Putnam (1995) identified the importance of teachers being asked to reconsider fundamental beliefs, especially the belief that they should be transmitters of knowledge and are responsible for covering a specified amount of content, whether students understand that content or not. Dialogue with colleagues is important in helping teachers move to new understandings about theories and beliefs (Franke, Carpenter, Levi, & Fennema, 1998; Joyce & Showers, 2002; Richardson & Placier, 2001).

Effective instruction often requires that teachers modify what they have learned in order to address variations in student needs and the learning environment. An understanding of the theory underlying a given instructional strategy learned through professional development enables teachers to use that strategy flexibly and adaptively.

> Principle 7: The way teacher learning is facilitated should mirror the instructional approaches they are expected to master and allow teachers to experience the consequences of newly learned capabilities.

Showing or telling teachers what to do is not enough. Teachers should experience the different types of instruction they are expected to implement (Borko, 2004; Cobb et al., 1991; Desimone et al., 2002). For example, if we want teachers to learn how to use cooperative learning to enhance students' computational skills, professional development should use cooperative learning to develop teachers' new expertise.

There is substantial evidence that teachers often "underimplement" new practices they have presumably learned. One reason for this is that they erroneously believe they are doing what the new practice requires (Cohen & Hill, 2000; Spillane et al., 2002). Change in teaching can be facilitated by giving teachers experience reflecting, ideally with colleagues, on the differences between what they have been doing and the new practice (Richardson & Placier, 2001).

It follows that professional development should attend to educators' needs to adapt their learning to their own students and contexts. Thus, one of the surest ways to foster lasting change in teaching practice is to give teachers the opportunity to see positive results in their students. This should help overcome suspicions that research is irrelevant to teachers' particular contexts and day-to-day responsibilities. Teachers are more engaged participants when they see clear benefits between what they are learning and their own classroom situations. Such engagement is more likely when it is informed by theory in which the educator involved has confidence.

Principle 8: Professional development should be continuous and ongoing, involving follow-up and support for further learning, including support from sources external to the school that can provide necessary resources and new perspectives.

Borko (2004) observed that knowledge changes faster than practice. Initially, the depth of practice is shallow, and the deepening of practice requires support over time that builds both cognitive understanding and practical knowledge and provides time to work with others to create the professional community needed to sustain difficult practice (Clair, Adger, Short, & Millen, 1998). As Kazemi and Franke (2003) concluded in summarizing several studies,

Teachers need [time] to strengthen their content knowledge and their instructional practices by participating in intellectual communities in which they work on content and pedagogy over a period of time, allowing themselves enough time to develop norms for interaction, navigate tensions and conflict within the group, and build confidence to make dilemmas of practice public. (p. 5)

As what is learned from professional development is implemented, learners often discover what they need to know and be able to do to be effective. If this need for learning, resources, and support is not met, increased professional competence and student achievement are unlikely to be experienced and the motivation to continue to implement the new practice and engage in additional professional development will be affected.

The research is clear that extensive opportunities to learn over time contribute to teacher effectiveness, especially when these opportunities are a continuing part of the implementation process and supported by sources external to the school (Garet et al., 2001; Hodges, 1996; Miller et al., 1994; Parsad, Lewis, & Farris, 2001; WCER, 2004–2005). However, it is important to note that it is not the amount of time teachers spend on a given topic that affects what they know and are able to do (American Educational Research Association [AERA], 2005; Garet et al., 2001), but the quality of the professional development they experience. Lauer (2001) found, for example, that total number of teachers' professional development days is unrelated to student performance; what matters is whether they had the opportunity to learn and implement new practices collaboratively.

While most professional development should be school based, educators also need to enrich this learning with new ideas and knowledge gained from sources beyond the school (Lieberman & Miller, this volume; Smylie, Allensworth, Greenberg, Harris, & Luppescu, 2001). Innovations are constrained when informed only by those who share similar ideas and experiences (Smylie, 1995).

The development of a capability for and commitment to new approaches to facilitating student learning takes time, including time to establish trust and shared meanings with those inside and outside the school organization. In a study of student grouping, Barr et al. (1992) found that district- and school-level educators took 4 years to deliberate and make changes.

Significant change in educational practice seldom occurs quickly; it is the result of programs designed with a 3- to 5-year professional development component. Ongoing support is especially critical in the first 2 years of implementation. Unfortunately, the public expects to see quick changes in schools and concrete evidence of almost immediate improvements in student achievement (Farkas & Friedman, 1995).

Principle 9: Professional development should be connected to a comprehensive change process focused on specific goals for improving student learning.

Professional development should be integrated with a comprehensive change process that deals with impediments to and facilitation of student learning (Desimone et al., 2002; Guskey, 1995;

Little, 1993; Smylie, 1995). The primary goal of professional development is, of course, to change or enhance teachers' instructional practices. Change in practice involves not only change in capabilities and motivation but also increased opportunity and support. It follows that to the extent that change is being pursued in coherent ways—professional development is aligned with curriculum, standards, and assessment—the effects of professional development are likely to be more robust (AERA, 2005; Desimone et al., 2002). Well-intentioned professional development can be undermined when teachers experience conflicting professional development activities that pull them in different directions or overload them with competing demands (Clair et al., 1998).

Educators must practice what they learn. Too often, they are asked to learn new things they cannot act upon because there is no organizational commitment to continuous experimentation and improvement. Teachers need time and opportunities to investigate why some practices might be better than others, see models of such practices, and personally develop these practices. School- and district-level support are essential components of this process (Joyce & Showers, 2002; NCRTE, 1991). Some district-level types of support for comprehensive change efforts include adequate funding, technical assistance, sustained central office follow-through, avoidance of quick fixes, and providing teachers adequate time to learn, plan, and implement new practices (Hodges, 1996).

> Principle 10: Evaluation of professional development should incorporate multiple sources of information on (a) outcomes for students and (b) the instruction and other processes that are involved in implementing the lessons learned.

Evaluation of the effectiveness of professional development experiences should be seen as essential to teacher learning. This takes us back to Principle 1, which seeks to focus professional development on the results of analyses of student outcomes and the reasons for progress, or lack of progress, in narrowing the gap between goals and student performance. Learning about the efficacy of various approaches to enhancing teacher capacity and motivation will inform both the process and the content of professional development and is an integral part of the problem-solving process that leads to continuous improvement. Assessment of the effects of professional development should incorporate multiple sources of information on (a) outcomes for students and (b) processes that are involved in implementing the lessons learned through professional development (Guskey, 1995; Joyce & Showers, 2002; Little, 1993; NCRTE, 1991; Tillema & Imants, 1995).

While third-party research and the periodic involvement of outside consultants may be desirable ways to evaluate the effectiveness of professional development, engaging teachers and school administrators on a continuing basis builds understanding and commitment to improvement at the school level. Such assessment must be nonthreatening, be conducted throughout various stages of implementation, allow sufficient time for change to occur, assess change in teaching as well as change in student learning, and help teachers think more carefully about their classroom practice (Hodges, 1996). Knowing the extent to which professional development has influenced student achievement contributes to the design of and incentives for further learning.

HOW CONFIDENT CAN ONE BE IN THE DESIGN PRINCIPLES?

While empirical research on the relationship between specific aspects of professional development listed above and student achievement is positive, it is limited. In addition to the available research, there are three other reasons the learner-centered design principles can be used with confidence to both develop and evaluate various approaches to professional development:

1. The 10 design principles are consistent with what we know about how people learn (for authoritative reviews of that research, see Alexander & Murphy, 1998; Bransford et al., 1999; Murphy & Alexander, 2006).

2. There is uncommon agreement among researchers about the centrality of the principles for effective professional development. This does not mean that researchers use the same terms to describe the principles identified here or that most researchers would list all 10 principles. But it is unlikely that one could find significant research that contradicts the principles identified here.

3. There is substantial consensus among policy and professional groups about the essential characteristics of professional development. These characteristics are reflected in the 10 learner-centered design principles (see American Federation of Teachers, 1995; Learning First Alliance, 2000; National Foundation for the Improvement of Education, 1996; National Governor's Association, 1995; National Research Council, 1996; National Staff Development Council, 2004; U.S. Department of Education, 1995).

CONCLUSION

The implementation of learner-centered professional development defined by the principles discussed in this chapter will require major changes in how professional development is delivered, how schools are structured, and the cultures and belief systems that perpetuate long-standing practices. Such changes are, however, warranted by their positive effects on teaching—the most powerful school-based influence on student learning.

Quality professional development, by itself, will not produce significant changes in student achievement. When professional development is thought of as a discreet program, a series of formal scheduled events, or is otherwise disconnected from authentic problem solving, it is unlikely to have much influence on teacher or student learning. Instead of treating professional development as a delivery system, schools need to provide educators with ongoing opportunities to learn as they collectively address the challenges posed by the inevitable gap between high standards and actual student performance. Unless sustained learner-centered professional development becomes a reality, there is little chance of schools as institutions becoming professional learning communities capable of continuous improvement in student achievement.

NOTE

1. A caution about the research: Few studies link variations in professional development directly to student achievement. Many studies, and most of those cited in this chapter, do measure the effects of professional development on teacher beliefs and behaviors that other research has shown to positively affect student learning. Most studies examine the

effects on small numbers of teachers and are carried out by advocates of the particular behaviors or professional development strategies being examined. Nonetheless, there is remarkable agreement among researchers on the essential elements of effective professional development.

REFERENCES

Alexander, P. A., & Murphy, P. K. (1998). The research base for APA's learner-centered psychological principles. In N. L. Lambert & B. L. McCombs (Eds.), *Issues in school reform: A sampler of psychological perspectives on learner-centered schools* (pp. 25–60). Washington, DC: American Psychological Association.

American Educational Research Association. (2005). *Teaching teachers: Professional development to improve student achievement.* Washington, DC: Author.

American Federation of Teachers. (1995). *Principles for professional development.* Washington, DC: Author.

Barr, R., Anderson, C. S., & Slaybaugh, J. E. (1992). Deliberations about grouping in Crete-Monee. In W. T. Pinl & A. A. Hyde (Eds.), *Effective staff development for school change* (pp. 65–93). Norwood, NJ: Ablex.

Borko, H. (2004). Professional development and teacher learning: Mapping the terrain. *Educational Researcher 33*(8), 3–15.

Borko, H., & Putman, R. T. (1995). Expanding teachers' knowledge base: A cognitive psychological perspective on professional development. T. R. Guskey & M. Huberman (Eds.), *Professional development in education: New paradigms and practices* (pp. 35–66). New York: Teachers College Press.

Bransford, J., Brown, A., & Cocking, R. (Eds.). (1999). *How people learn: Brain, mind, experience. and school.* Washington, DC: National Academy Press.

Bryk, A. S., Rollow, S. G., & Pinnell, G. S. (1996). Urban school development: Literacy as a lever for change. *Educational Policy, 10*(2), 172–201.

Carpenter, T. P., Fennema, E., Peterson, P. L., Chiang, C. P., & Loef, M. (1989). Using knowledge of children's mathematics thinking in classroom teaching: An experimental study. *American Journal of Educational Research, 26*(3), 499–531.

Center on English Learning and Achievement. (2002). *Effective professional development begins in the classroom.* Center on English Learning and Achievement, State University of New York at Albany.

Clair, N., Adger, C., Short, D., & Millen, E. (1998). *Implementing standards for English language learners: Initial findings from four middle schools.* Providence, RI: Education Alliance, the LAB at Brown University.

Cobb, P., Wood, T., Yackel, E., Nichols, J., Wheatley, G., Trigatti, B., & Perlwitz, M. (1991). Assessment of a problem-centered second grade mathematics project. *Journal of Research in Mathematics Education, 22,* 13–29.

Cohen, D. K., & Hill, H. C. (2000). Instructional policy and classroom performance. The mathematics reform in California. *Teachers College Record, 102*(4), 9–26.

Corcoran, T. C. (1995). *Helping teachers teach well: Transforming professional development.* Rutgers University, New Brunswick, NJ: Consortium for Policy Research in Education.

Darling-Hammond, L. (2000). Teacher quality and student achievement: A review of state policy evidence. *Education Policy Analysis Archives, 8*(1), 1–50.

Desimone, L. M., Porter, A. C., Grant, M. S., Yoon, K. S., & Birman, B. F. (2002). Effects of professional development on teachers' instruction: Results from a three-year longitudinal study. *Educational Evaluation and Policy Analysis, 24*(2), 81–112.

Eraut, M. (1995). Developing professional knowledge within a client centered orientation. In T. R. Guskey & M. Huberman, *Professional development in education: New paradigms and new practices* (pp. 227–252). New York: Teachers College Press.

Farkas, S., & Friedman, W. (1995). *Professional development for teachers: The public's view.* New York: Public Agenda for the National Foundation for the Improvement of Teaching.

Franke, M. L., Carpenter, T. P., Levi, L., & Fennema, E. (1998, April). *Teachers as learners: Developing understanding through children's thinking.* Paper presented at the annual meeting of the American Educational Research Association, San Diego.

Fullan, M. (2001). *The new meaning of educational change:* (3rd ed.). New York: Teachers College Press.

Garet, M. S., Porter, A. C., Desimone, L., Birman, B. F., & Yoon, K. S. (2001). What makes professional development effective? Results from a national sample of teachers. *American Educational Research Journal, 38*(4), 915–945.

Greenwald, R., Hedges, L., & Laine, R. (1996). The effect of school resources on student achievement. *Review of Educational Research, 66*(3), 361–396.

Grossman, P., Wineberg, S., & Woolworth, S. (2001). Toward a theory of teacher community. *Teachers College Record, 103,* 942–1012.

Guskey, T. R. (1995). Professional development in education: In search of the optimal mix. In T. R. Guskey & M. Huberman (Eds.), *Professional development in education: New paradigms & practices* (pp. 114–132). New York: Teachers College Press.

Hargreaves, A. (1995). Development and desire: A postmodern perspective. In T. R. Guskey & M. Huberman (Eds.), *Professional development in education: New paradigms & practices* (pp. 9–34). New York: Teachers College Press.

Hodges, H. L. B. (1996). Using research to inform practice in urban schools: 10 key strategies for success. *Educational Policy 10*(2), 223–252.

Joyce, B., & Showers, B. (2002). *Student achievement through staff development* (3rd ed.). Alexandria, VA: Association for Supervision and Curriculum Development.

Kazemi, E., & Franke, M. L. (2003). *Using student work to support professional development in elementary mathematics.* Seattle: University of Washington, Center for Teaching and Policy.

Kennedy, M. (1998, April). *The relevance of content in inservice education.* Paper presented at the annual meeting of the American Educational Research Association, San Diego.

King, B., Newmann, F., & Youngs, P. (2003). Enhancing school capacity through professional development. *WCER Highlights, 15*(1), 3, 7.

Knapp, M., McCaffrey, T., & Swanson, J. (2003, April). *District support for professional learning: What research says and has yet to establish.* A paper presented at the annual meeting of the American Educational Research Association, San Diego.

Lauer, P. A. (2001). *Preliminary findings on the characteristics of teacher learning in high performing, high needs schools.* Aurora, CO: Mid-Continent Research for Education and Learning.

Learning First Alliance. (2000). *Every child reading: A professional development guide.* Washington, DC: Author.

Little, J. W. (1993). Teacher's professional development in a climate of educational reform. *Educational Evaluation and Policy Analysis, 15*(2), 129–151.

Loucks-Horsely, S. (1995). Professional development and the learner-centered school. *Theory Into Practice, 34*(4), 265–271.

Louis, K. S., Marks, H. M., & Kruse, S.D. (1996). Teachers' professional community in restructuring schools. *American Educational Research Journal 33*(4), 757–798.

McCaffrey, D., Lockwood, J., Koretz, D., & Hamilton, L. (2003). *Evaluating value-added models for teacher accountability.* Santa Monica, CA: Rand.

McLaughlin, M. W., & Talbert, J. E. (2006). *Building school-based learning communities: Professional strategies to improve student achievement.* New York: Teachers College Press.

Miller, B., Lord, B., & Dorney, J. (1994). *Summary report: Staff development for teachers. A study of configuration and costs in four districts.* Newton, MA: Education Development Center.

Murphy, K. P., & Alexander, P. A. (2006). *Understanding how students learn: A guide for instructional leaders.* Thousand Oaks, CA: Corwin Press.

National Center for Research on Teacher Education. (1991). *Final report.* East Lansing: Michigan State University.

National Commission on Teaching & America's Future. (1996). *What matters most: Teaching for America's future.* New York: Author.

National Foundation for the Improvement of Education. (1996). *Teachers take charge of their learning.* Washington, DC: National Education Association.

National Governor's Association. (1995). *Transforming professional development for teachers: A guide to state policymakers.* Washington, DC: Author.

National Research Council. (1996). Standards for professional development for science teachers. *Science education standards* (chap. 4). Washington, DC: National Academy Press.

National Staff Development Council. (2004). *Standards for staff development.* Oxford, OH: Author.

Newmann, F. M., & Wehlage, G. G. (1995). *Successful school restructuring. A report to the public and educators by the Center on Organization and Restructuring of Schools.* Madison: University of Wisconsin-Madison.

Parsad, B., Lewis, L., & Farris, E. (2001). *Teacher preparation and professional development: 2000.* Washington, DC: National Center for Educational Statistics.

Peterson, P., McCarthey, S., & Elmore, R. (1996). Learning from school restructuring. *American Educational Research Journal, 33*(1), 119–153.

Pink, W. T. (1992). A school-within-a-school for at-risk youth: Staff development and program success. In W. T Pink & A. A. Hyde (Eds.), *Effective staff development for school change* (pp. 33–63). Norwood, NJ: Ablex.

Pink, W. T., & Hyde, A. A. (1992). Doing effective professional development. In W. T Pink & A. A. Hyde (Eds.), *Effective staff development for school change* (pp. 259–292). Norwood, NJ: Ablex.

Rice, J. K. (2003). *Teacher quality: Understanding the effectiveness of teacher attributes.* Washington, DC: Economic Policy Institute.

Richardson, V., & Placier, P. (2001). Teacher change. In V. Richardson (Ed.), *Handbook of research on teaching* (4th ed., pp. 905–950). Washington, DC: American Educational Research Association.

Rosenholtz, S. (1989). *Teachers' workplace: The social organization of schools.* New York: Teachers College Press.

Sanders, W. L., & Horn, S. P. (1998). Research findings from the Tennessee Value-Added Assessment System (TVAAS) database: Implications for educational evaluation and research. *Journal of Personnel Evaluation and Education, 12*(3), 247–256.

Schmoker, M. (2002). Up and away. *Journal of the National Staff Development Council 23*(4), 10–13.

Sergiovanni, T. (2005). *Strengthening the heartbeat: Leading and learning together.* San Francisco: Jossey-Bass.

Smylie, M. A. (1995). Teacher learning in the workplace: Implications for school reform. In T. R. Guskey & M. Huberman (Eds.), *Professional development in education: New paradigms & practices* (pp. 92–113). New York: Teachers College Press.

Smylie, M. A., Allensworth, E., Greenberg, R. C., Harris, R., & Luppescu, S. (2001). *Teacher professional development in Chicago: Supporting effective practice.* Chicago: Consortium for Chicago School Research.

Southeast Center for Teaching Quality. (2003). How do teachers learn to teach effectively? *Quality Indicators From Quality Schools, 2*(7), 2–7.

Spillane, J. P., Reiser, B. J., & Reimer, T. (2002). Policy implementation and cognition: Reframing and refocusing implementation research. *Review of Educational Research 72*(3), 393–414.

Tillema, H. H., & Imants, J. G. M. (1995). Training for the professional development of teachers. In T. R. Guskey & M. Huberman (Eds.), *Professional development in education: New paradigms & practices* (pp. 135–150). New York: Teachers College Press.

U.S. Department of Education. (1995). *Building bridges: The mission and principles of professional development.* Washington, DC: Author.

Wisconsin Center for Educational Research. (2004–2005). What "travels" in mathematics reform. *WCER Highlights, 16*(4), 5, 7.

CHAPTER NINE

Organizational Conditions That Enhance Teaching and Learning

Kenneth Leithwood

T he context in which today's teachers work is extraordinarily demanding, in no small measure because of the pressure on schools to be more publicly accountable for what students learn. Both state and (especially) national policies, principally the No Child Left Behind Act of 2001, account for this pressure. Advocates of these policies often assume that greater teacher motivation and commitment will be the outcome of their policies and that is exactly what is needed to "fix" schools (e.g., McDonnell, 2005; Ostroff, 1992). Empirical evidence in justification of this position is remarkably thin, however.

This chapter is premised on a different view, for which there is ample empirical evidence. The vast majority of teachers are extraordinarily committed to their students already (Dannetta, 2002).

AUTHOR'S NOTE: Parts of this chapter are based on Leithwood and Steinbach (2003).

So, increasing overall levels of teacher commitment and motivation should be the least of our worries; eroding such motivation and commitment is the more relevant concern. Schools will improve to the extent that the conditions in which teachers work allow them to use their existing capacities well and to further enhance those capacities, while at least having neutral effects on their existing commitment and motivation. Of course, getting better at the job is the most direct route to higher motivation. People like to do what they are good at.

A handful of conditions within the classroom and across the school have the potential to significantly improve teachers' capacities and, with them, student learning. Classroom conditions include workload complexity, student grouping practices, and curriculum and instruction. Key conditions at the school level include workload volume, school structures and procedures, partnerships with parents and the wider community, school culture and sense of community, student retention and promotion policies, and instructional program coherence.

CLASSROOM CONDITIONS

Workload Complexity

Teachers' feelings of stress, morale, and commitment to their schools are significantly influenced by the perceived complexity of their work. These feelings, in turn, demonstrably influence teachers' classroom performance and the learning of their students (e.g., Kushman, 1992; Ostroff, 1992). From teachers' perspectives, complexity increases when they are required to teach in areas for which they are not certified or otherwise not well prepared and when their students are uncooperative and achieve relatively poorly. Complexity is perceived to be increasingly manageable, however, when teachers are given a significant degree of autonomy over classroom decisions. This allows them to do the job the best way they know how. Manageability is also increased, in their view, by an atmosphere throughout the school that encourages learning, sometimes called "academic press," and when instructional resources are readily available.

Student Grouping

At any point over at least the last 50 years, a synthesis of available empirical evidence would have suggested, quite unambiguously, that students having difficulty at school, especially those disadvantaged by their socioeconomic backgrounds, learn more when they are working in heterogeneous rather than in homogeneous ability groups (e.g., Yonezawa, Wells, & Serna, 2002). Relatively high expectations for learning, a faster pace of instruction, peer models of effective learning, and a more challenging curricula are among the reasons offered for this advantage. Despite this evidence, over this same period, the bulk of teachers and administrators have enacted practices that separate students by ability. Their argument is that homogeneous grouping produces greater learning by allowing for the concentration of instructional resources on the same set of learning problems. Implementing heterogeneous grouping practices in classrooms has been regarded by many teachers as very difficult. Nevertheless, this is one of the rare examples of professional "common sense" being just plain wrong.

Curriculum and Instruction

A considerable amount of evidence suggests that the best curriculum for socially, economically, or culturally disadvantaged children would be the "rich curriculum" typically experienced by relatively advantaged students. In reality, struggling children often experience a curriculum focused on basic skills and knowledge, lacking much meaning for any group of students. In a comprehensive synthesis of empirical evidence, Brophy (n.d.) touched on the main features of a "rich curriculum," in which the instructional strategies, learning activities, and assessment practices are clearly aligned and aimed at accomplishing the full array of knowledge, skills, attitudes, and dispositions valued by society.

The content of a rich curriculum is organized around a set of powerful ideas. These ideas are "internally coherent, well connected to other meaningful learning, and accessible for application" (Brophy, n.d., p. 7). Skills are taught with a view to their application in particular settings and for particular purposes. In addition, these skills include general learning and study skills, as well as those specific to subject domains. Such metacognitive skills are especially beneficial for less able students who might otherwise have difficulty monitoring and self-regulating their own learning. "Deep understanding" is the goal for all students (Leithwood, McAdie, Bascia, & Rogrigue, in press).

Brophy's (n.d.) synthesis of research also suggests that effective instruction is conducted in a highly supportive classroom environment, embedded in a caring learning community. In this environment, most class time is spent on curriculum-related activities, and the class is managed to maintain students' engagement in those activities. Effective instruction also includes questions "planned to engage students in sustained discourse structured around powerful ideas," and teachers provide the assistance students need "to enable them to engage in learning activities productively" (pp. 8–9).

Children from diverse cultures may also require "culturally responsive" teaching (Jagers & Carroll, 2002; Riehl, 2000). Such teaching is based on the premise that students' diverse cultures pose opportunities instead of problems for teachers. Teachers adopting this perspective identify the norms, values, and practices associated with the often diverse cultures of their students and adapt their instruction to acknowledge, respect, and build on them.

SCHOOL CONDITIONS

Workload Volume

During the school year, teachers work an average of 50 to 53 hours per week, completing a long list of tasks. Only about half of that time is devoted to instruction tasks (e.g., Dibbon, 2004). Teachers' commitment to their schools and feelings of stress and morale, which influence instructional performance and student learning, are eroded when teachers perceive their workloads to be unfair in comparison with the work of other teachers in their own schools or across the district—when the overall number of pupils for which they are responsible becomes excessive, the size of their classes is perceived to make unreasonable demands on the time required for preparation and marking, and this situation seriously erodes the opportunities for providing differentiated instruction for their students. Excessive paperwork (filling in forms, collecting information for others, etc.) and the burden of nonteaching demands, such as hall monitoring, bus duty, and lunchroom supervision, add to perceptions that workload volume is excessive and has negative effects on teaching and learning (Byrne, 1991).

School Structures and Procedures

The primary purpose for school structures is to foster the development and maintenance of conditions, especially cultures, which support the work of teachers and the learning of students. Not all school structures are alterable, at least not easily or in the short term, however. This is especially the case for school location. Evidence suggests that the work of teachers is enhanced in schools located in suburban rather than urban locations. A considerable amount of evidence also suggests that struggling students in particular benefit from being part of relatively small organizations (e.g., Lee, 2000; Lee, Bryk, & Smith, 1993). For elementary schools, the optimum size seems to be about 250 to 300 students, whereas 600 to 700 students appears to be optimal for secondary schools. Smaller schools increase the chances of student attendance and schoolwork being monitored. In smaller schools, the likelihood of students having a close, ongoing relationship with at least one other significant adult in the school, an important antidote to dropping out, is also much greater. Smaller school organizations tend to have more constrained and more focused academic programs and are more communal in nature, with teachers assuming more personal responsibility for the learning of each pupil (Lee, Ready, & Johnson, 2001; National Research Council & National Institute of Medicine, 2004).

All other structural attributes of schools influencing the quality of teachers' work are potentially quite malleable and can easily outweigh the negative effects of larger school sizes and urban locations. Positive contributions to teachers' work are associated with structures that provide teachers with opportunities to collaborate with one another (such as common planning times), work in small teams, prepare adequately for their classroom instruction, access ongoing professional development, and participate in school-level decisions (Tschannen-Moran & Barr, 2004). Physical facilities that permit teachers to use the types of instruction they judge to be most effective increase teachers engagement in their schools and desire to remain in the profession; this is also the case when the school has well-developed and stable programs on which to build when new challenges present themselves (Tsui & Cheng, 2002).

Three features associated with school procedures also influence the quality of teaching and learning through their effects on teachers' sense of individual and collective efficacy (Tschannen-Morin & Barr, 2004) as well their job satisfaction and organizational commitment (Dannetta, 2002). These features include quality of communication in the school, how well the school's plans for improvement match teachers' views of what the school's priorities ought to be, and provision of regular feedback to school working groups about the focus and quality of their progress.

School Culture and Sense of Professional Community

A small but compelling body of evidence suggests that pupils benefit when teachers in a school form a "professional learning" subcommunity (Louis & Kruse, 1995; Newmann & Associates, 1996). Participation in such communities promotes instructional program coherence across the school. It also stimulates growth in teachers' instructional skills, enhances teachers' sense of mastery and control over student learning, and builds teachers' sense of responsibility for student learning. School communities and cultures enhance teaching and learning when the goals for teachers' work are clear, explicit, and shared; when there is little conflict in teachers' minds about what they are expected to do; and when the atmosphere in the school is generally positive and friendly. Mutual trust among faculty is also a key feature of schools that are successful in making significant improvement (Bryk & Schneider, 2002).

Teaching and learning are also enhanced when student behavior is under control and collaboration among teachers is encouraged. Teachers also thrive when the cultures of their schools value and support their safety and the safety of their students and when there are high expectations for students and a strong academic press evident to students and teachers across the school. School cultures that help teachers to find their work meaningful (e.g., clear and morally inspiring goals) also have a positive influence on teachers' affective dispositions and subsequent performance in class.

Partnerships With Parents and the Wider Community

Creating a widely shared sense of community among all school stakeholders is important for several reasons. First, the affective bonds between students and teachers associated with a sense of community are crucial in engaging and motivating students to learn in schools of any type (Lee et al., 1993). A widely shared sense of community is also important as an antidote to the unstable, sometimes threatening, and often insecure world inhabited by a significant proportion of economically deprived families and children. A collective sense of belonging for those living in these challenging circumstances provides psychological connections and identity with and commitment to others (Beck & Foster, 1999, p. 350); individuals who feel secure and purposeful as a result are, in turn, less susceptible to the mind-set of fatalism and disempowerment that often arises from repeated episodes of loss (Mitchell, as cited in Beck & Foster, 1999). Success at school depends on having goals for the academic, personal, and vocational strands of one's life, as well as a sense of self-efficacy about the achievement of those goals. Feelings of fatalism and disempowerment discourage both the setting of such goals and the development of self-efficacy about their achievement.

The contributions of parent partnerships to student learning vary enormously across the alternative forms that those partnerships may take. These forms range from parent involvement in the instruction of their own children, at one extreme, to direct participation in school decision making, at the other (e.g., Epstein, 1996; Epstein et al., 2002). No matter the student population, involving parents primarily in the instruction of their own children is most likely to contribute to children's learning (Leithwood & Menzies, 1998).

Creating meaningful partnerships with parents in economically poor communities is often quite difficult (Griffith, 2001; Hatton, 2001). As Crosby (1999) pointed out, it is difficult to "mandate parent involvement with people whose time is totally consumed in a struggle to survive" (p. 303). But when the educational culture of the student's home is weak, the student benefits from the school's direct efforts to influence that culture in ways that acknowledge the circumstances faced by the student's family.

The nature of the school's relationship with the wider community also influences teaching and learning through its effect on teachers' job satisfaction as well as teachers' decisions about whether to remain in the school and in the profession. When the reputation of the school in the local community is positive and there is considerable support by parents and the wider community for the efforts and directions of the school, teachers' work with students is enhanced (Ingersoll, 2001).

Retention and Promotion Policies

While student retention by course has long been a common practice in secondary schools, social promotion by grade has been a common policy in elementary schools until quite recently. Over the past decade, however, policymakers in many jurisdictions have enacted a "tough love" strategy for raising student performance, which often includes retaining students at grade until they meet minimum passing standards, often judged by the results of end-of-grade exams. Over all groups of elementary students, retention policies rarely produce improved learning and often have negative effects on learning as well as students' attitudes toward school and learning (Darling-Hammond, 1998; Foster, 1993; McCoy & Reynolds, 1999; Reynolds, 1992; Shepard & Smith, 1990; Westbury, 1994).

Some of this evidence seems contradictory, however, because retention policies have dramatically different effects on different groups of pupils. For pupils with a relatively robust sense of academic self-efficacy, the raising of standards with clear sanctions for failure can be positively motivating. A robust sense of academic self-efficacy typically results in more effort as a response to the threat of failure (Bandura, 1986). So, those who have traditionally done well at school, acquired high levels of academic self-efficacy in the process, but are not be trying as hard as they could may well benefit from such policies. In contrast, those who have often struggled at school and frequently experienced failure are likely to have developed a low sense of academic self-efficacy. For them, the most likely response to the threat of retention is to give up and, at the secondary level, to drop out of school altogether (Haney, 2001).

Instructional Program Coherence

While the amount of evidence about instructional program coherence is modest, Newmann, Smith, Allenswork, and Bryk (2001) reported impressive effects on pupils' achievement in reading and mathematics in elementary schools serving communities experiencing high rates of poverty, social stress, and racial diversity. For purposes of this exceptionally well-designed study, *instructional program coherence* was defined as "a set of interrelated programs for students and staff that are guided by a common framework for curriculum, instruction, assessment, and learning climate and that are pursued over a sustained period" (Newmann et al., 2001, p. 297).

In contrast to excessive numbers of unrelated, unsustained improvement initiatives in a school, instructional coherence contributes to learning by connecting students' experiences and building on them over time. As pupils see themselves becoming more competent, their motivation to learn is also likely to increase. Similar effects can be expected for teachers as they work collaboratively toward implementing a common instructional framework.

CONCLUDING REFLECTIONS: ON LEADERSHIP

It is tempting to argue that efforts to improve teaching and learning are most effective when they focus directly on the relationships between teachers and students and that talented teachers will do good work within any kind of school organization. This argument, however, flies in the face of evidence that even the most well-meaning and enthusiastic teachers are unable to sustain serious changes in their practices in the context of school organizations that are, usually inadvertently, hostile to those changes (Louis & Miles, 1990; Randi & Corno, 1997). The institutionalization of significant change requires its advocates to become organizational "designers."

We have known for many years, however, that organizational designs alone make little difference to the quality of teaching and learning in schools. School leadership is key—a catalyst for creating the conditions described in this chapter (Hallinger & Heck,

1996; Leithwood, Seashore Louis, Anderson, & Wahlstrom, 2004). But the context for leadership is a powerful determinant of the forms of leadership that will be useful. This assertion encourages the view that leadership is situational and context dependent (Duke, 1987; Shamir & Howell, 1999). When staff members experience lack of leadership, the problem may be one of fit. For example, Susan brings to her new job boundless energy, ambitious visions, and a strong commitment to school reform. But Susan succeeds Tony, who had the same qualities and was successful in helping staff initiate a large bundle of changes in the school during the 3 years of his tenure. The staff are in the midst of refining their knowledge, "working out the kinks" in these changes, and recovering from the ubiquitous "implementation dip" (Fullan, 1991). The support they need, at this point, is "close-to-the-elbow" technical assistance (Louis & Miles, 1990) and a stable school environment, with limited distractions from their efforts to consolidate the changes they have made. They also need help in assessing whether these changes are paying off as anticipated. From Susan's perspective, this is seems like dull work that does not take advantage of her strengths.

As a minimum, then, efforts to describe school leadership must acknowledge the importance of situation and context; this means allowing for variation in leadership style and forms of enactment. It is possible to do this, however, and still endorse a particular model of leadership when the model fits the broad challenges being experienced by many reforming and restructuring schools and when considerable variation in behavior within the model is possible. Evidence suggests that a *transformational model of leadership* is a good match for the times (Leithwood et al., in press).

Roberts's (1985) synopsis of transformational leadership sounds a lot like what Susan is keen to offer:

> This type of leadership offers a vision of what could be and gives a sense of purpose and meaning to those who would share that vision. It builds commitment, enthusiasm, and excitement. It creates a hope in the future and a belief that the world is knowable, understandable, and manageable. The collective action that transforming leadership generates empowers those who participate in the process. There is hope, there is optimism, there is energy. In essence, transforming

leadership is a leadership that facilitates the redefinition of a people's mission and vision, a renewal of their commitment, and the restructuring of their systems for goal accomplishment. (p. 1024)

Research concerning the meaning of transformational leadership in practice indicates that it is multidimensional (e.g., Podsakoff, MacKenzie, Moorman, & Fetter, 1990). Transformational leadership is concerned, as is Susan, with developing a vision, fostering acceptance of group goals, and providing intellectual stimulation. But it is also concerned with providing support to individual staff members as they grapple with changing their practices; it monitors high-performance expectations in the face of learning new behaviors; and it also includes setting an example for staff to follow that is consistent with the values espoused by the district or school. Each of these dimensions of transformational leadership can be carried out through a variety of quite different, specific behaviors.

When leaders use transformational practices to improve the school and classroom conditions described in this chapter, all students and all teachers are the winners.

REFERENCES

Bandura, A. (1986). *Social foundations of thought and action.* Englewood Cliffs, NJ: Prentice Hall.

Beck, L., & Foster, W. (1999). Administration and community: Considering challenges, exploring possibilities. In J. Murphy & K. S. Louis (Eds.), *Handbook of research on educational administration* (pp. 337–358). San Francisco: Jossey-Bass.

Brophy, J. (n.d.). *Teaching: A special report reprinted by the Laboratory for Student Success.* Philadelphia: Mid-Atlantic Regional Educational Laboratory, Temple University Center for Research in Human Development and Education.

Bryk, A., Schneider, B. (2002). *Trust in schools: A core resource for improvement.* New York: Russell Sage Foundation.

Byrne, B. M. (1991). Burnout: Investigating the impact of background variables for elementary, intermediate, secondary, and university educators. *Teaching and Teacher Education, 7*(2), 197–209.

Crosby, E. A. (1999). Urban schools: Forced to fail. *Phi Delta Kappan, 81*(4), 298–303.

Dannetta, V. (2002). What factors influence a teacher's commitment to student learning? *Leadership and Policy in Schools, 1*(2), 144–171.

Darling-Hammond, L. (1998). Alternatives to grade retention. *School Administrator, 55*(7), 18–21.

Dibbon, D. (2004). *It's about time: A report on the impact of workload on teachers and students.* St. Johns, Canada: Memorial University of Newfoundland.

Duke, D. L. (1987). *School leadership and instructional improvement.* New York: Random House.

Epstein, J. (1996). Perspectives and previews on research and policy for school, family, and community partnerships. In A. Booth & J. Dunn (Eds.), *Family-school links* (pp. 209–246). Mahwah, NJ: Lawrence Erlbaum.

Epstein, J., Sanders, M., Simon, B., Salinas, K., Jansorn, N., & Voorhis, F. (2002). *School, families & community partnerships: Your handbook for action.* Thousand Oaks, CA: Corwin Press.

Foster, J. E. (1993). Review of research: Retaining children in grade. *Childhood Education, 70*(1), 38–43.

Fullan, M. (1991). *The new meaning of educational change.* Toronto, Canada: OISE Press.

Griffith, J. (2001). Principal leadership of parent involvement. *Journal of Educational Administration, 39*(2), 162–186.

Hallinger, P., & Heck, R. (1996). The principal's role in school effectiveness: An assessment of methodological progress, 1980–1995. In K. Leithwood & P. Hallinger (Eds.), *International handbook of educational leadership and administration* (pp. 723–783). Dordrecht, The Netherlands: Klüwer Academic.

Haney, W. (2001). Response to Skrla et al: The illusion of educational equity in Texas: A commentary on "accountability for equity." *International Journal of Leadership in Education, 4*(3), 267–275.

Hatton, E. (2001). School development planning in a small primary school: Addressing the challenge in rural NSW. *Journal of Educational Administration, 39*(2), 118–133.

Ingersoll, R. (2001). Teacher turnover and teacher shortages: An organizational analysis. *American Educational Research Journal, 38*(3), 499–534.

Jagers, R. F., & Carroll, G. (2002). Issues in educating African-American children and youth. In S. Stringfield & D. Land (Eds.), *Educating at-risk students: Vol. 101. Yearbook of the National Society for the Study of Education* (pp. 49–65). Chicago: University of Chicago Press.

Kushman, J. (1992). The organizational dynamics of teacher workplace commitment: A study of urban elementary and middle schools. *Educational Administration Quarterly, 28*(1), 5–42.

Lee, V. (2000). School size and the organization of secondary schools. In M. T. Hallinan (Ed.), *Handbook of the sociology of education* (pp. 327–344). New York: Klüwer/Plenum.

Lee, V., Bryk, A., & Smith, J. B. (1993). The organization of effective high schools. In L. Darling-Hammond (Ed.), *Review of research in education, 19* (pp. 171–267). Washington, DC: American Educational Research Association.

Lee, V., Ready, D., & Johnson, D. (2001). The difficulty of identifying rare samples to study: The case of high schools divided into schools-within-schools. *Educational Evaluation and Policy Analysis, 4,* 365–379.

Leithwood, K., McAdie, P., Bascia, N., & Rogrigue, A. (in press). *Teaching for deep understanding.* Thousand Oaks, CA: Corwin Press.

Leithwood, K., & Menzies, T. (1998). Forms and effects of school-based management: A review. *Educational Policy, 12*(3), 325–346.

Leithwood, K., Seashore Louis, K., Anderson, S., & Wahlstrom, K. (2004). *How leadership influences student learning: A review of research for the Learning From Leadership Project.* New York: Wallace Foundation.

Leithwood, K., & Steinbach, R. (2003). Successful leadership for especially challenging schools. In B. Davies & J. West-Burnham (Eds.), *Handbook of educational leadership and management* (pp. 25–43). London: Pearson Longman.

Louis, K., & Kruse, S. (1995). *Professionalism and community: Perspectives on reforming urban schools.* Thousand Oaks, CA: Corwin Press.

Louis, K., & Miles, M. B. (1990). *Improving the urban high school: What works and why.* New York: Teachers College Press.

McCoy, A. R., & Reynolds, A. J. (1999). Grade retention and school performance: An extended investigation. *Journal of School Psychology, 37*(3), 273–298.

McDonnell, L. (2005). Assessment and accountability from the policymaker's perspective. In J. Herman & E. Haertel (Eds.), *Uses and misuses of data for educational accountability and improvement: Vol. 104. Yearbook of the National Society for the Study of Education* (pp. 35–54). Malden, MA: Blackwell.

National Research Council & the National Institute of Medicine. (2004). *Engaging schools: Fostering high school students' motivation to learn.* Washington, DC: National Academies Press.

Newmann, F., Smith, B., Allensworth, E., & Bryk, A. (2001). Instructional program coherence: What it is and why it should guide school improvement policy. *Educational Evaluation and Policy Analysis, 23*(4), 297–321.

Newmann, F. M., & Associates. (1996). *School restructuring and authentic student achievement.* San Francisco: Jossey-Bass.

Ostroff, C. (1992). The relationship between satisfaction, attitudes, and performance: An organizational level analysis. *Journal of Applied Psychology, 77,* 963–974.

Podsakoff, P., MacKenzie, S., Moorman, R., & Fetter, R. (1990). Transformational leader behaviors and their effects on followers' trust in leader satisfaction and organizational citizenship behaviors. *Leadership Quarterly, 1*(2), 329–351.

Randi, J., & Corno, L. (1997). Teachers as innovators. In B. J. Biddle, T. L. Good, & I. F. Goodson (Eds.), *The international handbook of teachers and teaching* (Vol. II, pp. 1163–1221). Dordrecht, The Netherlands: Klüwer.

Reynolds, A. J. (1992). Grade retention and school adjustment: An explanatory analysis. *Educational Evaluation and Policy Analysis, 14*(2), 101–121.

Riehl, C. (2000). The principal's role in creating inclusive schools for diverse students: A review of normative, empirical, and critical literature on the practice of educational administration. *Review of Educational Research, 70*(1), 55–81.

Roberts, N. C. (1985). Transforming leadership: A process of collective action. *Human Relations, 38,* 1023–1046.

Shamir, B., & Howell, J. M. (1999). Organizational and contextual influences on charismatic leadership emergence and effectiveness. *Leadership Quarterly, 10*(2), 257–283.

Shepard, L. A., & Smith, M. L. (1990). Synthesis of research on grade retention. *Educational Leadership, 47*(8), 84–88.

Tschannen-Moran, M., & Barr, M. (2004). Fostering student achievement: The relationship between collective teacher efficacy and student achievement. *Leadership and Policy in Schools, 3,* 187–207.

Tsui, K. T., & Cheng, Y. C. (2002). School organizational health and teacher commitment: A contingency study with multi-level analysis. *Educational Research and Evaluation, 5*(3), 249–268.

Westbury, M. (1994). The effect of elementary grade retention on subsequent school achievement and ability. *Canadian Journal of Education, 19*(3), 241–250.

Yonezawa, S., Wells, A. S., & Serna, I. (2002). Choosing tracks: "Freedom of choice" in detracking schools. *American Educational Research Journal, 39*(1), 37–67.

CHAPTER TEN

Continuous School Improvement

Willis D. Hawley and Gary Sykes

O rganizations of all kinds are being urged to master the processes associated with the phrase *continuous improvement.* The phrase is meant to suggest that organizations work in steady, systematic fashion to improve their results. Typically, this emphasis also includes greater attention to distinct measures or indicators of outcomes, so there is renewed interest in developing good indicators that not only signal to external audiences how well the organization is doing but also supply information to members that help them make improvements in teaching and learning.

The essence of this process can be captured in a model outlined in the following pages. This model sets forth a series of steps that schools work through on a continuing basis. In broad outline, the process is initiated when schools come together as communities to determine their schoolwide goals, together with associated values and standards. At the outset, they also determine what assessments they will use to supply evidence of the desired learning (including those assessments mandated by state and federal policy); then, they examine the gap between their goals and the evidence of outcomes, taking into account other evidence as well (for example, such things as attendance rates). Next, the school community examines relevant evidence and deliberates on what problems or issues are contributing to the differences between goals for student learning and assessed outcomes. Once the school has made a determination about the nature of the problem(s), a search for practices that might improve the results is undertaken, which includes the identification of human and financial resources that would be needed to implement the most promising alternatives. Needed resources are developed, or plans for their development are initiated. Finally, members of the school community select and implement the practices they believe will result in improvements, testing the efficacy of and modifying the practices as implementation proceeds. Then, the cycle continues.

Two features of this model seem particularly important. One is reliance on evidence as the basis for forward progress. The model emphasizes that schools gather a range of evidence, particularly evidence of student learning, and use it to inform decision making. The second is the collaborative culture that supports this process. This culture is vital to the success of the model, so its use may require some "reculturing" of the organization, as described in more detail below.

A MODEL OF CONTINUOUS SCHOOL IMPROVEMENT

A cycle represented by four phases inscribes the school improvement process. Inevitably, use of such a model in any particular school is likely to raise many issues that a basic description does not cover. Figure 10.1 represents the model in its essential form.

Figure 10.1 oversimplifies the processes involved in continuous school improvement. Within each box (phase) is a complex set of activities that need to be adapted to particular contexts. Many of the context variables have to do with the culture of the organization and its experience with success in implementing change initiatives. Nonetheless, this conceptualization is a reasonable summary of the literature on the dynamics of positive organizational change (e.g., Fullan, 2001; Leithwood & Louis, 1998). It is particularly appropriate to understanding the challenges faced by school leaders as a result of the increasing emphasis on holding schools accountable for continuing improvement in student achievement.

Figure 10.1 Four-Phase Cycle of Continuous Improvement

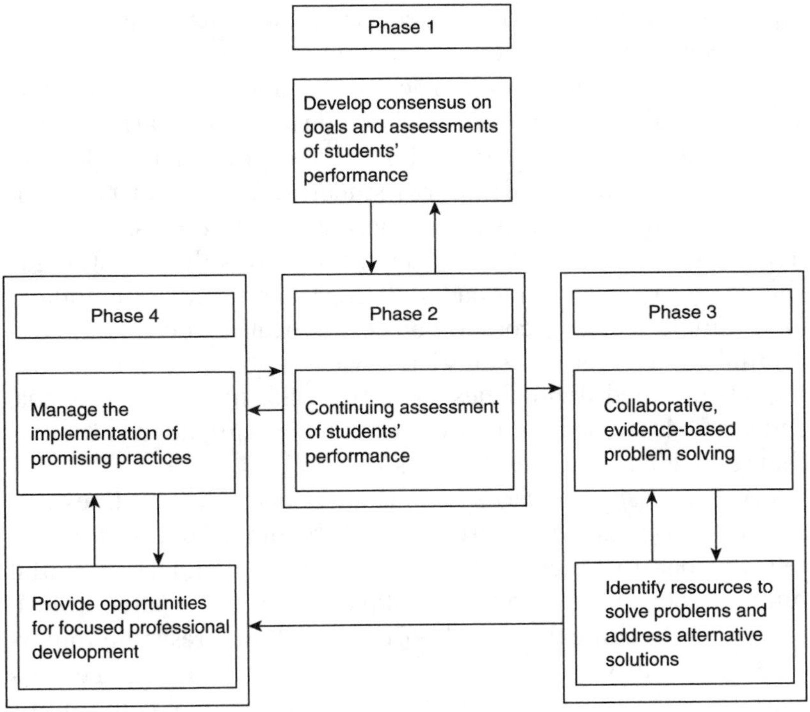

```
                    ┌──────────────────┐
                    │     Phase 1      │
                    └──────────────────┘
                    ┌──────────────────┐
                    │ Develop consensus│
                    │ on goals and     │
                    │ assessments of   │
                    │ students'        │
                    │ performance      │
                    └──────────────────┘

┌─────────────┐   ┌──────────────────┐   ┌─────────────────┐
│   Phase 4   │   │     Phase 2      │   │     Phase 3     │
├─────────────┤   ├──────────────────┤   ├─────────────────┤
│ Manage the  │ ← │ Continuing       │ → │ Collaborative,  │
│ implementa- │   │ assessment of    │   │ evidence-based  │
│ tion of     │   │ students'        │   │ problem solving │
│ promising   │   │ performance      │   │                 │
│ practices   │   │                  │   │                 │
│             │   └──────────────────┘   │                 │
│ Provide     │                          │ Identify        │
│ opportuni-  │ ←──────────────────────  │ resources to    │
│ ties for    │                          │ solve problems  │
│ focused     │                          │ and address     │
│ professional│                          │ alternative     │
│ development │                          │ solutions       │
└─────────────┘                          └─────────────────┘
```

Phase 1: Develop Consensus on Values, Goals, Standards, and Assessments of Student Performance

Gaining Agreement About Priority Goals

The logical starting point for school improvement is to determine the goals of learning and to achieve a workable consensus around them. As a first order of business, schools continuously engage in the process of clarifying their *core values*—those matters that call forth their deepest passions, commitments, and caring responses. Values come first and foremost, even before their technical representation in learning goals, standards, and assessments. Achieving value clarity and consensus, however, is a great accomplishment in a school, because value conflicts and ambiguity are the norm. Ambiguity over core values is often useful in submerging conflicts and keeping the peace. But the cost is correspondingly high. Without value clarity and consensus, organizations have lost one important basis for productive action.

A second crucial matter concerns focus. More effective schools avoid the trap of trying to include too many learning goals and spreading their efforts too thinly across them. Particularly in schools serving poor and minority students, schools must concentrate learning very tightly around a *core set of objectives*. This does not mean basic skills alone. In fact, the idea is that all students should be engaged with broad and deep learning goals, including, for example, reading comprehension as well as decoding, conceptual as well as procedural knowledge of mathematics, and inquiry-oriented approaches to science. So, in achieving focus, consensus is needed on a core set of challenging academic goals that schools can reach with their students.

A third issue concerns the meaning of *consensus*. Does this mean that all teachers must agree all the time? Such a standard sets the bar too high. Yet consensus does include substantial numbers of teachers and other stakeholders (e.g., parents) in a school. At the same time, a school cannot allow a resistant minority to impede progress, holding the majority hostage. Leaders work to build a viable consensus within the school community, bringing along those who dissent or encouraging them to leave the community. Furthermore, leaders take care not to create a false consensus that papers over fundamental disagreements or impose a hasty "consensus" on a faculty, engendering passive resistance and resentment. Genuine consensus requires that real disagreements among faculty are surfaced and discussed. Tensions between the need for genuine dialogue and debate, on the one hand, and timely consent as the basis for collective action, on the other, are managed skillfully throughout the continuous-improvement cycle.

Securing Agreement About How Priorities Will Be Assessed

At the same time that schools seek to identify common goals for students—and this is crucial—successful schools also develop agreement on what counts as learning and how this is to be assessed. Here, the complexities come in several varieties. One concern is just how specific and detailed the learning objectives must be. The standard today generally has pushed toward greater specification among learning objectives as coordinated across grade levels. For example, third-grade teachers need to know what to expect from second-grade teachers and, in turn, what they must accomplish for the fourth-grade teacher. And there needs to be agreement on time allocations and coordinated activity across the subjects in the curriculum (i.e., reading, writing, mathematics, science, social studies, etc.).

Goals that are not anchored in evidence of accomplishment cannot serve to guide improvement. So, schools must reach agreement on the characteristics of such evidence, including how to use it in public ways. Each of these qualifications requires further description.

Today, most schools are held accountable to external assessments of various kinds. Taken alone, however, such assessments do not provide a solid base of evidence around which to develop instructional improvements. The timing of the assessments, the feedback provided, and the lack of information on untested aspects of the curriculum call for schools to supplement such evidence with additional assessments that supply formative feedback, that are "curriculum embedded," and that complement quantitative evidence with qualitative information. Schools then face the crucial task of developing such complementary forms of assessment even as they attend to external, mandated testing. In effect, then, the new standard is that schools have worked out a proper balance between external, high-stakes accountability and the internal assessments useful to improved teaching and learning.

While teachers have always developed their own practical means for gauging student learning within their own classrooms, the new requirement is that such assessments become part of the public, objective, and collective practice of the school rather than being private, subjective, and idiosyncratic. In effect, this commitment makes good on the aphorism that "it takes a school to educate a child," meaning that each student's progress through school is not simply the serial responsibility of first this teacher, then that one, but rather of the collective. This requires a new social and technical practice in the school. The technical aspect concerns the assessment methods that are adopted—how student work is judged according to rubrics, for example. The social aspect concerns how teachers come together to work out common assessment practices and then to engage in assessment in public forums, in which teachers display student work and other evidence of learning for their colleagues to consider and to evaluate. In successful schools, leaders effectively manage the transition from private, individual assessment to public, collective assessment, and this is a significant aspect of school reculturing, for it alters some of the most basic norms that typically regulate the practice of teaching.

Agreement on goals and assessments must be accompanied by a shared instructional vision that includes guidance on the evidence that the school will routinely collect and use in efforts to make a range of improvements. Such evidence must supply a well-rounded picture of how the school is doing. Consequently, the school community must carefully consider what this evidence consists of, from among a potentially large set of indicators. For example, in many schools, relevant evidence might include matters such as daily attendance figures; rates of student mobility; course-taking patterns of students, including advanced placement and honors courses; graduation rates; rates of grade retention; and evidence of nonacademic outcomes concerning the general health and well-being of students.

Summary of Phase 1

The essential tasks at the outset of the continuous-improvement process are to establish the central goals and standards for the school and then to select a set of indicators that balance reasonableness with completeness so that the total set does not overwhelm the school's capacity to attend to them all. Skillful work on this issue is a matter for schoolwide deliberations. An additional point is that work on these goals and assessments may be phased in over time, according to a school's strategic plan, so that one year, the faculty works on reading and mathematics, next on science and social studies, and so on. Developing a strategic plan along these lines is a critical responsibility for the whole school community.

Phase 2: Continuously Assess Student Performance

The work of developing consensus on standards and assessments initiates the school improvement process. In many schools, teachers already feel that the demands of testing are driving out time for instruction and are putting undue emotional pressures on students. So, the injunction to "continuously assess" may engender resistance and misunderstanding. There is, however, considerable evidence indicating that schools that are most effective develop a rich means of regularly assessing student learning for purposes of schoolwide improvement (Cawelti & Protheroe, 2001; McLaughlin & Talbert, 2006; Newmann & Wehlage, 1995; Teddlie, 1999).

What continuous assessment means in specific terms will vary from school to school, as a profusion of methods are available, including the use of running records, "tuning protocols," looking at student work, lesson study, the inquiry cycle, and many others (for practical discussion of what assessment practice might look like, see Black, Harrison, Lee, Marshall, & Wiliam, 2004; for examples of new forms of assessment that provide teachers with useful knowledge about what students are learning, see Allen, 1998; Darling-Hammond, Ancess, & Falk, 1995; Lieberman & Miller, 2001; McDonald, Mohr, Dichter, & McDonald, 2003). The particular procedures that a school adopts matter less than how they embody the basic principles of evidence-based decision making. The first principle is that assessment must be integrated or aligned with goals and standards, so that the information provided is directly relevant to the learning that is desired. The second principle is that the information be supplied in timely and transparent fashion so that teachers can use it in their work. The third principle is that such assessments are public and collective. Teachers come together as a community to work out assessments that all will participate in, and the school must create regular opportunities for teachers to present and discuss evidence of student learning in public forums. Effective schools schedule time for such collaborative assessment practice, making it integral to the work day and work week. Furthermore, building school capacity to make use of evidence is likely to be a priority for schoolwide initiatives, including professional development.

Successful schools develop complementary formal and informal assessments and build these into the flow of instruction and other school improvements. Problem solving begins with evidence of the gap between goals and standards and learning outcomes. What does the evidence reveal? Consider, for example, a range of possible outcomes of an analysis of student literacy in relation to high-priority goals. Reading achievement seems acceptable over-all, but disaggregated results show substantial gaps between poor and minority students in the school and their White, middle-class counterparts. Or while certain component literacy skills look solid, others are deficient (e.g., students can decode text but when asked comprehension questions, they often stumble). Or more contentiously, third-grade results look solid, but fourth-grade achievement is deficient. Or teachers' informal assessments of learning do not confirm what external test results show.

Because the model calls for new uses of assessment, which implies new learning on the part of school participants, leaders in successful schools actively create opportunities for the needed pro-fessional learning as an integral part of an overall approach to assessment. Furthermore, the school schedule must provide com-mon time to examine assessment information, and school social norms must encourage teachers to open both their teaching and their students' learning to public scrutiny. Norms of trust, reci-procity, risk taking, and conflict management rather than avoid-ance, autonomy, and privacy must be gradually established in the school's culture.

This second phase in the model proposes that schools signifi-cantly improve the ways that they work with evidence as the fundamental basis for progress. Assessment becomes a central, driving force in the school, moving front and center. To accommo-date this shift, schools reconsider how time is organized, how cul-tural norms support assessment work, and how learning about and from assessment is acquired and made part of the regular working knowledge of teachers and administrators. Schools learn how to work with evidence—particularly assessment of student learning, but including a wide range of indicators related to school functioning.

Phase 3: Engage in Collaborative, Evidence-Based Problem Solving

How do schools use evidence of student learning to make improvements? The next phase in the process takes up this issue, and four matters are essential: problem solving based on assess-ment of student learning and other evidence, schoolwide collabo-ration, the identification of promising policies and practices, and selecting courses of action strategically.

The Importance of Schoolwide Collaboration

Effective problem solving in schools brings all concerned interests together to look at results, formulate a shared theory or understanding, consider potential responses, identify needs for new resources and capabilities, and move into action in response. The productive school community collaborates in the process of problem solving so that the process is widely regarded as legitimate, different perspectives are welcomed, actions resolved upon are widely accepted, and the move to implementation is embraced wholeheartedly. Throughout, the aim is to develop a shared understanding of the problem(s) and to mobilize the school to respond wisely and vigorously.

Collaborative problem solving is enhanced by several conditions (see Little, this volume; Leithwood, this volume). Finding adequate time is obviously a major issue. Human relations are critical: teachers who trust each other, norms that support constructive criticism, and methods for joining and resolving disputes. Structures need to be in place that create forums for the work of problem sensing and decision making, such as regular team meetings among teachers at the same grade level or department meetings within high schools and middle schools. Often useful are school connections to inside and outside sources of expertise and scrutiny coupled with a willingness to learn from such sources. As well, schools work to secure the authority to proceed with actions that might violate existing policies and practices; in so doing, they master the micropolitics of their districts and their communities.

In schools in which conditions to support collaborative problem solving are not in place, leaders must skillfully manage two agendas simultaneously: establishing the supportive conditions while engaging in the process ("building the bus while driving it"). The imperative of raising student performance does not allow for "time-outs." If schools are to meet the challenge of continuous improvement, engagement with both the model and the conditions that support it will be necessary.

Problem Framing

A first step in problem solving involves the framing of the problem. *Framing* simply means that the school must come to an agreement on the nature of the problem. For example, if a school uncovers evidence that achievement growth stalls for minority students as they proceed through the grades, how shall such a problem be interpreted? What is the "theory" of the problem? Does the school invoke inadequate parent support? Is the "safety net" of second- and third-chance learning opportunities insufficient? Is there a cultural fit between the curriculum and certain students? Are there deficiencies in the instruction teachers are providing? Are resources to support student learning adequate? Critical to the problem-solving process is the conduct of inquiry and deliberation in response to problems, in which various "theories" may be considered and tested, even including the gathering of additional information that might inform decisions.

There are many ways to frame problems (see Bolman & Deal, 2003). An approach that directly engages alternative policies and practices assumes that school improvement occurs against a backdrop of a number of broad beliefs about the reasons many schools are not more effective. Taken together, these possible explanations illustrate the kinds of starting points that school communities may consider as they confront discrepancies between their goals for students and evidence of student learning.

Alignment of Instructional Guidance. One account of the fundamental problems confronting schools reckons that many schools lack a system of instructional guidance that aligns standards for learning, curriculum content, assessment, instructional practice, second-chance learning (e.g., summer and afterschool programs), teacher learning opportunities, and performance sanctions and incentives (Murphy, 2003). Technical aspects of improvement seek to establish better coordination among these factors.

Coherence and Focus. A second, related account emphasizes not only technical alignment but also programmatic coherence and a tight focus on just those programs and initiatives that advance core mission and goals (Newmann, Smith, Allensworth, & Bryk, 2001). This account reckons that many schools have adopted too many disparate initiatives that fail to "hang together" in support of the basic academic mission, necessitating choices not only about what will be emphasized but also about what will be de-emphasized. In this account, reform occurs not only by addition but also by subtraction or reduction, as the school focuses, relentlessly in some cases, on its primary priorities in ways that are consistent across grades and subjects.

Collaborative Culture. Yet another account highlights the importance of shared values, dispositions, and beliefs, chiefly concerning commitments to high goals for all students, together with social resources such as interpersonal trust and caring relationships with students that facilitate collaborative improvement processes (Bryk & Schneider, 2002; Leithwood & Louis, 1998; Sergiovanni, 2005). In this reckoning, schools often are lacking in core beliefs among staff, together with facilitating social relationships. In addition to working on issues of instructional alignment and programmatic coherence, schools must cultivate the social resources associated with the construct of "a learning community."

Cognitive Demand. A fourth general explanation for student learning has to do with the delivered curriculum. What students are taught obviously influences the opportunities they have to learn, and these opportunities may differ substantially in their content and rigor (Oakes, Quartz, Ryan, & Lipton, 2000). The curriculum itself may ask too little of students. Or even when the curriculum is rigorous, teacher expectations for student performance may be too low. For example, the low performance of students in lower-achieving groups within schools or inside classrooms is often associated with low "cognitive demand." In particular, "tracking" of students typically creates unequal access to knowledge.

Resource Adequacy and Mobilization. A fifth account draws attention to the adequacy and allocation of resources of various kinds. According to this perspective, resource inadequacies and inequities often plague low-performing schools (Betts, Rueben, & Danenberg, 2000; Miles & Darling-Hammond, 1998). Among school resources that enjoy a reliable relationship with outcomes are small class sizes and, especially, caring and highly competent teachers. Time is another such resource, harking back to an earlier generation of research that emphasized the importance of "engaged time" and "time on task." Issues of resource availability, allocation, and use draw attention to how school leadership effectively mobilizes as well as acquires resources of various kinds.

Social Capital. Finally, many have argued that the influences on students' learning in families and communities are so powerful that improvements within schools are inevitably limited in their effects (Rothstein, 2004). This account asserts that what is needed are more effective social policies—including those affecting housing, health, income maintenance, and social disorganization. For their part, schools need to build partnerships with families and community organizations that reflect a holistic approach to the facilitation of student learning (see Epstein et al., 2002; Warren, 2005).

Such a multifaceted consideration of the challenges facing improvement is daunting, but these accounts help to frame the range of possibilities that schools may examine. Any given school often confronts more than one of these possible explanations for student underperformance. Notice also that some such problems can pose serious threats to the social order of the school, because the discipline of evidence-based continuous improvement opens teaching to public scrutiny, and this surely represents a threat should teachers not be producing expected results.

In consequence, the process of problem framing must be direct, fearless, and deliberate. Schools might naturally gravitate to external explanations that avoid the hard questions. Typical examples include lack of parental support, inadequate resources, and stifling regulations, but these are at best partial explanations. Schools must look directly to curriculum and instruction for both problems and solutions. The task of inquiry is to determine what factors in this practice might be impeding learning and then to consider what might be done in response. Such possibilities might trace to the instruction that is provided by some or all of the teachers; cultural aspects of the school, including how well adults work with each other and with students; structural aspects of the school, including how various special programs are integrated with the regular program; personnel issues, including the stability of students and staff; or aspects of parental and community relationships. Many other factors might be named and framed.

Identifying "Promising" Practices and Programs

Once the school community has examined the evidence and reflected together on how to frame one or more problems, the task is to identify practices, principles, and programs for the school to adopt and implement. The search for solutions to problems is difficult because schools are flooded with ideas—some good, others less useful, and some counterproductive. How, then, might leaders search effectively? The starting point is a firm grasp of the problem(s) that the school has framed, together with core values. The search focuses just on those improvement ideas that directly address the problems in ways that are consistent with the school's values.

A first step here is to become familiar with programs that have been developed and validated through the research process in a manner similar to adoption of innovations in other fields. School leaders, however, cannot simply consult a menu of "promising practices," match the right one to the particular problem(s) that the school has framed, and then move smoothly into adoption and use. Rather, they must use judgment in working out the "fit" of practices, programs, and principles to their particular schools and the students they serve.

Note too that the phrase *promising practices* often refers to professional consensus among experts in the field, based on such criteria as best-evidence syntheses, which take into account the weight and character of evidence on a wide range of important matters related to the problems to be solved. Such knowledge may not be fully validated according to strict scientific principles, but it still serves as valuable guidance. Educators must become familiar with the character of evidence that undergirds particular programs in order to assess merit in relation to their schools' needs.

Problem solvers search for solutions not only in research but also through networks of expert colleagues, professional organizations and publications, district leaders, authoritative Web sites, local universities, and the experiences and practices of successful schools. The search is wide initially, then deep around those ideas that appear most promising. As well, search generates a set of alternatives that pose contrasts so that schools can weigh the relative value of alternatives. Contrast cases have the benefit of bringing out features of reforms that might otherwise remain submerged from view: for example, "Connected Math" or "Everyday Math"? "Open Court" or "Success for All"? Choices of these kinds must be appraised carefully by administrators and teachers alike.

Managing the Adoption Challenge

Next, school leaders engage the whole school community in the process of selecting the strategy or practice they wish to adopt. While search for alternative solutions might be delegated in order to conserve organizational energy, selection is participatory and deliberative, for adoption decisions have serious consequences for all members of the school community. To decide, the school community considers the questions dealing with evidence and fit to the problem, the cultural context of implementation, and the resources available. Here are some examples of these questions:

Evidence and Fit

- What is the evidence that the reform produces intended results? How well does the evidence apply to our particular school?
- Have other schools like ours experienced success with the program or practice? What do we know about such other experiences?
- How well does the reform address the problem(s) that have been framed?

Cultural Context

- How well does the reform fit with our core values and commitments?
- How stable and enduring is the support for this reform likely to be within the school and its larger community (including the district)?
- Will this practice require organizational restructuring and, if so, will that bring on resistance or require different relationships among faculty, staff, and students?

Available Resources

- Does the staff have the capacity needed to employ the practice successfully?
- Is there a need for additional financial resources, and, if so, where will we get them?
- Does the reform include practical tools and materials that supply guidance to teachers in implementation?

From a school's perspective, these questions suggest that "promising practices" are grounded in relative, not absolute, considerations—relative to a school's values, the problems and challenges it seeks to address, the burdens it must bear in putting the reform into practice, and the resources needed to implement the practice.

If answers to questions about evidence and feasibility such as those posed above are negative, considerations turn to whether these potential difficulties can be addressed and how serious the challenges are to effective implementation. The school then must decide whether resources or conditions needed can be secured and how long that would take. This inquiry leads to a decision to go forward, to modify the practice, or to search for other more feasible solutions to the problem(s) that have been identified.

A school committed to continuous improvement will attend to the challenge of implementing the program in its unique setting before implementation begins, taking up questions of how to adapt the program wisely to the particular characteristics of the school. In this process, the school will also consider how to supplement the "promise" of the program with local knowledge in order to produce the best result. So conceived, the process is more nearly one of "adaptation" than simple "adoption," particularly if the practice or program is complex.

Phase 4: Implement Promising Practices

From Adoption to Implementation

Once a school has made the decision to adopt (or invent) a reform, it must take up the challenges of implementation. There is a long history in American education of ideas developed by leading thinkers—Dewey, Bruner, Vygotsky, and many others—that become "lost in translation," picked up in schools in ways that produce misguided practice. So, there are four possible results: good idea/effective use; good idea/poor use; poor idea/effective use; and poor idea/poor use. Each is a possible outcome for schools that adopt new ideas, so we can see the relationship between the adoption problem (Is the idea good or not?) and the implementation problem (Is the idea effectively put into practice?). The ideal is to make a good selection and then implement the reform effectively, continuously evaluating the efficacy of the new initiative and modifying practices and strengthening conditions and resources as experience warrants.

Teacher Learning and Continuous School Improvement

While new organizational arrangements and outside funding or internal resource reallocation may be necessary, at its heart, *school improvement almost always calls for enhancing the knowledge, skills, and dispositions of teachers (and supporting staff)*. The "implementation problem," then, invariably involves a teacher learning challenge. Whatever course of action a school adopts, success usually hinges on providing support and resources for teachers to strengthen existing expertise or to learn new practices. Teachers' knowledge and skills are at stake as well as their beliefs and attitudes, their motivations, their willingness to commit, and their capacity to apply new knowledge to their particular schools and classrooms (see Elmore, 2003).

School improvement initiatives are often accompanied by some, though often inadequate, opportunities for professional development. In the continuous-improvement process, professional development is driven by the analysis of student needs, is targeted on specific skills needed by individuals and groups of teachers, and is ongoing and integral to the implementation process (see Hawley & Valli, this volume; Lieberman & Miller, this volume). Conditions influencing teacher learning are established within the school to support continuous improvement, including attention to matters such as schedules, teacher assignments, use of meetings, resource development, cultivation of leadership, formation of teams, and related matters.

It is not unusual for members of an organization to resist change on the grounds of feasibility and to underestimate their own capacity. Virtually all definitions of leadership include the facilitation of change by encouraging and supporting the development of commitments and capacity.

The Importance of Strategic and Flexible Leadership

Managing the implementation process calls for great skill on the part of leadership. Problems of various kinds need to be anticipated. For example, change can mean overload so that teachers burn out and lose confidence and commitment. If reform is not carefully managed and well supported, it can turn into more work for teachers without evidence of corresponding rewards. Schools might adopt reforms in nominal fashion without really digging in to understand what they mean for instruction. In such cases, the tendency is to adopt procedural aspects of reform without understanding their deep intent, thereby weakening their influence on teaching and learning. When deep understanding is lacking or is not widely shared, teachers and administrators may genuinely believe that they are engaged in improvement, when little change is actually taking place (Spillane, 2004). Finding no effect of the "change," educators may abandon promising practices. Reformers often underestimate the resources—time, money, technical assistance—required for deep change. When reforms are hurried, teachers are not provided with the ongoing support they need to make changes; reform leaders do not stay the course; and improvements are short-circuited.

Conditions in schools often work against steady, problem-focused learning on the part of teachers. The school may not be organized to provide common planning time for teachers to collaborate. Scale is another consideration. Large schools face a more complex task than do smaller schools in mobilizing teacher learning around reforms. School culture again comes into play: for example, norms and taken-for-granted assumptions that support risk taking and mutual trust, help seeking and giving, and related social processes. And community support and understanding is another factor influencing the prospects for learning-oriented improvements.

Continuing Evaluation

To determine whether the reform is "working," the school gathers evidence on student performance, particularly around those aspects the school had framed as problematic. At this point in the process, the school considers several hypotheses about the results. If improvements are not forthcoming, then three possibilities exist. One is that the school framed the problem(s) incorrectly. Another is that the school identified the right problem(s) but adopted the wrong reform. And a third is that the school correctly identified the problem(s) and the solution but implemented the reform imperfectly or adapted it inadequately to the particular circumstances of the school. In practice, the results might be due to some mix of these hypotheses. So, the school must engage in inquiry to determine next steps: reframe the problem(s), engage in solution search, or problem solve around implementation difficulties that have emerged. But the bottom line is pragmatic: Has the reform benefited student learning?

When the continuous-improvement model is used well, by definition, efforts to enhance student learning will be successful. But even successful improvements need to be continually examined with an eye toward even better results. Always, there is a return to the evidence of student learning.

FINAL THOUGHTS

The continuous-improvement model specifies that schools begin with attention to goals, assessments, and the larger issue of "evidence." This is common sense (you can't plan a trip unless you know where you want to go), but in strategic terms, there may be a need to carefully work up to these matters, because they represent a very high accomplishment in many schools, achieved against the drag of custom, tradition, and settled accommodations among faculty. In consequence, leaders—new leaders in particular—may want to adopt the philosophy of "small wins." For example, a leader or leadership team may believe that tracking and grouping practices limit the opportunities of some students but that immediate, schoolwide attention to this issue might prove divisive. Consequently, the initial move might call for volunteers on the faculty to experiment with detracking in certain courses or grades, with reports to the full faculty on the results. "Small wins" simply means that leadership engages the school community initially on matters that do not stir up controversy and that will result in victories that the whole staff can celebrate. It also means taking the "temperature" of a faculty to determine how cohesive the group is and what they perceive their needs to be, and then devoting attention to fulfilling such needs in order to establish a base of good will.

Many schools must learn how to focus more clearly and insistently on student learning. The image to hold in mind is creative problem solving. If educators complain that those outside of schools are meddling overmuch in what goes on inside of them, the best antidote would be a rapidly multiplying set of schools in which the local school community had seized its own destiny and was making steady improvements in teaching and learning—not at a sacrifice of all else, but in a serious and well-rounded way. Society must trust educators to do the right things; educators must earn that trust. The idea of evidence-based continuous improvement is advanced in this spirit, as a call for greater self-determination and self renewal in schools and as one means for schools to do the work they are charged with. This model is not the answer. But it is a framework that schools can use in working toward the answer that is best for them.

REFERENCES

Allen, D. (Ed.). (1998). *Assessing student learning. From grading to understanding.* New York: Teachers College Press.

Betts, J., Rueben, K., & Danenberg, A. (2000). *Equal resources, equal outcomes? The distribution of school resources and student achievement.* San Francisco: Public Policy Institute of California.

Black, P., Harrison, C., Lee, C., Marshall, B., & Wiliam, D. (2004, September). Working inside the black box: Assessment for learning in the classroom. *Phi Delta Kappan,* pp. 8–21.

Bolman, L., & Deal, T. (2003). *Reframing organizations* (3rd ed.). San Francisco: Jossey-Bass.

Bryk, A. S., & Schneider, B. (2002). *Trust in schools: A core resource for school improvement.* New York: Russell Sage Foundation.

Cawelti, G., & Protheroe, N. (2001). *High student achievement: How six school districts changed into high performance systems.* Arlington, VA: Educational Research Service.

Darling-Hammond, L., Ancess, J., & Falk, B. (1995). *Authentic assessment in action: Studies of schools and students at work.* New York: Teachers College Press.

Elmore, R. (2003). *School reform from the inside out.* Cambridge, MA: Harvard University Press.

Epstein, J., Sanders, M., Simon, B., Salinas, K., Jansorn, N., & Voorhis, F. (2002). *School, family, and community partnerships* (2nd ed.). Thousand Oaks, CA: Corwin Press.

Fullan, M. (2001). *The new meaning of organizational change* (3rd ed.). New York: Teachers College Press.

Leithwood, K., & Louis, K. S. (Eds.). (1998). *Organizational learning in schools.* Lisse, The Netherlands: Swets & Zeitlinger.

Lieberman, A., & Miller, L. (Eds.). (2001). *Teachers caught in the action: Professional development that matters.* New York: Teachers College Press.

McDonald, J., Mohr, N., Dichter, A., & McDonald, E. (2003). *The power of protocols: An educator's guide to better practice.* New York: Teachers College Press.

McLaughlin, M. W., & Talbert, J. E. (2006). *Building school-based learning communities: Professional strategies to improve student achievement.* New York: Teachers College Press.

Miles, K. H., & Darling-Hammond, L. (1998). Rethinking the allocation of teaching resources: Some lessons from high-performing schools. *Educational Evaluation and Policy Analysis, 20*(1), 9–29.

Murphy, J. (2003). *Leadership for literacy: Research-based practice, preK–3.* Thousand Oaks, CA: Corwin Press.

Newmann, F., Smith, B., Allensworth, E., & Bryk, A. (2001). Instructional program coherence: What it is and why it should guide school improvement policy. *Educational Evaluation and Policy Analysis, 23*(4), 297–321.

Newmann, R., & Wehlage, G. (1995). *Successful school restructuring: A report to the public and educators.* Madison: Center on Organization and Restructuring of Schools, Wisconsin Center for Educational Research, University of Wisconsin.

Oakes, J., Quartz, K. H., Ryan, S., & Lipton, M. (2000). *Becoming good American schools: The struggle for civic virtue in educational reform.* San Francisco: Jossey-Bass.

Rothstein, R. (2004). *Class and schools. Using social, economic, and educational indicators to close the Black-White achievement gap.* New York: Teachers College Press.

Sergiovanni, T. (2005). *Strengthening the heartbeat: Leading and learning together in schools.* San Francisco: Jossey-Bass.

Spillane, J. (2004). *Standards deviation: How schools misunderstand educational policy.* Cambridge, MA: Harvard University Press.

Teddlie, C. (Ed.). (1999). *The international handbook of school effectiveness research.* New York: Falmer Press.

Warren, M. (2005). Communities and schools: A new view of urban education. *Harvard Educational Review, 75*(2), 133–173.

CHAPTER ELEVEN

Essential Principles for Teaching and Learning for a Multicultural Society

James A. Banks, Peter Cookson, Geneva Gay,
Willis D. Hawley, Jacqueline Jordan Irvine,
Sonia Nieto, Janet Ward Schofield, and
Walter G. Stephan

As the population of the United States becomes more diverse racially and ethnically, it is increasingly important that schools serve the needs of all students and that schools prepare students to learn with and from persons whose race, ethnicity, and language are different from their own. This reality led the Carnegie Corporation to support efforts by an interdisciplinary "Multicultural Education Consensus Panel" of researchers to synthesize research that would be useful to educators and policymakers in designing practices and policies to prepare their students to live and work in a multicultural society. This chapter updates the initial publication of the Multicultural Education Consensus Panel.[1] The findings of the panel are updated and summarized here as design principles that can serve as guides to productive responses to the challenges and opportunities presented by the racial, ethnic, and language diversity of schools in ways that enhance both intercultural competence and academic achievement.

Current concern about school improvement has focused almost exclusively on how to increase student performance on standardized tests. Of course, students' academic achievement, measured broadly, is critically important to individuals and to the United States, but schools have other essential—and complementary—responsibilities. One of the most important of these is to reduce racial and ethnic discrimination and provide all students with the dispositions and skills needed to learn with and from others. Moreover, racial and ethnic discrimination, whether overt or subtle, significantly undermines the opportunities and motivation of all students who are the victims of discrimination to pursue ambitious educational goals. Simultaneously, the persistence of discrimination sets an unacceptable example of institutional behavior for all students. Moreover, discrimination results in racial and ethnic separation within schools, thereby denying all students the benefits of learning with and from students different from themselves (Hawley, in press). Schools can make a significant difference in the lives of students and are a key to maintaining a free and democratic society. Democratic societies are fragile and are works-in-progress. Their existence depends upon a thoughtful citizenry that believes in democratic ideals and is willing and able to participate in the civic life of the nation.

This chapter might have been called "Beyond Effective Schools." Students of all races and ethnic groups benefit from schools with conditions that enable them to engage in continuous improvement (see Hawley & Sykes, this volume; Leithwood, this volume; Teddlie, 1999). Twelve "design principles for a multicultural society" outlined here focus on the special opportunities and challenges that are related to the racial and ethnic diversity of schools and the United States. These principles are presented in five categories: (1) teacher learning, (2) student learning, (3) intergroup relations, (4) assessment, and (5) school governance, organization, and equity.

TEACHER LEARNING

Principle 1: Professional development programs should help teachers understand the complex characteristics of ethnic groups within U.S. society and the ways in which race, ethnicity, language, and social class interact to influence student learning and behavior.

Continuing education about diversity is especially important for teachers because of the increasing cultural, racial, and ethnic gaps that exist between teachers and students in the United States. Effective professional development programs should help educators to (a) uncover and identify their personal attitudes toward racial, ethnic, language, and cultural groups; (b) acquire knowledge about the histories and cultures of the diverse racial, ethnic, cultural, and language groups within the nation and within their schools; (c) become acquainted with the diverse perspectives that exist within different ethnic and cultural communities; (d) understand the ways in which institutionalized beliefs within schools, universities, and popular culture can perpetuate stereotypes about racial and ethnic groups; (e) acquire the knowledge and skills needed to develop and implement an *equity pedagogy*, defined by Banks (2004) as instruction that provides all students with an equal opportunity to attain academic and social success in school; (f) understand how to use the cultural values and life experiences of students to enrich their learning and the learning of others; and (g) develop a repertoire of instructional competencies for teaching students in diverse schools and classrooms.

Professional development programs should help teachers understand the complex characteristics of ethnic groups and how variables such as social class, religion, region, generation, extent of urbanization, race, and gender strongly influence ethnic and cultural behavior. These variables influence the behavior of groups both singly and interactively. Social class is one of the most important variables that mediate and influence educational behavior and outcomes (Rothstein, 2004). However, institutional and interpersonal racism continues to affect students of color in every social class group, although it does so in complex ways that to some extent, but by no means always, reflect social class status (Steele & Aronson, 1995).

If teachers are to increase learning opportunities for all students, they must be knowledgeable about the social and cultural contexts of teaching and learning. Although students are not solely products of their cultures and vary in the degree to which they identify with them, some distinctive cultural behaviors are associated with ethnic groups (Boykin, 1986; Nieto, 2005). Teachers should become knowledgeable about the distinctive cultural backgrounds of their individual students. They should also acquire the skills needed to translate that knowledge into effective instruction and an enriched curriculum, while guarding against cultural stereotyping (Gay, 2000).

Teaching should be culturally responsive to students from diverse racial, ethnic, cultural, and language groups. Making teaching culturally responsive involves strategies such as constructing and designing relevant cultural metaphors and multicultural representations to help bridge the gap between what students already know and appreciate and what they will be taught. Culturally responsive instructional strategies transform information about the home and community into effective classroom practice.

Rather than relying on essentialized and generalized notions of ethnic groups that can be misleading, effective teachers use knowledge of their students' cultures and ethnicity as a framework for inquiry. They also use culturally responsive activities, resources, and strategies to organize and implement instruction (Au, 2006; Gay, 2000).

STUDENT LEARNING

Principle 2: Schools should ensure that all students have equitable opportunities to learn and to meet high standards.

Schools can be thought of as collections of opportunities to learn (Darling-Hammond, 1997). A good school maximizes the learning experiences of all students. One might judge the fairness of educational opportunity by comparing the learning opportunities students have within and across schools. The most important of these opportunities to learn are (a) teacher quality (indicators include experience, preparation to teach the content being taught, participation in high-quality professional development, verbal ability, and teacher rewards and incentives); (b) a safe and orderly learning environment; (c) time actively engaged in learning; (d) student-teacher ratio; (e) a rigorous curriculum; (f) grouping practices that avoid tracking and rigid forms of student assignment based on past performance; (g) sophistication and currency of learning resources and information technology used by students; and (h) access to extracurricular activities.

Although the consequences of these different characteristics of schools vary with particular conditions, the available research suggests that when two or more cohorts of students differ significantly in their access to opportunities to learn, differences in the quality of education also exist (Dreeben & Gamoran, 1986). Such differences affect student achievement and can undermine the prospects for positive intergroup relations.

The content that makes up the lessons students are taught influences the level of student achievement. This is hardly surprising, but the curricula students experience and the expectations of teachers and others about how much of the material students will learn vary from school to school. In general, students who are taught more rigorous curricula learn more than their peers with similar prior knowledge and backgrounds who are taught less rigorous curricula. For example, early access to algebra leads to greater participation in higher math and increased academic achievement.

> Principle 3: The curriculum should help students understand that knowledge—whether the source is research, books and articles, teachers, or the media—is socially constructed and reflects personal experiences as well as the social, political, and economic contexts of the times and places in which the knowledge was formulated and shared.

In curriculum and teaching units and in textbooks, students often study historical events, concepts, and issues only or primarily from the points of view of the powerful (Banks, 2006). The perspectives of the less powerful are frequently silenced, ignored, or marginalized. This kind of teaching privileges mainstream students, who most often identity with the victors or dominant groups, and causes many students of color to feel left out of the American story.

Concepts such as the "discovery of America," the "Westward movement," and "pioneers" are often taught primarily from the points of view of the European Americans who constructed them. The curriculum should help students to understand how these concepts reflect the values and perspectives of European Americans as well as their experiences in the United States. Teachers should help students learn how these concepts can have very different meanings for groups indigenous to America and for groups such as African Americans, who came to America in chains, or to immigrants from many countries who work in arduous and low-paying jobs.

Teaching students the different and often conflicting meanings of concepts and issues for the diverse groups that make up the United States will help students to better understand the complex factors that contributed to the birth, growth, and development of the nation; to develop empathy for the points of views and perspectives that are normative within various groups; to communicate effectively with diverse groups and individuals; and to increase their ability to think critically and collaboratively solve complex problems.

> Principle 4: Schools should provide all students with opportunities to participate in extra- and cocurricular activities that develop knowledge, skills, and attitudes that increase academic achievement and foster positive relationships among students of different racial and ethnic groups.

Research evidence that links student achievement to participation in extra- and cocurricular activities is increasing in quantity and consistency (Braddock, 1999; Eccles & Barber, 1999; Gootman, 2000). Significant research supports the proposition that participation in afterschool programs, sports activities, academic associations (e.g., language clubs), and school-sponsored social activities contributes to academic performance, reduces high school dropout rates and discipline problems, and enhances interpersonal skills among students from different ethnic backgrounds. Gutiérrez and her colleagues, for example, found that "nonformal learning contexts," such as afterschool programs, are useful in bridging home and school cultures for students from diverse groups (Gutiérrez, Baquedano-Lopez, Alvarez, & Chiu, 1999).

Braddock (1999) concluded that involvement in sports activities was particularly beneficial for African American male high school students. When designing extracurricular activities, educators should give special attention to recruitment, selection of leaders and teams, the cost of participating, allocation of school resources, and opportunities for cooperative, equal-status intergroup contact.

INTERGROUP RELATIONS

Principle 5: Schools should create or make salient superordinate crosscutting group memberships in order to improve intergroup relations.

Creating *superordinate groups,* groups with which members of all existing racial and ethnic groups in a situation identify, improves intergroup relations (Gaertner, Rust, Dovidio, Bachman, & Anastasio, 1994; Pettigrew, 2004). When membership in superordinate groups is salient, other group differences become less important. Creating superordinate groups stimulates liking and cohesion, which can mitigate preexisting animosities.

In school settings, many superordinate group memberships can be created or made salient. For example, it is possible to create superordinate groups through extracurricular activities. Also, many existing superordinate group memberships can be made more salient: the classroom, the grade level, the school, the community, the state, and even the nation. The most immediate superordinate groups are likely to be the most influential (e.g., students or members of the school chorus, rather than Californians), but identification with any superordinate group can decrease prejudice.

Principle 6: Students should learn about stereotyping and other related biases that have negative effects on racial and ethnic relations.

We use categories in perceiving our environments because categorization is a natural part of information processing. But the mere act of categorizing people as "in-group" and "out-group" members can result in stereotyping, prejudice, and discrimination (Tajfel & Turner, 1986). Specifically, making distinctions between groups often leads to perceiving the "other" group as more homogenous than one's own group and to an exaggeration of the extent of the perceived group differences. Thus, categorizing leads to stereotyping and to behaviors influenced by those stereotypes.

Intergroup contact can counteract stereotypes if the situation allows members of each group to behave in a variety of ways across different contexts so that their full humanity and diversity are displayed. In some intergroup relations programs, members of minority and majority groups are asked to discuss what it feels like to be the target of stereotyping, prejudice, and discrimination (Kamfer & Ventner, 1994). Sharing this type of information informs students of the pain and suffering their intentional or even thoughtless acts cause. It can also create empathy for the "other" group and undercut stereotyping and prejudice. Negative stereotypes can also be modified in situations by providing in-group members with information about multiple out-group members who disconfirm stereotypes across a variety of situations (Johnston & Hewstone, 1992).

Principle 7: Students should learn about the values shared by virtually all cultural groups (e.g., justice, equality, freedom, peace, compassion, and charity).

Teaching students about the values that virtually all groups share, such as those described in the United Nations Universal Bill of Rights, can provide a basis for perceived similarity that can promote favorable intergroup relations (Kohlberg, 1981; Stephan & Stephan, 2004). In addition, the values themselves serve to undercut negative intergroup relations by discouraging injustice, inequality, unfairness, conflict, and a lack of compassion or charity. The value of egalitarianism deserves special emphasis, since a number of theories suggest that it can help to undermine stereotyping and prejudice and to restrict the direct expression of racism (Gaertner & Dovidio, 1986; Katz, Glass, & Wackenhut, 1986).

Principle 8: Teachers should help students acquire the social skills needed to interact effectively with students from other racial, ethnic, cultural, and language groups.

One of the most effective techniques for improving intercultural relations is to teach members of the cultural groups the social skills necessary to interact effectively with members of another culture (Bochner, 1994). Students need to learn how to perceive, understand, and respond to group differences. They need to learn not to give offense and not to take offense.

For example, the *intercultural sensitizer*, a technique initially developed for intercultural training, can be used to present instances in which members of different groups regard the behavior of out-group members as offensive or antagonistic (Cushner & Landis, 1996). Intercultural sensitizers consist of a series of written vignettes, in which members of one cultural group engage in behaviors that are typically misunderstood by members of another cultural group. Intercultural sensitizers teach students more appropriate interpretations of behaviors of individuals belonging to groups different from themselves. Students also need to be helped to realize that when members of other groups behave in ways that are inconsistent with in-group norms, these individuals are not necessarily behaving antagonistically (Kamfer & Venter, 1994). Other techniques that involve sharing experiences of intergroup interactions and related issues have also been found to improve intergroup relations (Nagda & Derr, 2004). Intergroup dialogues can go a long way toward demystifying the behavior of out-group members and creating more accurate perceptions.

Conflict resolution is a skill that can be taught in schools in order to improve intergroup relations (Deutsch, 1993). A number of school districts throughout the United States are teaching students to act as mediators for disputes among other students. This type of mediation holds promise as one approach to resolving certain intergroup conflicts in schools. Moreover, an orderly and safe school environment fosters high student achievement.

Principle 9: Schools should provide opportunities for students from different racial, ethnic, cultural, and language groups to interact socially under conditions designed to reduce fear, anxiety, and status differences.

Among the primary causes of prejudice are anxiety and fear (Gaertner & Dovidio, 1986; Stephan, 1999). Anxiety and fear lead members of social groups to avoid interacting with out-group members and cause them discomfort when they do (Stephan &

Renfro, 2002). Fears about members of other groups often stem from concern about realistic and symbolic threats to the in-group, for instance, that the in-group will lose some or all of its power or resources or that its very way of life will be undermined. Many such fears have little basis in reality or are greatly exaggerated.

To reduce uncertainty and anxiety concerning interaction with out-group members, the contexts in which interaction takes place should be relatively structured; the balance of members of the different groups should be as equal as possible; the probabilities of failure should be low; and opportunities for hostility and aggression should be minimized. Issues of perceived status inequality should also be addressed (Cohen, 2004; Pettigrew, 2004).

Providing factual information that contradicts misperceptions can also counteract prejudice based on a false sense of threat. Stressing the value similarities that exist between groups should also reduce the degree of symbolic threat posed by out-groups and thus reduce fear and prejudice.

ASSESSMENT

Principle 10: Teachers should use multiple culturally sensitive techniques to assess complex cognitive and social skills.

Evaluating the progress of students from diverse racial, ethnic, and social class groups is complicated by differences in language, learning characteristics, and cultures. Hence, the use of a single method of assessment will likely further disadvantage students from particular social classes and ethnic groups.

Teachers should adopt a range of formative and summative assessment strategies that give students an opportunity to demonstrate mastery. These strategies should include observations, oral examinations, performances, and teacher-made as well as standardized measures and assessments. Students learn and demonstrate their competencies in different ways. The preferred mode of demonstrating task mastery for some is writing, while others do better speaking, visualizing, or performing; some are stimulated by competitive and others by cooperative learning arrangements; some prefer to work alone, while others like to work in groups. Consequently, a variety of assessment procedures and outcomes that are compatible with different learning, performance, work, and presentation styles should be used to determine if students are achieving the levels of skill mastery needed to function effectively in a multicultural society.

Assessment should go beyond traditional measures of subject matter knowledge and include complex cognitive and social skills. Effective citizenship in a multicultural society requires individuals who have the values and abilities to promote equality and justice among culturally diverse groups.

SCHOOL GOVERNANCE, ORGANIZATION, AND EQUITY

Principle 11: A school's organizational strategies should ensure that decision making is widely shared and that members of the school community learn collaborative skills and dispositions in order to create a caring learning environment for students.

School policies and practices are the living embodiment of a society's underlying values and educational philosophy. They also reflect the values of those who work within schools. Whether in the form of curriculum, teaching strategies, assessment procedures, disciplinary policies, or grouping practices, school policies embody a school's beliefs, attitudes, and expectations of its students (Nieto, 1999). This is true whether the school is one with extensive or limited financial resources, with a relatively monocultural or a richly diverse student body, or located in a crowded central city or an isolated rural county.

School organization and leadership can either enhance or detract from developing learning communities that prepare students for a multicultural and democratic society (Hawley, in press). Schools that are administered from the top down are unlikely to create collaborative, caring cultures. Too often, schools talk about democracy but fail to practice shared decision making. Powerful multicultural schools are organizational hubs that include a wide variety of stakeholders, including students, teachers, administrators, parents, and community members. The racial and ethnic diversity of the staff is celebrated and represented in leadership groups and social interactions.

There is convincing research evidence that parental involvement is critical in enhancing student learning (Epstein et al.,
2002). A just and effective multicultural school is receptive to
working with all members of the students' communities.

Principle 12: Leaders should ensure that all public schools,
regardless of their locations, are funded equitably.

School finance equity is a critical condition for creating just
multicultural schools. Inequities in the funding of public education are startling (Kozol, 2005). Two communities adjacent to
one another can provide wholly different support to their public
schools, based on property values and tax rates. Students who live
in poor communities are punished because they must attend
schools that are underfunded compared with schools located in
more affluent communities. Moreover, variations within districts
of funding and the quality of physical facilities often reflect the
income levels of the communities served by the schools.

The relationship between increased school expenditures and
school improvement is complex (Burtless, 1994). When investments are made in ways that significantly improve students'
opportunities to learn, such as increasing teacher quality, reducing class size in targeted ways, and engaging parents in their
children's education, the result is likely to be improved student
knowledge and skills.

The failure of schools and school systems to provide all
students with equitable resources for learning will, of course,
work to the disadvantage of those receiving inadequate resources
and will usually widen the achievement gap between schools.
Since achievement correlates highly with student family income
and persons of color are disproportionately low income, inequities
in opportunities to learn contribute to the achievement gap
between White students and students of color.

CONCLUSION

Effective multicultural schools help students from diverse racial,
cultural, ethnic, and language groups to experience academic
success. Academic knowledge and skills are essential in today's
global society; however, they are not sufficient. Students must also

develop the knowledge, attitudes, and skills needed to interact positively with people from diverse groups and participate constructively in their nation's civic life. Students must be competent in intergroup and civic skills to function effectively in today's complex and ethnically polarized nation and world.

Diversity in schools in the United States is both an opportunity and a challenge. The nation is enriched by the ethnic, cultural, and language diversity among its citizens and within its schools. However, when diverse groups interact, intergroup tension, stereotypes, and institutionalized discrimination can and do exist. When these conditions occur and are not addressed, the academic achievement and learning opportunities of all students are undermined. Schools must find ways to respect and utilize the diversity of their students as well as help to create a unified nation-state to which all U.S. citizens have allegiance. Structural inclusion into the nation-state and power sharing will engender feelings of allegiance among diverse groups. *E pluribus unum*—"out of many, one"—is the delicate goal toward which our nation and its schools should strive. We offer these design principles with the hope that they will help educational policymakers and practitioners realize this elusive and difficult but essential goal of a democratic and pluralistic society.

NOTE

1. The Multicultural Education Consensus Panel, chaired by James A. Banks, was cosponsored by the Center for Multicultural Education (CME) at the University of Washington and the Common Destiny Alliance at the University of Maryland. This chapter updates the more extensive 2001 report, *Diversity Within Unity: Essential Principles for Teaching and Learning in a Multicultural Society,* available from the CME at http://www.depts.washington.edu/centerme.home.htm.

REFERENCES

Au, K. (2006). *Multicultural issues and literacy achievement.* Mahwah, NJ: Lawrence Erlbaum.

Banks, J. A. (2004). Multicultural education: Historical development, dimensions, and practice. In J. A. Banks & C. A. M. Banks (Eds.), *Handbook of research on multicultural education* (pp. 1–24). New York: Macmillan.

Banks, J. A. (2006). *Cultural diversity and education: Foundations, curriculum, and teaching* (5th ed.). Boston: Allyn & Bacon.

Bochner, S. (1994). Culture shock. In W. Lonner & R. Malpass (Eds.), *Psychology and culture* (pp. 245–242). Boston: Allyn & Bacon.

Boykin, A. W. (1986). The triple quandary and the schooling of Afro-American children. In U. Neisser (Ed.), *The school achievement of minority children: New perspectives* (pp. 57–92). Hillsdale, NJ: Lawrence Erlbaum.

Braddock, J. (1999). Bouncing back: Sports and academic resilience among African-American males. *Education and Urban Society, 24,* 113–131.

Burtless, G. (Ed.). (1994). *Does money matter? The effect of school resources on student achievement and adult success.* Washington, DC: Brookings.

Cohen, E. G. (2004). Producing equal-status interaction amidst classroom diversity. In W. G. Stephan & W. P. Vogt (Eds.), *Education programs for improving intergroup relations, theory, research, and practice* (pp. 37–54). New York: Teachers College Press.

Cushner, K., & Landis, D. (1996). The intercultural sensitizer. In D. Landis & R. S. Bhagat (Eds.), *Handbook of intercultural training* (2nd ed., pp. 185–202). Thousand Oaks, CA: Sage.

Darling-Hammond, L. (1997). *The right to learn.* San Francisco: Jossey-Bass.

Deutsch, M. (1993). Cooperative learning and conflict resolution in an alternative high school. *Cooperative Learning, 13,* 2–5.

Dreeben, R., & Gamoran, A. (1986). Race, instruction, and learning. *American Sociological Review, 51,* 660–669.

Eccles, J. S., & Barber, B. L. (1999). Student council, volunteering, basketball, or marching band: What kind of extracurricular involvement matters? *Journal of Adolescence Research, 14,* 10–43.

Epstein, J. L., Sanders, M. G., Simon, B. S., Salinas, K. C., Jansorn, N. R., & Voorhis, F. L. V. (2002). *School, family, and community partnerships* (2nd ed.). Thousand Oaks, CA: Corwin Press.

Gaertner, S. L., & Dovidio, J. F. (1986). The aversive form of racism. In J. F. Dovidio & S. L. Gaertner (Eds.), *Prejudice, discrimination, and racism* (pp. 61–90). Orlando, FL: Academic Press.

Gaertner, S. L., Rust, M. C., Dovidio, J. F., Bachman, B., & Anastasio, P. A. (1994). The contact hypothesis: The role of a common in-group identity on reducing intergroup bias. *Small Group Research, 25,* 224–249.

Gay, G. (2000). *Culturally responsive teaching: Theory, research, and practice.* New York: Teachers College Press.

Gootman, J. A. (Ed.). (2000). *After-school programs to promote child and adolescent development: Summary of a workshop.* Washington, DC: National Academy Press.

Gutiérrez, K. D., Baquedano-Lopez, P., Alvarez, H. H., & Chiu, M. M. (1999). Building a culture of collaboration through hybrid language practices. *Theory Into Practice, 38*, 87–93.

Hawley, W. D. (in press). Designing schools that use student diversity to enhance learning for all students. In G. Orfield & E. Frankenberg (Eds.), *Lessons in integration: Realizing the promise of racial diversity in America.* Charlottesville: University of Virginia Press.

Johnston, L., & Hewstone, M. (1992). Cognitive models of stereotype change. *Journal of Experimental Social Psychology, 28*, 360–386.

Kamfer, L., & Venter, J. L. (1994). First evaluation of a stereotype reduction workshop. *South African Journal of Psychology, 24*, 13–20.

Katz, I., Glass, D. C., & Wackenhut, J. (1986). An ambivalence-amplification theory of behavior toward the stigmatized. In S. Worchel & W. G. Austin (Eds.), *Psychology of intergroup relations* (2nd ed., pp. 103–117). Chicago: Nelson-Hall.

Kohlberg, L. (1981). *Essays on moral development.* New York: Harper & Row.

Kozol, J. (2005). *The shame of the nation: The restoration of apartheid schooling in America.* New York: Crown.

Nagda, B., & Derr, A. S. (2004). Intergroup dialogues: Embracing difference and conflict, engendering community. In W. G. Stephan & W. P. Vogt (Eds.), *Education programs for improving intergroup relations: Theory, research, and practice* (pp. 133–152). New York: Teachers College Press.

Nieto, S. (1999). *The light in their eyes: Creating multicultural learning communities.* New York: Teachers College Press.

Nieto, S. (Ed.). (2005). *Why we teach.* New York: Teachers College Press.

Pettigrew, T. F. (2004). Intergroup contact: Theory, research, and new perspectives. In J. A. Banks & C. A. McGee-Banks (Eds.), *Handbook of research on multicultural education* (2nd ed., pp. 770–781). San Francisco, CA: Jossey-Bass.

Rothstein, R. (2004). *Class and schools: Using social, economic, and educational reform to close the Black-White achievement gap.* Washington DC: Economic Policy Institute.

Steele, C. M., & Aronson, J. (1995). Stereotype threat and the intellectual test performance of African Americans. *Journal of Personality and Social Psychology 69*, 791–811.

Stephan, C. W., & Stephan, W. G. (2004). Intergroup relations in multicultural education programs. In J. A. Banks & C. A. McGee-Banks (Eds.), *Handbook of research on multicultural education* (2nd ed., pp. 782–798). San Francisco: Jossey-Bass.

Stephan, W. G. (1999). *Reducing prejudice and stereotyping in schools.* New York: Teachers College Press.

Stephan, W. G., & Renfro, C. L. (2002). The role of threats in intergroup relations. In D. Mackie & E. R. Smith (Eds.), *From prejudice to intergroup emotions* (pp. 191–208). New York: Psychology Press.

Tajfel, H., & Turner, J. C. (1986). The social identity theory of intergroup behavior. In S. Worchel & W. G. Austin (Eds.), *Psychology of intergroup relations* (2nd ed., pp. 33–47). Chicago: Nelson-Hall.

Teddlie, C. (Ed.). (1999). *The international handbook of school effectiveness research.* New York: Falmer Press.

CHAPTER TWELVE

Local School Districts and Instructional Improvement

Richard F. Elmore

THE PROBLEMATIC ROLE OF LOCAL SCHOOL DISTRICTS

Most public educators would find it difficult to imagine a world without local school districts, as much as they might wish that districts were better organized and better run, more helpful, and less politically unstable and obtrusive. While educators take local school districts for granted, policymakers, I think, regard them as increasingly problematical. One result of the current period of educational reform could well be a substantial erosion of the traditional role of local school districts in the governance of education, and maybe even an elimination of local school districts in all but symbolic form and function.[1]

Briefly, the problem is this: Over the past 20 years or so, states have gradually increased their share of educational funding, largely as a result of increased judicial and political pressure for equalization of local school expenditures and pressure from school districts themselves for increasingly ambitious definitions of what constitutes an "adequate" educational program. A major consequence of this gradual fiscal centralization of school finance at the state level has been increasing salience of elementary and secondary education as a state political issue and, not surprisingly, increasing pressure for accountability in the expenditure of state education funds.

Governors and state legislators have become more active agents of education reform, as much out of fiscal and political necessity as out of their own interests in the issue. The growth of the state role has been accompanied, since at least the mid-1980s, by a substantial retrenchment in federal policy, signaled by a decrease in the federal share of school funding and a shift in federal policy toward a more facilitative and less obtrusive role. Formal authority for education, then, has gradually migrated away from localities and the federal government toward states (see, for example, Goertz, Floden, & O'Day, 1996; Massell & Fuhrman, 1994).

This migration of education policy and governance toward the states has been accompanied by an increasing willingness of states to intervene directly in schools, either bypassing local school districts altogether or giving them a limited and circumscribed role. The No Child Left Behind Act of 2001 (NCLB), the federal policy governing compensatory education and accountability, now requires states to develop and enforce standards with progressively severe sanctions to turn around failing schools. In the wake of NCLB, every state now has the capacity to collect school-level student performance data directly, using school districts as little more than test administration contractors, and to report school-level results at the state level. Some states, such as Kentucky and South Carolina, have experimented with reward programs, independently identify schools as being in various stages of trouble on academic performance measures, and have the authority to intervene in both districts and schools to remediate poor performance (Ladd, 1996). Over time, this direct state-to-school connection will probably increase for at least two reasons: First, state policymakers are becoming less patient with educators' explanations for limited evidence of increased student performance in the face of substantially increased state expenditures. Second, local districts have been relatively defensive in the face of aggressive state reforms, responding to state initiatives for school improvement with attempts to protect their roles, rather than playing more assertive roles in defining the reform agenda through their own school improvement efforts.

At the same time that states, under aggressive federal pressure, have tightened the state-to-school accountability connection, they have shown themselves willing to initiate policies that directly challenge the monopoly of local school systems over the provision of public education. Many state charter school laws, for example, in Massachusetts, authorize state agencies to charter schools directly, without any local participation, or provide appeal mechanisms that permit schools to be chartered over the opposition of local districts (Finn, Bierlein, & Manno, 1996; Millot, 1995; Wohlstetter, Wenning, & Briggs, 1995). Since the late 1980s, a number of states have introduced school choice policies, such as postsecondary options for secondary school students, vouchers for school dropouts, interdistrict choice programs, and private school voucher programs for poor, inner-city students, that allow students to move fluidly among schools of various types without regard to local jurisdictional boundaries. These programs reach only a relatively small fraction of students, but their effects have been disproportionately large on perceptions of the role of local school systems. State legislators have gotten used to viewing local school districts and school boards as a special interest, focused mainly on maintenance of monopoly control of public schools and, in their view, balancing the interests of students and their parents against local institutional interests. Not surprisingly, local institutional interests are often the losers in these decisions.

In this political and economic climate, it is understandable that the emerging theme of education reform involves standards for student academic performance, formulated on a statewide basis, under prescriptive federal policies, backed by rewards and sanctions that operate directly on schools, treating school districts as agents of accountability for federal and state policies. Standards-based reforms take as their point of departure the perceived failure of public schools to deliver reliable, high-quality instruction to aid students in basic academic subjects. The distinguishing characteristic of American schools has become the vast difference in the quality of teaching and learning delivered to students (within districts from school-to-school and between districts) between those with high and low proportions of students in need. These variations in student learning pose a highly conspicuous problem of state policymakers because they threaten the rationale for increased state expenditures on education.

If there is to be a reemergence of the local role in education, it will not take the form of an assertion of the traditional doctrine of local control of schools. Local districts, by becoming more fiscally dependent on states, have lost much of the power of the argument for local democratic control of schools. State legislators and governors have gotten used to making decisions that affect schools directly, and, in doing so, they juxtapose the institutional interests of local districts and the collective interests of professional educators against the individual interests of parents and students. State policymakers are not likely to retreat from this view, especially as pressure increases on them to account for the results of increased state expenditures. A redefinition of the local role in education will have to focus on what I have called the principle of *value added to student performance*. Like it or not, for better or for worse, the currency of the realm in education policy making has become student academic performance. States have gotten better and better at collecting school-level data on student performance and at connecting their data collection systems to state accountability systems that reward and penalize schools. They have become less and less dependent on districts to perform these functions for them. We might argue about the design of these state accountability systems, about the educational values represented in their student performance measures, or about their effects on students and schools, and these arguments are legitimate. But the basic reality of education policy is, and will continue to be, that educators and the schools they work in will be judged largely by their effect on student learning. Local school districts will increasingly be judged—and, I think, criticized—on the basis of whether they add value to student learning.

Kenneth Leithwood has developed, in his chapter for this volume, a set of principles for continuous improvement of schools. One way of thinking about the future role of local school districts is to say that they will become the prime enablers of the school-level actions that Leithwood describes. Local school systems would organize, for example, to provide assistance to schools in clarifying their missions and goals, in reframing their cultures and structures around student learning, in collecting and using information about teaching and learning, in articulating state and district policy in ways that connect to the experience and needs of people in schools, and in creating a stable environment for planning and deliberate action. I think Leithwood's perspective on school improvement is a useful way of reframing the district role, and I would therefore recommend that district-level administrators pay attention to the school-level conditions that relate to good teaching and learning and redefine their role in terms of those actions, rather than in terms of their own bureaucratic routines and institutional interests.

There is evidence that some local districts have developed effective strategies for managing school improvement on a large scale, although data on student performance suggest that these districts are a small minority. Districts that engage in effective management of school improvement tend to judge the performance of district and school administrators on the basis of their contributions to student achievement; they set clear expectations that principals will be directly involved in curriculum and instruction in schools and will develop the competencies to make this involvement constructive; they use staff development as a deliberate instrument of instructional improvement and focus it on clearly defined district priorities; and they emphasize active involvement in instructional improvement at all levels of the district, rather than bureaucratic routine and structure (Hallinger & Murphy, 1982; Murphy & Hallinger, 1986, 1988; Murphy, Hallinger, Peterson, & Lotto, 1987).

Many school districts fail to engage in constructive action around school improvement, however, not because they have bad intentions or even because they don't engage in activities that school people regard as constructive. School districts often fail to add value to student performance because they lack a coherent theory about how to influence teaching and learning in productive ways. This is the problem I would like to take as the focus for my contribution to this volume.

THE INSTRUCTIONAL CORE
AND SOME WAYS OF IMPROVING IT

The single most persistent problem of educational reform in the United States is the failure of reforms to alter the fundamental conditions of teaching and learning for students and teachers in schools in anything other than a small-scale and idiosyncratic way (Elmore 1996a, 2004). Reforms wash over schools in successive waves, creating the illusion of change on the rolling surface of policy making, but deep under this churning surface, the fundamental conditions of teaching and learning remain largely unchanged in all but a small proportion of classrooms and schools (Cuban, 1984). As pressure mounts from states for increased school-level accountability for student academic performance, the problem of producing changes in teaching and learning on a large scale will become more visible and ultimately more troublesome for local school districts.

Sustained and continuous improvement in instruction on a large scale requires local educational policymakers and administrators to think and act in ways very different than those in the past. Local board members and administrators have traditionally thought of themselves as responsible for the structure of relations between themselves and the schools they oversee and of relations among teachers within schools and between schools and their clients. Hence, local policymakers and administrators have tried to influence how schools go about their work by restructuring central office functions and school site decision making. The most common forms of restructuring have consisted of site-based management, which exerts more control over decisions affecting instruction in the hands of teachers, principals, and representatives of parents and the community, and changes in the internal structure of schools that permit teachers to work more collaboratively with each other. There is substantial evidence, both historical and contemporary, that these changes in structure do not, by themselves, result in large-scale changes in teaching and learning (Elmore, 1996a; Elmore, Peterson, & McCarthey, 1996; Malen, Ogawa, & Kranz, 1990; Tyack & Cuban, 1995; Wohlstetter et al., 1995).

The reason for this gap between changes in structure and changes in teaching and learning is, in my judgment, relatively straightforward. Structural change allows teachers, principals, and community stakeholders to work together in new ways, but it does not, by itself, change the *knowledge* that these actors bring to bear on the problem of instruction.

Teaching is hard work. Teachers develop their approaches to teaching out of their prior experience as students and out of their experience in solving problems on a daily basis in their classrooms. These approaches to teaching tend to be relatively stable once they are established, and they are relatively immune, except in rare cases, to exhortations from policymakers and administrators to teach differently. Teachers are now being asked by education reformers to teach more ambitious content to larger and larger numbers of students, but these reforms do not provide teachers with access to the knowledge or support they need to practice differently. Simply changing the structure of relationships in schools does not change the knowledge of practice that teachers bring to their work. The primary problem of school reform, then, is knowledge and its development, use, and deployment in the classroom. Local school districts are currently not well equipped to address this problem; their long-term survival depends on their skill in addressing this problem.

Every organization has certain core processes that define its work. In schools, these core processes consist of decisions about what is taught and to whom, how students are grouped for purposes of instruction, how content is allocated to time, how teachers relate to each other in their work with students, and how student learning is judged by students, teachers, and external authorities (Elmore, 1995). Changes in schools, or in the structures that surround them, that do not affect these core processes do not affect teaching and learning. Knowledge about how to affect change in schools that does not bear on these core processes is knowledge that is not directly useful in helping teachers solve the basic problems of their daily work. Education reforms that do not give first priority to knowledge about these core processes—how they develop, how they affect what students learn, and how they affect what teachers teach—are unlikely to have any effect on student performance.

Challenging new standards for what all students should know and be able to do in reading, writing, and mathematics, for example, can't be implemented in large numbers of classrooms without grappling with the knowledge that teachers need in order to change the core processes of schooling. Do new standards require new curricula? If so, where will it come from, and how will teachers learn the new practices it entails? Do new standards require that students be grouped in new ways to provide them access to new curricula? If so, what sorts of grouping practices are most likely to work? Do some students require more time than others to master the academic skills represented in standards? If so, how would time be used differently for different types of students, and what would be the implications of different uses of time for the way teachers' work is organized? Do new standards require that teachers relate to each other more explicitly across grade levels, academic subjects, and groups within grade levels? If so, what kinds of coordination are required, and how will they occur? Do new standards require new ways of assessing student learning and using the results of assessment to change instruction when it appears not to be working for certain kinds of students? If so, where will these new assessment practices come from? Each of these changes in the core carries with it substantial requirements for new knowledge, and their success depends on the mobilization of knowledge in forms that teachers can use in the course of their daily work.

Furthermore, changing the core processes of schooling requires an explicit theory of how teachers learn to teach and a translation of that theory into constructive actions in school systems and schools. Most school systems currently operate on the assumption that teachers arrive, early in their careers, equipped to teach whatever they are expected to teach. Insofar as teachers acquire new knowledge in the course of their careers, they typically do so either through single, one-shot, district-provided staff development workshops or through graduate courses in schools of education. Both of these types of training are typically delivered in isolation from the teacher's classroom and often focus on topics that have only marginal relevance to the immediate demands of classroom practice. They operate on what might call the "take-back" theory of teacher learning: Teachers acquire bits and pieces of knowledge from a variety of sources that they are expected to "take back" to their classrooms and implement. According to the take-back theory of teacher learning, it is the teacher's sole responsibility to make sense of knowledge acquired outside the classroom and to figure out how to apply it in his or her daily work. Furthermore, it is usually the teacher's responsibility to mesh the competing demands of new knowledge delivered from a variety of sources. It is not unusual, in my experience, for a single elementary school teacher to have to figure out how to make math manipulatives, writing journals, self-esteem improvement, assertive discipline, and substance abuse education somehow cohere in a given school day.

This view of teacher learning reflects the largely confused and inept approach that most school districts take to professional development. In most local school systems, teacher professional development is organized as a separate staff function in the central office, detached from the line responsibilities by which schools are administered on a daily basis. Topics for professional development tend to reflect the current "reforms du jour" and usually lack a coherent focus on a single topic over a sustained period of time. What teachers receive by way of new knowledge, then, is a welter of disconnected bits and pieces that are largely disconnected from the administrative relationships that are intended to influence their daily work.

Ann Lieberman and Lynne Miller's contribution to this volume gives an account of the current state of knowledge about the practice of professional development. My interest in the problem of professional development is in how it relates to sustained improvement of instruction. If professional development is to play a role in sustained instructional improvement, it should meet certain basic requirements. It probably should, for example, be based on the premise that teachers learn to teach—and they are likely to learn to change their teaching practice—by engaging in new forms of practice in the presence of people who have some expertise in that practice, by observing others engaging in new forms of practice, and possibly by observing themselves on videotape and analyzing their practice with others. Professional development probably should be based on the premise that changing instruction requires coherence and focus in professional development—working, for example, on a manageable set of new practices in a sustained way over time until they become part of a relatively stable set of repertoires with which a teacher is comfortable. Professional development probably should be based on the premise that administrators at the district level and school level are responsible for creating the conditions necessary to support sustained engagement in improvement, for example, by reducing competing demands on teachers to respond to "reforms du jour" and focusing attention on a limited set of practices that are consistent with broader, systemwide expectations for student learning. And professional development should provide for feedback and redesign of professional development activities by teachers, based on their experience in adapting new practices to the demands of diverse classrooms. The basic theory of teacher learning here is that teachers learn to teach by teaching, but not just by improvising as solo practitioners; they learn by practicing in the presence of others and analyzing their own practice against the observed practice of others. I have seen this model work in a particularly powerful way in an urban school system (Elmore, 1996b).

There may be other theories of teacher learning that are equally powerful and promising as a basis for sustained instructional improvement. I do not pretend to know the full range of possible theories that are available. My point is a broader one: It is impossible to affect teaching and learning in any sustained way across a system of schools unless the people running the system have a coherent theory of how teachers learn and are willing to base their own actions and the organization and management of the system on that theory.

These are the fundamental challenges, then, of reframing the local district's role: basing district- and school-level decisions on an understanding of the core activities of schools and on a defensible theory of how teachers learn to teach. I offer the following principles as guidance for administrators and teachers who are interested in pursuing this path.

1. *If it's not teaching and learning, why are we doing it?* One fundamental condition for a new district role understands that everyone's job should be evaluated on the basis of its connection to the core activities of schooling and its contribution to value added to student performance. Much of the policy making and administrative activity that occurs in districts has only a remote connection to teaching and learning, and much of it complicates the jobs of teachers and principals who bear the main responsibility for instruction by creating a penumbra of distractions from the core problems of schooling. It is reasonable to expect that any action at the district level should be evaluated in terms of the value it adds to instruction; if it fails that standard, then it should bear a very large burden of proof.

2. *Reciprocal accountability, for performance and capacity.* As performance expectations for student learning become more explicit and more binding on schools, policymakers and

administrators have a reciprocal obligation to provide the capacities necessary for school-level actors to meet these expectations. I would go so far as to say that no performance standard should be binding on teachers and principals unless system-level policymakers and administrators meet their reciprocal responsibilities to provide the knowledge, professional development, and resources students should know and be able to do. Likewise, every professional development activity should have to meet the test of whether it connects with a specific problem of classroom practice confronting teachers in meeting expectations for student learning and whether it embodies an approach that results in the adaptation of practice to specific classroom settings.

NOTE

1. For criticism of the role of local districts and proposals for reform, see Hill (1995) and Finn (1991).

REFERENCES

Cuban, L. (1984). *How teachers taught. Constancy and change in American classrooms.* New York: Longman.

Elmore, R. (1995). Teaching, learning, and school organization: Principles of practice and the regularities of schooling. *Educational Administration Quarterly, 31,* 355–374.

Elmore, R. (1996a). Getting to scale with good educational practice. *Harvard Educational Review, 66,* 1–26.

Elmore, R. (1996b). *Staff development and instructional improvement in Community School District #2, New York City.* Cambridge, MA: Consortium for Policy Research in Education, Harvard University.

Elmore, R. (2004). *School reform from the inside out: Policy, practice, and improvement.* Cambridge, MA: Harvard Educational Publishing Group.

Elmore, R., Peterson, P., & McCarthey, S. (1996). *Restructuring in the classroom: Teaching, learning, and school organization.* San Francisco, CA: Jossey-Bass.

Finn, C. (1991). *We must take charge: Our schools and our future.* New York: Free Press.

Finn, C., Bierlein, L., & Manno, B. (1996). *Charter schools in action: A first look.* Washington, DC: Hudson Institute.

Goertz, M., Floden, R., & O'Day, J. (1996). *The bumpy road to education reform* (Policy Brief No. RE-20). Philadelphia: Consortium for Policy Research in Education.

Hallinger, P., & Murphy, J. (1982). The superintendent's role in promoting instructional leadership. *Administrator's Notebook, 30*(6), 1–4.

Hill, P. (1995). *Reinventing public education.* Santa Monica, CA: Rand.

Ladd, H. (Ed.). (1996). *Holding schools accountable.* Washington, DC: Brookings Institution.

Malen, B., Ogawa, R., & Kranz, J. (1990). What do we know about SBM? A case study of the literature. In W. Clune & J. Witte (Eds.), *Choice and control in American education: Vol. 2. The practice of choice: Decentralization and school restructuring* (pp. 289–342). Philadelphia: Palmer Press.

Massell, D., & Fuhrman, S. (1994). *Ten years of state education reform.* Philadelphia: Consortium for Policy Research in Education.

Millot, M. D. (1995). *What are charter schools? An introduction to the concept and statutes.* Seattle: University of Washington, Institute for Public Policy and Management.

Murphy, J., & Hallinger, P. (1986). The superintendent as instructional leader: Findings from effective school districts. *Journal of Educational Administration, 24,* 213–236.

Murphy, J., & Hallinger, P. (1988). Characteristics of instructionally effective school districts. *Journal of Educational Research, 81,* 175–181.

Murphy, J., Hallinger, P., Peterson, K., & Lotto, L. (1987). The administrative control of principals in effective school districts. *Journal of Educational Administration, 25,* 161–192.

Tyack, D., & Cuban, L. (1995). *Tinkering. Toward utopia: Reflections on a century of public school reform.* Cambridge, MA: Harvard University Press.

Wohlstetter, P., Wenning, R., & Briggs, K. (1995). Charter schools in the United States: The question of autonomy. *Educational Policy, 9,* 331–358.

Index

CORWIN
PRESS

The Corwin Press logo—a raven striding across an open book—represents the union of courage and learning. Corwin Press is committed to improving education for all learners by publishing books and other professional development resources for those serving the field of PreK–12 education. By providing practical, hands-on materials, Corwin Press continues to carry out the promise of its motto: **"Helping Educators Do Their Work Better."**

Great Public Schools for Every Child

Our Mission Statement

To fulfill the promise of a democratic society, the National Education Association shall promote the cause of quality public education and advance the profession of education; expand the rights and further the interests of educational employees; and advocate human, civil and economic rights for all.